Practical Magic:

A Translation of Basic Neuro-Linguistic Programming into Clinical Psychotherapy

by Stephen R. Lankton, A.C.S.W.

Meta Publications
P.O. Box 565
Cupertino, California 95015

Library of Congress Card Number 80–50148
I.S.B.N. 0–916990–08–7

DEDICATIONS

This book is dedicated in memory of the late Milton H. Erickson M.D. and to:

Sunsets on the Gulf of Mexico,
Shooting stars,
Roman candles at midnight, and
My parents who fully believe:
   "you can accomplish anything
   you set your mind to."

ACKNOWLEDGEMENTS

Many thanks for the time, effort, and encouragement I received with this manuscript from my New York friends—Dorinda Hoarty, Nancy Winston, and Paul Lounsbury, who initially went over this presentation every which way during its original draft and gave both their time and themselves to enhance the final work for you, the reader. Similar thanks to Tom Codon of Big Sur, California. The original typing and indexing work of Linda Doremus, Jean Grifka and Joseph Grifka was much appreciated. Magical thanks to the Alabama Angel for her help in locating the lost manuscript! And note that Irene Abizaid was the co-therapist for the therapeutic metaphor example. Finally, I want to acknowledge a special thanks to my former trainers, clients, and trainees around the country who provided the opportunities for learning that were the broad foundation leading to this work. Especially, I want to mention my indebtedness and thanks to the exceptional Milton H. Erickson, M.D. of Phoenix, Arizona, and to John Grinder and Richard Bandler of California, all of whom allowed and supported my making an in-depth study of their individual work and material for several years prior to this writing. And last, to my wife, Carol, and my son, Ryan, for support and aid in preparation.

Table of Contents

FOREWORD

I returned to the beach today.

Yesterday this beach experienced the largest and worst storm in the coast's history but today the water is calm because storms come and go. There are many reminders that the sea gives us about this pattern of coming and going. The tides come in and recede. The moon sets. The sun rises. Waves swell and wash. Then, the sun sets and the moon rises in its place. Day and night make cycles to which the Earth is bound.

I watch the rounded wave flatten on the sand and then recede. Today the sands of the shoreline are very flat. There is no rolling beach as there had been yesterday. As I watch the wave roll back into the water that makes the coast, I notice thousands or millions of tiny bubbles that come and disperse. I don't know where the bubbles go but as they become increasingly rare my ears hear their crackling effervescence and I watch them disperse in a random fashion among the waves.

Even this random dispersal of bubbles seems to have a pattern as they roll over a transparent film of water. The transparent film of water is all that remains of the wave. The bubbles disperse in an entropic fashion, increasingly more slowly. They slide back into the gulf as they are greeted by the next incoming wave.

I feel the cool chill of the whitecap break on my ankles as I pull my foot through the water. I can't see the water that holds and transports those tiny bubbles because the film of water is transparent and paper-thin. I see just the bubbles move and yet my mind takes this stimulus and creates a concept of the water's presence as an integral part of the phenomena before me.

Ideas are like waves. Explanations have life cycles, too. It seems that everything is expressed in rhythmical cycles. The nervous system must adjust to a swing between awareness and sleep, between a cycle of standing vertical and reclining horizontally, and within the bounds of the pulse of the heart and the lungs. The mind, too, seems to follow these comings and goings. The mind grasps an idea and then releases it.

This book that you are holding constitutes an important part of my integration of several contemporary psychotherapies with the orientation taught me by Milton H. Erickson and the modeling principles used by Richard Bandler and John Grinder in their work which subsequently led to their development of neuro linguistic programming. This book constitutes an important piece of my understanding of psychological level communication and its use in therapy.

I anticipate that the readers will grasp and release these ideas for themselves as they make their own integration of this material into their personal styles and preferred orientations. I expect that this book will serve as a reference point just as the ocean serves as a place to which a person can return again and again to be renewed in a certain understanding.

Steve Lankton
Panama City Beach, Florida
September, 1979

INTRODUCTION

It is an undeniable pleasure to write this introduction to Steve Lankton's book, *Practical Magic.* I approached the manuscript with curiosity as to what its author would accomplish, knowing him to be an inquisitive and far-reaching individual. I'm satisfied that this book exquisitely fulfills its intentions of demonstrating Mr. Lankton's expertise in translating the fundamentals of Neuro-Linguistic Programming (NLP) into the language of psychotherapy.

NLP is so alien to psychotherapy that only a psychotherapist of Steve Lankton's caliber could have exacted the essential fundamentals for making such a meaningful translation. Mr. Lankton is a native speaker of the language of psychotherapy and has traveled into our Meta Land. He returned to psychotherapy with information and skills with which he has built a bridge such that native speakers of each language can better communicate with one another. That is what makes this book so valuable to the psychotherapist. A former student of NLP, Steve Lankton has provided for the world of psychotherapy what Berlitz provides for the infrequent traveler, a handguide that makes the basics available, usable, and also provides the sincere learner an opportunity to decide whether to engage in further endeavors to become a fluent speaker of the experiential language of NLP. The tourist will be grateful, the seasoned traveler will find this the doorway to extensive learning. The native speaker of NLP will respect its simplicity and knowledgable exemplification and each of us will fully appreciate its usefulness in bringing those outside our domain closer to understanding what our experience is.

Neuro-Linguistic Programming is quite a new field. Developed by Richard Bandler, John Grinder, myself, Judith DeLozier, Robert Dilts, David Gordon and others, it contains a wealth of behavioral technology that is useful to the psychotherapist as well as

being applicable to any endeavor involving communication —
sales, education, management, etc. I personally have come to concentrate on the training of expert practitioners and trainers of pure
NLP and fully appreciate how this book will instill desire in many
of you to depart from psychotherapy to endeavor into the rigorous
training experiences necessary to become certified in the field of
Neuro-Linguisitc Programming.

Every psychotherapist will find this an easy doorway to the technology of NLP. It is another example of how even the more basic
levels of NLP can enrich the competency of psychotherapists who
practice in the arts of change. Steve Lankton's book demonstrates
how far basic NLP can take psychotherapists toward the magical
and pragmatic results NLP has to offer. From the basic patterns he
has created a fundamental translation and it will become the gate-
way for psychotherapists to the precision and thoroughness of
NLP. We, from the field of NLP, salute him, support him, and await
the inevitable numbers of desirable immigrants this book will
bring to us from across the bridge.

Leslie Cameron Bandler

PREFACE

The client is a 43 year old male, heavy set. He sits rigidly in front of you. His eyes move down and to his right before looking into yours. His cheeks and neck begin to redden as he says to you, "Those kids irritate me so much I just want to slap them." He mimes a slap with his right hand and asks, "Do you know what I mean?" He pauses. As therapist, you observe his expression, gestures, and skin color changes. You hear his voice rise on the word "just" and then return to a low gravelly tone. You have been offered an unprecedented opportunity to respond to this man. You can't help but respond as even no response is a response. The question is: how? What do you do and say next and what outcome are you after with this man?

Perhaps, as therapist, you would "intuitively" select your next response. No doubt, though, you would have in mind a general therapeutic framework. However few, the dictates of this framework would result in a particular content to your response and, in addition, likely alter the nature of the transactions between you and the client thereafter. A caseworker might ask the man for an in-depth assessment of each of his children and that intervention might be a good therapeutic choice. A Gestalt Therapist said that he would ask the client to describe the incident in the present tense, imagining his children on the empty chair in front of him and addressing them as though they were present. This, too, might be a good choice. A woman who practices Bioenergetics told me that she would direct the client to experience his body and help him to become "grounded" in a secure sense of the "here and now." This, too, might be a therapeutically sound choice. There are lots of therapies and all of them would offer additional choices.

This book is primarily about choices during treatment. A reader might well ask, "Treatment of what?" In the latter part of the 20th century, the answer might be "neurosis" or "character armor" or "impasses." Since theories of psychology are only ways of talking about human behavior—that is, metaphor—words like "neurosis" and "impasse" are useful as labels born from a recent historical framework of thought. Some of the distinctions and approaches made available by the early psychoanalytic metaphors have already dropped out of clinical and common usage. Others have been retained and expanded upon because their use facilitates obtaining certain results and because they make behavior understandable.

One possible approach to changing behavior is to determine and use those conditions which exist when it does change. Those of us interested in creating change devise intriguing theories about how it happens. When we do explain, we explain with metaphors. Most metaphors of personality, behavioral change, and therapy introduce new words, techniques and emphases. Despite seeming or actual disagreements among these explanations, though, they each learn and borrow from one another. Even though there seems to be a vast difference in the behavior of therapists from different schools, there are many common formal processes that occur between the various approaches.

In this volume I pinpoint some of the common patterns of creating change as they exist in most of the current psychotherapies. I will also present the basics of Neuro-linguistic Programming, a model, rather than theory, of behavioral change and subjective experience. Using modeling principles, I will make explicit common patterns that are minimally necessary for you, as therapist, to effect powerful and lasting change in your clients. I believe that as you learn these patterns step by step you will find yourself becoming equipped with a myriad of new therapeutic choices that will greatly enhance your existing repertoire of proven skills and the fine choices you already have available.

Preparing a Journey

All journeys are similar. When a person sets out for a journey, he can expect some things with some certainty. Some journeys are circular and bring the traveler back to his original destination. Others place the traveler in new circumstances never before encountered and he becomes a pioneer. All journeys are full of surprises; they are occasions for growth, changes of scenery, people and wildlife. If the traveler is the type who is motivated to seek wisdom, he seeks it in his journey, sensing that there are limits to that which he can learn in his own land. He sets about the task of packing, of gathering information about the journey ahead, the road conditions, the weather conditions, what kinds of people he is likely to meet. Eagerly, he inquires of those returning from other journeys similar to his own and he remembers his own past journeys and the learnings that he acquired on those. At last, preparations are complete and the traveler is excitedly underway, noticing each detail and change in the terrain, the weather, the vegetation, animal activities, and the customs of the people whom he visits. He puts these factors together in a fabric of his own understanding which become his own personal memories, his own personal growth, and provide for the enrichment of his life in his later years. Regardless of what the traveler finds, he has that confident and cautious wisdom that he or she will be able to mold them into useful learnings, tales to be told to his children, to their children and grandchildren, into artifacts and curios to adorn the hut for years and maybe generations to come. The task of preparation is a specific and methodical task for those travelers who are adept at their trade.

INTRODUCTION TO CHANGE AND COMMUNICATION

There is a broad range of opportunities for applying the tools of NLP to clinical pyschotherapy. Allow me to whet your appetite with some brief sketches.

In Ann Arbor, Michigan, a woman employed as a social worker suffered chronic depression each year during the autumn. Her daughter had died several years earlier and, although she had grieved for the daughter, her depression continued. In the course of a single half-hour session she was able to re-organize her resources to overcome this trauma. She has not experienced distress in the two fall seasons since.

In Jackson, Michigan, a secretary in her fifties who had sought medical and chiropractic treatment for a continuous hip and leg pain was given total relief in a single hour-long appointment. She had experienced such pain on the job and at home that it had almost completely occupied her conscious attention. Immediately after the session the pain was gone and has not returned.

In the same city a newly married postal worker in her twenties was unable to have sexual relations with her husband. As she and he entered the bedroom she experienced fears, doubt, and anxiety that she could not explain. No home remedy was working to improve their conjugal relations and she was considering divorce. During our session it was discovered that the sexual content of her difficulty seemed to be rooted in an early "traumatic" experience wherein her father had associated fear with sexual thoughts by informing her of "what can happen to girls" who get assaulted and raped. This material had been out of her consciousness and was not needed for our purposes, although she identified the memory within the first twenty minutes of the interview. The changes she sought were gained in the course of the remaining hour. Both she and her husband expressed thanks and the difficulties have not returned after two years.

A rather vivacious woman in her twenties complained of lack of enjoyment in sexual conduct and lack of orgasm. During a two day treatment marathon in Ann Arbor, Michigan, she made all the changes that were necessary. She later reported joyfully, "You have cured me of something that five other therapists failed to do in six years." What was done? Using the change patterns described in rigorous detail later in this text the author and the client identified the associations and bad feelings that were part of her first experiences during sexually oriented social behavior. These were changed by either breaking them into smaller and more manageable bits of information, or were enhanced by associating them with further memories that constituted useful and pleasant resources.

The back pain that she experienced as she began sexual contact was converted into a signal that could initiate judging and comparing her current activity with her ideal and acceptable self-image. When this arrangement was made to her satisfaction, various pleasurable sensations were remembered and the process of remembering and enjoying these memories was learned and made to occur at her will.

Finally, her interpersonal behavior was enhanced as she learned to produce a melodious voice tone and relaxed facial expression to this entire range of learnings.

When she was asked to check the completeness of the work in fantasy, both her self-report and her subtle unconscious behaviors indicated that the changes were in fact sufficient and pleasant. Double checks were done to insure that she had the self-image she wanted and needed, that she knew how to engage in social small-talk, that she could be appropriately intimate, that she would not inhibit her building excitement during orgasm, and that she in fact had information about birth control and hygiene. Her report of success came two weeks later in the presence of her previous therapist. He and her social network were pleased for her. She reports (with a smile) that things are going just fine for her.

The wife of a prominent international government consultant in Washington, D.C. became the client along with her husband. She had been taking 400mg. of Meloril and Thorazine for the last 12 years. If she decreased her medication she hallucinated the voices of various religious figures and what she thought to be the voice of the devil. These voices would tell her to do various things most of which had to do with bringing life to the dead. The medication and weekly visit to a psychiatrist had the problems in check but created what was a rather embarrassing and disappointing family life. Peggy, in her fifties, was very friendly and spent twelve hours working with the author in the period of three days in her home. The changes consisted of a reorganization of the thinking process that was accompanied by the hallucinations. The thinking process of her husband was identified and taught to her instead. Her previous history included some unfortunate deaths and some unreliable information from various family members. All of these early trauma and mis-information exchanges were reviewed in dissociation with certain alterations. The dissociations allowed her to make more adequate use of the information and wisdom of her early family life without the danger of being overwhelmed by the intense feelings and misinformation that the memories contained. Rehearsal of the thinking structure used by her husband (after it was identified and copied) allowed her immediately to have confidence in her ability to "join the human race" and "do things right." All of the changes were systematically generalized into areas outside of the home. Each opportunity was taken to add the mechanisms of self-expression and self-control in all areas of her current and potential life. The day the author left, Peggy was selected for jury duty. She subsequently has reduced her medication to less than 100 mg. a day and is still dropping. She looked into returning to school and employment and is currently planning each. She and her husband (who was also seen briefly to prepare him for the change) are socializing and being peers for the first time in over a decade. She is, at the time of this writing, traveling alone from East to West coast making friends with her children and acquaintances from the past. She wrote and said, "Thank you for giving me back my life."

Hypnosis was used as the modality to assist a boy from Illinois with his asthma. His father was a psychiatrist and his mother was a professional in another field. His sister and brother were also overachievers and the client was the youngest in the household. During a class demonstration, the boy and his father participated in activities lasting about two hours. The special instructions to the father were delivered in metaphor and concerned his changing role. He had been burdened with the role of overinvolvement and rescuing in the family and had made the current family structure resemble the family from which he came. In his youth he had been in the role of attending to his brother and his brother's illness. The psychiatrist signaled agreement with the avenues of change proposed in the metaphors that were designed for his situation the night before.

The youth was placed into a trance and told several stories about young Indians who are in the transition period of their life. They must go into the desert (the boy played in the woods often) and find a totem or Katchina that would be their guide and from which they would get their name. While the boy heard the stories he indicated that he had identified with the Indian boy and was imagining himself in the desert about to sleep and dream under the desert stars. The author arranged the stories to be of a stressful nature both psychologically and physically (asthma attacks are triggered by such stress in this family) and the boy showed adequate participation in the metaphor. When the Indian boy (and the client) were very ready for the appearance of the Katchina, the author placed two Katchina dolls (from the folklore of Plains Indians) in the hands of the boy. He was instructed to open his eyes. When he did he was faced with the decision: "which one did the Indian boy pick?" One was the "whipper of children" the other was "the long haired dancer." One choice means returning to the tribe as a brave and one means returning to the tribe under the care of the squaws. The client considered carefully. The time allowance was given, the trance was maintained and the metaphors were completed. The boy was awakened. What had he done? The situation was arranged at the process level so that the change was free of specific reality or historical material. The next time the boy experiences either type of stress he will "flash" in his mind the pictures of the dolls he held in his hand and he will, in so doing, bring into his awareness a profound sense of relaxation that was attached to that memory and which constituted the major body state during the trance.

The father reported over a year later that the boy had no further asthma attacks, that he mentioned the Katchinas only once or twice in the duration, and that he was becoming a man in some ways that delighted and surprised the father.

It is not possible to know if the treatment was the curing factor in this person's life or not. It is very certain however, that this boy will associate to deep relaxation when ever he pictures those dolls. Whether he picked the "right" one or not is unimportant! It is also certain that he will picture those dolls during many types of stress. Most important the entire incident has provided a metaphor and perhaps a real experience for the boy's "rites of passage" into the part of manhood that he considers special just as the Indian brave considers his own specialness.

In Kentucky, a family therapist in his fifties was suffering chronic depression that he had attempted to change with various therapists for years. We worked for less than an hour and he experienced relief that utterly surprised and delighted him. During the session he recalled having acquired his difficulties during the American economic depression. Since many years of psychotherapy had failed to bring him relief, he was resigned to his depression. While working with the author his face softened, he began to smile, and, as he put it, "to bubble." I arranged for the change to generalize to his relations with his wife and integrate into the marriage. Both husband and wife thanked me and expressed their relief and satisfaction.

A psychiatrist in California was having marital difficulties identified by his wife but apparently outside of his awareness. A single therapy session created changes in his grooming, recreational, and "courting" behavior. The wife expressed her delight and the husband was not threatened or intimidated in any way. Subsequently, both have aggressively sought and used additional opportunities for marital enrichment.

The details of the clinical work in these cases would occupy a chapter each. They are here to indicate the versatile applications available to the creative therapist with the change patterns of Neuro-Linguistic Programming. The cases are taken from various socio-economic groups, in different geographical locales, with a varying degree of client "naivete." The problems range from situational adjustments to somatic, marital, emotional, and cognitive difficulties. The transcripts elsewhere in this writing also involve problems from several of these arbitrary "diagnostic" realms.

Neuro-Linguistic Programming (NLP) is the study of the structure of subjective experience. It was created by behavioral modelers John Grinder and Richard Bandler and intersects with the theoretical material of several fields including Cybernetics, Linguistics, Psychotherapy, and personality theory. NLP makes explicit patterns of behavior and change that have previously been only intuitively understandable. But before we launch our discussion, we need first to make a special emphasis on the difference between a theory and a model.

A theory is a tentative statement that attempts to explain or interpret *why* things relate as they do. A model, however, is a pattern or copy of already existing phenomena which, as designed, can be imitated or recreated. As such, a model ignores realms visited by the theoretician. Theories are speculative thought and not advanced for the purpose of replicating events. Consider, for instance, the difference of approach in trying to imagine *why* Henry Ford was motivated to mass produce automobiles and studying *what* elements and *which* sequences are necessary to do so. In the latter case, if we are thorough in our observations, noting all of the factors involved in mass producing cars, we can build a model from which anyone could achieve the same outcome as Ford. This, of course, is exactly what his competitors did. So a model deals only with what can be observed and can be expected to replicate certain portions of the observed event. Models are necessarily limited to the purpose for which they are designed.

Any model of human experience is designed to be specific and empirical. It is based on what we can see, hear, feel, smell, etc. Since it is not a theory, a model is content free and can thus provide you with very specific criteria for making therapeutic interventions with your clients. Traditionally the word "syntax" has referred to the structure of our language system. In this model I will expand its use to include not only language but all the other systems through which human beings receive and represent their experience. Just as a writer can use his knowledge of the structure of language to effect certain outcomes in print, you as a therapist, with a precise knowledge of the verbal and non-verbal "grammar" of your clients, can set and co-create very specific goals on their behalf.

Many clinicians have had the experience of attending the workshop of a therapeutic "wizard"—a profoundly effective agent of change—and have been appropriately impressed with that person's skills and presence. The trainee, through a kind of intuitive modeling, is able to imitate the skills of the leader perhaps for the duration of the workshop and perhaps for a week after he returns. Then, typically, the impact of the new skills and possibilities for creating change begins to ebb and fade and the trainee finds that he is only a little wiser for the encounter with the wizard. It is, again, like the already accomplished poet who reads the work of someone more skilled; he can revere and understand some of the latter's accomplishment but, from reading, not necessarily be able permanently to attain a new level of skill. Intuitive modeling is often not enough.

What is missing is a way for the trainee systematically to package and absorb the syntax of the leader's communication skills. The modeling principles used here accomplish this and lead the student to a way of "organizing" his intuition. You, as a therapist, can, cognitively *and* intuitively, imitate, learn and even teach the powerful change work of any successful communicator that you encounter.

Obviously, I believe that you will see, hear, and feel the reward of studying and applying the grammar of human communication as presented in this text. This book is designed to add to your learning by presenting a few conceptual pieces at a time and connecting each piece to the sensory experience implicit in the clinical examples. Next I must begin with an introduction of the basic building blocks that you will need to understand and use communication tools in clinical practice. Throughout the book I will present and expand upon what I believe to be the minimal pieces necessary to be useful to you as serious clinicians.

Input System

Everyone has, at most, five sensory systems through which he contacts physical reality. These senses, the eyes, ears, skin, nose, and tongue are the input systems or input channels. Clinical therapy tends to underemphasize the importance of the sensory data exchanged between people and between people and environments. This is largely owing to a lack of helpful linguistic labels, or markers for this subtle phenomena of sensory input. This book, of course, will help expand observation and skill in this area.

I assume that sensory input constitutes the "bottom line" on how people exchange communication. This model of communication and therapy must, therefore, begin with the noticing of sensory input channels, especially sensory distinctions made within the kinesthetic, visual and auditory channels.

Using these three sensory systems, input can be observed to be directed, conditioned, shaped, and even switched frequently by individuals themselves and by others around them.

This model of communication chooses to punctuate ongoing human experience at those momentary points when any sensory channel begins internal processing and stops using external "input."

Representational Systems

A representational system is a sensory processing system that
initiates and modulates behavior—sight, audition, feelings both
visceral and tactile, gustation, and smell memories. As Bandler and
Grinder state, in *The Structure of Magic,* Volume II:

> Each of us, as a human being, has available a number of
> different ways of representing our experience of the world. Fol-
> lowing are some examples of the representational systems each
> of us can use to represent our experiences.
>
> We have five recognized senses for making contact with the
> world—we *see,* we *hear,* we *feel,* we *taste* and we *smell.* In addition
> to these sensory systems, we have a language system which we
> use to represent our experience. We may store our experience
> directly in the representational system most closely associated
> with that sensory channel. We may choose to close our eyes and
> create a visual image of a red square shifting to green and then
> to blue, or a spiral wheel of silver and black slowly revolving
> counter-clockwise, or the image of some person we know well.
> Or, we may choose to close our eyes (or not) and to create a
> kinesthetic representation (a body sensation, a feeling), placing
> our hands against a wall and pushing as hard as we can, feeling
> the tightening of the muscles in our arms and shoulders, becom-
> ing aware of the texture of the floor beneath our feet. Or, we may
> choose to become aware of the prickling sensation of the heat
> of the flames of a fire burning, or of sensing the pressure of
> several light blankets covering our sighing bodies as we sink
> softly into our beds. Or we may choose to close our eyes (or not)
> and create an auditory (sound) representation—the patter of
> tinkling raindrops, the crack of distant thunder and its following
> roll through the once-silent hills, the squeal of singing tires on
> a quiet country road, or the blast of a taxi horn through the
> deafening roars of a noisy city. Or we may close our eyes and
> create a gustatory (taste) representation of the sour flavor of a
> lemon, or the sweetness of honey, or the saltiness of a stale
> potato chip. Or we may choose to close our eyes (or not) and
> create an olfactory (smell) representation of a fragrant rose, or
> rancid milk, or the pungent aroma of cheap perfume.

In other words, we are constantly taking in information from the
outside world through our sensory channels. Some of it we are

conscious of and some of it not. What we sense externally (whether conscious or unconscious) we translate into internal representations that, in turn, mediate our behavior. Consider the difference between seeing an appetizing dessert and hearing it described: both experiences involve different sensory channels yet either might trigger salivation. Hearing a pleasant tune may initiate foot tapping, singing along, or even the experience of seeing musical notes. How representational systems interact to comprise an individual's subjective experience will be one of our major focal points, especially in chapters 2 and 3. For now, it is enough to note that anytime a human being interacts with the external world, he will do so through sensory representations. Information will be taken in through all channels, processed through a few favored channels, and finally, fed back to the external world through behavior initiated in particular sensory modes. The sensory processing channel for which a person is most conscious will be called the primary representational system—a person's most highly valued and most conscious sensory channel at any point in time.

The Map is Not the Territory

Since a model concentrates on the structure of experience rather than on content, our bottom line of inquiry will always be sensory based. What does a client see? What does the client hear? What does the client feel? Smell? Taste? How exactly do these sensory events interact to form the client's presenting problem? What resources are needed to solve the problem and through which sensory system can they be accessed? The fact that a client is visualizing internally—"seeing in the mind's eye"—will be more significant to us than the actual content of the pictures.

The map is not the territory. We operate out of our sensory representations of the world and not on "reality" itself. How else could clients be coming into our offices with descriptions of pain, frustration, and limitations when other people find the world exciting, open-ended, and offering nothing but choices? It is not the "world" itself that dictates our fulfillment or unhappiness, it is each person's own *version* of it. Most (or perhaps all) of our behavior is mediated by internal constructions and experiential representations of our world. This includes the range of behavior from opening doors and starting the car to "bad habits," overly emotional reactions in harmless situations, and gross perceptual dis-

orders such as in psychosis. We are all, through our senses, crea-
tors of the world. Presenting the structure of that creation and
techniques for altering and expanding its borders and limitations
is the purpose of this book.

Representational System Predicates

To help you tune your senses toward discovering the structure
of a client's experience, I want to alert you to the fact that the
adverbs, adjectives, and verbs that people select while speaking
reveal which sensory system they are most conscious of at a point
in time. This class of words—called "predicates"—are not metaphorical when they are sensory related. That is, if someone tells
you that they "see what you mean," they are literally making meaning of what you say by accessing pictures internally. If someone
else reports that something "sounded good" or "came through as
clear as a bell" that person is literally informing you that he is
representing information to himself auditorily.

The following example, perhaps familiar to you, demonstrates
how two well-intentioned people can fail to make contact at the
first, and therefore most vital, step of communication.

Client: "I am so *hurt.* (Eyes look down to the right and left
hand moves to sternum). My husband left and (left hand presses
sternum) I *feel* helpless . . . so alone. I've never *felt* so much *pain,*
do you know what I mean?" Therapist: "Let me *see* if I understand this; I want to be *clear* on the source of your pain (eyes
move up and to the left). Would you *focus* in and get a *picture* of
your pain and we'll *see* if that tells you how to deal with it." Client: (pause) "I just tried to get a *hold* of a picture but I just *feel*
worse. I don't *feel* like you're in *touch* with my difficulty."

This therapist may come to conclude that the client is "resistant" and the client already considers the therapist insensitive. Now
this is a slight exaggeration, but not much.

The suffering client is aware of only that portion of sensory
experience called body sensations—her kinesthetic representational system. The well-intentioned therapist is responding
through another sensory modality; his is a visual representation of
experience.

All of us can recall pleasant associations we have with being at
the seashore. If you, right now, were to go to the beach in memory,

you would be able to remember some of the sights and/or sounds, feelings and smells at the water's edge. The taste of sand or salt water might also come back to you. What is unlikely is that all the parameters of the memory would return to you at the same time. Conscious attention is a limited, that is to say, selective phenomenon; its focus is constantly roving along the continuum of our sensory channels. If a client describes an incident that evoked anxiety, you can predictably expect to hear about only a fraction of what he experienced.

Since consciousness is limited, people are aware of only a fraction of their visual, kinesthetic, auditory, or olfactory modes of experience (George Miller, 1956). Particularly during times of stress, people tend exclusively to favor the use of one sensory system. You can discover which system a client is attending to at any moment in time by listening to the words he selects to describe experience. This selection usually occurs at an unconscious level, free of conscious "censorship". The list that follows is a typical set of predicates from the three most commonly used representational systems—visual, auditory, and kinesthetic.

Visual	Auditory	Kinesthetic
focus	listen	feel
see	yell	firm
clear	talk	touch
bright	hear	pressure
picture	harmony	tense
perspective	noisy	concrete
show	discuss	hurt
hazy	call	touchy
colorful	loud	irritated
pretty	shout	clumsy
peak	told	pushy
glimpse	mellifluous	relaxed

By tuning your ear to the predicates that people use you can learn a great deal about the sensory components of their experience. As you become skilled at this, you will notice that you are easily able to match the predicates of your clients, thereby making a powerful move toward greater contact and rapport. You will literally be speaking the client's language.

Generic Communication

Communication as a word is overused. Define communication as anything people do to have influence on another person's experience. If I am describing my vacation to you I want directly to influence you into having an idea of what it was like. I want your representations to approximate my representations. Indirectly, I will be giving information through the excitement in my voice tone, my facial expressions, hand gestures, posture, etc. All of these messages will be taken in by your senses, consciously or not, and will influence experience in you.

According to this writing, it is not possible *not* to influence someone's experience and produce a response. A response is considered to be anything from verbal output to skin color changes, eye movements, gestures, or breathing. I take any of these to be an indicator that a person's internal state has altered, that his experience has been influenced.

Whether a response occurs in awareness or out of awareness is secondary to our concern. Since consciousness is limited, we are really only cognizant of a fraction of the stimuli that we are continually responding to anyway. In any face to face encounter with another human being there will be a great deal of information exchanged and responses elicited, most of which will be unconscious.

Since it is impossible not to influence our clients' experience, we as therapists have to ask ourselves, "What influence do we want to have and for what purpose?" We can influence clients, verbally and non-verbally, in precise ways for desirable ends as well as through unconscious random means. We can influence certain experiences deliberately that will be of use in treatment or influence experience by accident, perhaps even eliciting behavior that traditionally has been labeled "resistance" (Reich 1945; Fenichel 1945). Part of the purpose of building a model of subjective experience is to enable us, as therapists, to generate new behaviors that will predictably co-create desirable outcomes in our clients as well as ourselves.

Feedback and Variety

The influencing of another person's experience is known to the communicator by means of his sensory input channels. In face to face interviews, the therapist will use his own eyes, ears, skin and nose. Other feedback mechanisms include all manner of measurements and tests. The value of the feedback, though, is related to the role it plays in modifying subsequent communications.

Once a person changes his behavior (voice tone, expression, gesture, skin color, posture, etc.) on the basis of sensory input, feedback and variety have been established. An important thing about feedback is that it must be relevant. It must use sensory input to notice differences that literally "make a difference." Feedback and variety of behavior which lead to more elegant, successful or adaptive outcomes are said to be intelligent behavior. This book is about increasing intelligence (Batson, 1972) in communication and change by specifying relevant input patterns to use in feedback and a variety of relevant paradigms of behavior to streamline and increase your own variety of well formed responses.

Internal Response to External Behavior

Each sensory stimulation triggers an internal representation which, in turn, initiates some sort of externally noticeable behavior (Arnold, 1959). Suppose a mother and daughter are encountering each other and the mother smiles. The daughter sees the smile—External Stimulus—and instantly represents the perception to herself. She does this unconsciously and the representation just happens to be an internal visual memory of having been disciplined by that smiling face (see illustration). The meaning the daughter extracts from this internal representation remains out of her awareness but it mediates her response to mother's present smile. The daughter is only conscious of the feeling of resentment and a desire to avoid her mother at the moment.

If the mother had intended favorably to influence the daughter then the message she intended was not the one received. The "meaning" a message has is determined by the response(s) it elicits rather than the intention the sender had when conveying it. Mother's presumed intentions in the above interaction had nothing to do with how her daughter responded to her. As therapists, too, we can approach our work with a client with the best of intentions but still have difficulty helping him make the changes he wants. If the mother is sensitive to the slightest changes in the daughters posture, face muscles, voice tone, expressions and gestures, she can use these indicators to adjust the communication and emphasis. These small changes from the daughter are indicators of the changing ideas and feeling states that the daughter experiences when she sees and hears the communication messages from mother. All of these slight changes are ideo-motor responses (Erickson, 1961) or, in other words, the motor indicators that ideas —internal representations—are changing. The mother's sensitivity to the internal change allows her to pace her communication to the readiness and the special needs and history of the daughter. This same principle easily translates into the realm of therapy, but first let's find out what happens when responsive communication and feedback are not used.

There are lots of ways in which communication messages can get distorted. In this case the daughter's remembered representation limited her present possible perception of her mother's smile. Also, as we shall see in Chapter 3, conflicting messages are frequently sent and received through several input channels at once. The incongruence can elicit from the receiver not only meanings that are made out of (beyond) conscious awareness but also and equally incongruent multi-channel response. For instance, a woman will say to a man, "I love you." while shaking her head back and forth to indicate, "no." The man may hear the words consciously and visually register the headshake out of awareness. Thus, his internal response to the words may initiate an appreciative smile and the words, "I know," a response that is accompanied by a harsh tonal shift as the words are spoken—the unconscious response to the head shake. This output can also be received on several channels and, in turn, elicit an equally incongruent response. This type of communication is a common source of marital disagreements, business misunderstandings and painful social interactions.

What is missing from the example of mother and daughter, and necessary to generate a more desirable outcome, is feedback. Mother's success in conveying the initial message to her daughter will largely depend upon whether she can sense the latter's response to her smile and be flexible enough in modifying her be-

ACTUAL RESPONSE VERSUS DESIRED RESPONSE

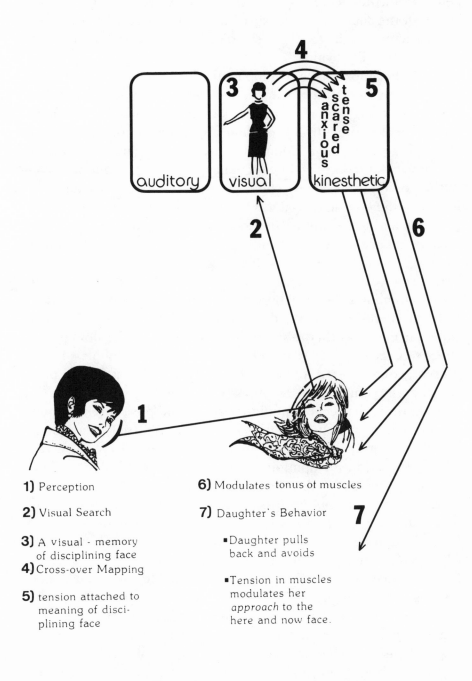

1) Perception

2) Visual Search

3) A visual - memory
of disciplining face

4) Cross-over Mapping

5) tension attached to
meaning of disci-
plining face

6) Modulates tonus of muscles

7) Daughter's Behavior

- Daughter pulls
back and avoids

- Tension in muscles
modulates her
approach to the
here and now face.

havioral output. With updated information—we will initially call this her intuitions about what Daughter experiences when she smiles—she can try varying her behavior. She can experiment and generate further feedback until she finally discovers what would count for the daughter as an expression of friendliness. The advantage to acting on the feedback she elicits over, say, redoubling her initial smiling is obvious.

Given the ambiguity and complexity of communication, it is too simple to say that Mother's unproductive smiling was a mistake or the *"wrong* thing to do." This is a content judgment that stymies further exploration. In a modeling approach to communication and change, we find it infinitely more useful therapeutically to emphasize "outcomes" while recognizing positive intent inherent in the communication. As clinicians, we owe it to our clients to influence them in beneficial ways. This includes being sensitive to feedback and being willing to modify our behavior whenever our sensory experience tells us that what we are already doing is not working. To this end, an explicit understanding of the sensory structure of experience and a formal model of the dynamics present in communication will be a great boon. Given that our contact with our clients already results in our influencing their subjective experience, we, as therapists, have only the choice of doing it as effectively as we can. With the concepts and techniques I will present, you can learn to create change easily, effectively and permanently in your clients as well as yourselves.

With these basic communicational presuppositions in mind (Input channels, Representational systems, Internal processing, Communication output, and Feedback), I want to turn to a presentation of what, in my opinion, are the most salient aspects of the clinical approach. I will follow that with a chapter on the most fundamental concepts and techniques that subsequently developed into NLP. Chapter 3 will discuss how maps of experience are formed and how incongruence comes into being and is structured. Chapters 4 and 5—Change Patterns and Strategies—will present further concepts and techniques that will enable you to make not only remedial changes in your clients—i.e. solving particular problems—but also to help them make wide ranging generative changes that alter the unifying patterns which comprise entire sets of problems. The chapters on Metaphor and Hypnosis will further suggest to both your conscious and unconscious mind that the map is not the territory and that personal and clinical versions of human experience are merely powerful stories. Techniques for tapping into this creative power and using it to embellish and expand a client's personal metaphor will be suggested. Finally, I will conclude with a presentation of some of the formal patterns of change that have been observed at work in a variety of therapeutic approaches. The chapter will present the process patterns that are, to many of us, *the* important aspect of the various therapeutic approaches. The content or theoretical story simply stands as an arbitrary, but often useful, way to organize observations and interventions. This chapter began with various case sketches and many of them were surprisingly short. The types of cases reviewed were of a broad variety and give the impression that there is an unending comprehensiveness to the applicability of the ideas that will be shared in this writing. As a word of caution, some facts emerge from my work to balance the "fantastic" with the practical. The mechanistic framework offered here is not a way to do therapy but rather a way to investigate what therapy does and how to maximize that it does do what we, as therapists, intend. Not all of the changes my clients seek occur in one session and sometimes I am not personally successful with a particular client who seeks my help. When a client is quite vague about the goals he seeks or when I find that I can not stretch my personal style initially to engage the client, the time that I spend in treating his concerns also increases. Still another reason for lengthy and continued contact occured in the case of "Betty" presented later in this book (p. 142). She was severely limited both psychologically and physically. Here, the treatment period included intense contact over several months. This writing is a testament about the ability to view therapy in a new and useful way. Therefore, it is also an attempt to help my trainees and readers stretch their personal styles and effectiveness rather than their clients' duration of treatment whenever and wherever that is possible. Those of you who subscribe to an existing theoretical orientation can use the process patterns to add to the many effective choices you already have available. Irrespective of the particular content in a personality theory, there are identical formal patterns that occur in most all of them, like regional dialects of the same language. Studying this book takes you on a journey of identifying and using those patterns at various levels of complexity and organization.

An Undertaking

The traveler never really stops gathering information throughout the journey, and he uses the gathered information to better understand those places through which he passes and those people who live there. In each land, the people place a different meaning upon the fire and the rains and the wind. At times he learns the ocean can be treacherous and dangerous; at other times it can be peaceful and restful; it brings death and destruction and it brings bounty. He experiences the winds and the sun, the rains and what he's learned of fire, the domesticated animals, and the seasons. Rains, for example, are celebrated by some and feared by others because of the floods and torment they bring. The traveler not only knows this information and uses it to understand each place he goes, but he shifts that information as he travels to different lands, recombining what he has in order to find compatibility and understanding with those among whom he is currently dwelling. And this attitude of constantly recombining, of constantly moving forward on the pathway and on the journey becomes a mental harbor in which the traveler nurtures and nurses his own learnings despite experiences with the farmers in their plains, the herdsmen in their hills, the hunters in the forests and the fishermen on the shore.

Seeking shelter in their homes and tents, lean-tos, grass huts and refreshing himself with their grains, mutton and rabbit, he changes clothes appropriate for each terrain. He begins to understand their various attitudes, perspectives and those things which touch them. Unencumbered by personal ties of those he meets, the traveler learns to take his attitude with him as a guiding principle, to respect those with whom he is dwelling, to help them increase their choices with the wisdom he has brought from the journeys he has traveled up to that point. The traveler knows well that each person dwelling in his respective land understands far more of the customs and the resources of that particular area than he does—a total stranger. And the traveler learns that he can increase their understanding and the fantasies and imagination that each of the people uses in his respective land. The farmer is secure because he is settled and established. The traveler can bring to him the excitement and creativity that comes by having few roots. The herdsmen feel peaceful in their quiet, routine lifestyles, joyous to commune with the sun by day and play music to the stars by night. To him, the traveler brings the wisdom of the cities. The traveler brings knowledge of those places in which women and men completely switch their roles and lifestyles. The fishermen are rugged because their life is hard. They are strong because the sea is tough. They are married to the sea because the sea is the source of life. They are tempered and challenged in their association with it. To them, the traveler brings the wisdom of tenderness and a respect for the land to which they are unaccustomed. None would trade places with the other but each exudes a mutual respect, knowing that he has chosen his vocation and his surroundings in that way which is most appropriate for utilizing his own strength and his own temperament.

CHAPTER I THE CLINICAL APPROACH

Process vs. Content

There is both a process and a content to any act of human communication. When two people are exchanging information via their sensory apparatus, the exchange has a non-verbal form or "grammar" as well as denoted and connoted meaning or substance. Most theories of personality and social science acknowledge the process portion of the exchange. They also peg its importance within the hierarchy of their model.

Psychiatrically, process is referred to as indicators of "latent communication" (Langs 1973, pp. 294–330). It is considered a secondary expression of neurotic symptoms and affect. In Communication Theory process is called "noise" as distinguished from the "signal" (content) portion of a communication (Shannon & Weaver, 1949). Noise is thought to qualify or be a statement *about* the message given by the signal. Process is higher up the ladder in therapeutic models like Gestalt, Psychodrama, and Family Therapy. Much of their effectiveness comes from their willingness to use actively the non-verbal portion of exchange. The theories grow or suffer somewhat from the attempts to label process as, "character armor," "layers of personality," "robotism," "group culture," "family rules," and so on.

I would like to suggest that in the ensuing discussions you put aside the theoretical implications of such terms. Each theory identifies and assesses process communication in its own way. This clinical approach drawn offers you not a theory but a model.

For instance I would attend to and build the relationship *between* mine and another person's voice tone and tempo, muscle tone, facial expression, gestures on both sides of the body, posture, skin color, pupil dialation and so forth. I would respond without labeling, judging or pegging any of the behaviors according to a theory or causality ("this should occur because . . ., if they stop then she will . . ., that can't happen since he. . . ."). At a recent training workshop for therapists, I encountered a woman outside in the hallway during a break. She looked at me and began shaking her head from right to left as she said, "Can I come in? Or is the workshop almost over?" I immediately matched her voice tone and tempo and the headshake and said, "Yes, the workshop is not over yet."

Many people would respond to this incongruence by nodding ("yes") insistently to compensate. Others might mirror her incongruence and experience a confusion. If she was a client, the therapist might "meta-comment," feedback her incongruence and ask her which was the message she "really" intended. Responding to each message in the same channel through which it was offered, as I did, was very satisfactory for both of us. She immediately changed her posture, smiled warmly and entered the workshop looking at ease despite having arrived late.

Responding in this way obviously requires more involvement and flexibility on the part of the therapist: I was systematically incongruent when I shook my head "no" and said "yes," but the result is an exchange that the client can intuitively understand, decode and use.

The one technique for responding to process that does pervade many therapies is "meta-commenting" (Haley, 1963). As stated, a meta-comment is communication about communication, as in "Are you aware that when you said you are happy you shook your left fist?" This is considered to be a useful "confrontation" in several therapeutic approaches. It is one choice and, in some cases, a good one. As it often implies a judgment of dishonesty, though, it can be just another content response to the client's process. The result is an increased defensiveness on the part of the client and a redoubled attempt on the part of the therapist to convince the client that a change is awaiting when he behaves differently. Of course, both the righteous and defensive become right in their own way* as what can often ensue is a power struggle with meta-commenting coming from both therapist and client (Haley 1963). It is rather paradoxical that most clinicians are trained in graduate

*See Chapter III on calibrated communication loops, page 91.

school about the importance of unconscious communication but are offered only one possible type of response to it with their clients.

Some schools of operational therapy, notably Gestalt and Psychodrama, teach their students to respond to non-verbal behavior by systematically stressing "awareness." It is held that if clients can become conscious of their non-verbal messages, they will have "choice" and their behavior can then change. This is the same principle behind meta-commenting: to insist a client be conscious of a portion of his process communication that is *chosen by the therapist.* Through awareness-directing techniques and various questions, the client's unconscious messages are transformed into grist for the conscious mind to grind upon the therapeutic mill.

Adhering to this principle places the therapist in a peculiar and unequal social position. It also fosters problems in treatment that are conventionally labeled as "resistance," "transference," and "counter-transference" (Robert Langs 1973). These problems can always, of course, be interpreted as another demonstration of the presenting difficulty of the client rather than a comment on the therapist's limited range of responses. . . .

You can produce profoundly different outcomes by responding to a client's many messages on the same level and through the same channels as they are offered. By adopting their verbal and non-verbal syntax you side-step a number of difficulties that are secondary to producing change. In NLP this concept and technique of meeting the client on her own ground is called "pacing." I often prefer to call it analog matching or simply "matching." From the detailed discussion in Chapter 3, you will begin to be able to apply this principle to your own behavior and respond with requisite variety to the many process level messages that your clients are constantly offering.

Respect for Character

Most systems of therapy and change espouse respect for the client's character. To me, the major ingredient is an appreciation for all the messages sent by a client. If communication is offered by a client that my senses or skill tell me is outside of the client's awareness, I respect that arrangement and do not try to force anything into consciousness. I have also found it unfailingly useful to assume that each person, consciously or otherwise, is always making the best choice available to them. "When people come to us in therapy expressing pain and dissatisfaction, the limitations which they experience are, typically, in their *representation* of the world and not the world itself" (*Magic,* vol. II, p. 3). That is, a client's choices are dictated by the form and accuracy of his personal map of existence, what he *believes* to be the possible range of choices in his life. Given whatever convictions a person has about the world, himself, other people, etc., I assume he makes the best possible choice out of what he knows. The fact that I as therapist, perceive the world differently—hopefully as a place richer with choice—may enable me to help expand my client's map of possibilities. I respect the fact, however, that he is already doing the best he can, given certain limitations.

The following example will illustrate my definition of respect when working with a client. Mrs. Sims presented her problems in a sharp tone of voice, with her head thrust forward, and her right index finger often pointing at me. She listed what she wanted from therapy very explicitly: she was leaving on vacation in two days and a) wanted to be rid of her chronic car sickness, b) her trouble reading while riding in a car, c) her past tendency to gain weight on vacation, and d) she wanted to lose weight and be relieved of a general sense of depression in her daily life. She did not name as one of her problems her "pushy" behavior or any concern that seemed directly related to it.

Since Mrs. Sims' demeanor was out-right challenging I decided to use metaphor as the modality of exchange between us. Telling stories that are isomorphic with a client's problems and include metaphoric solutions is an indirect but highly effective therapeutic manuever. Chapter 6 outlines this process in more detail. I decided with Mrs. Sims to construct a story that covered her immediate concerns and made reference to the future task of losing weight in her daily life and, in a highly indirect aside, her challenging behavior. This use of metaphor bypassed her usual conscious control and yet allowed her to fully participate in the behavioral changes unconsciously. I constructed and narrated several stories that systematically identified and evoked resources from her past that were appropriate to the changes she demanded. My initial nonverbal delivery matched her voice, tempo, breathing, posture and expression.

Two weeks later, she kept another appointment with me and reported that she was nearly all the way home from her vacation before realizing that she had not once been car sick and had been reading throughout the trip, sometimes for as long as five hours. She had gained no weight over the trip either. She said that she was very satisfied particularily since she had been very doubtful that my telling stories could make any kind of difference. She then began to demand, in the "pushy" way, that I now help her to lose more weight and get over a general sense of depression.

In the second session, rather than using metaphor, I directed my approach to her conscious mind. Because of the fruits from the first session, she was very willing to follow my suggestions and lines of inquiry. At one point, discussing the sources of her depression, Mrs. Sims "spontaneously" suggested that her "pushy" behavior might be why she did not have friends. She recalled arguments she had had with acquaintances when they had confronted her behavior. We proceeded from there and the results of the second session were very satisfactory to both of us.

The point is that this client would have been mishandled if, instead of attending to her immediate problems, I had delivered meta-comments about her "pushy" character. Later she revealed to me that she had walked out on her previous therapist because he had redefined her problem as one of "being too demanding." The changes I helped to effect were made while still respecting the way she expressed herself. When she first came to see me, Mrs. Sims wanted to keep her personality, not argue or defend it. Furthermore, her "pushiness" may have a good deal of survival value at the local hospital where she works. Meeting her on her own ground yielded a number of changes she was pleased with rather than "resistance" and mis-communication.

This case underlines the importance and value of respecting the character of the client. The therapeutic principle of "using everything the client presents you" is implicit in the work. The examples also illustrate how valuable it is to utilize the clients' responses to engage their own resources as much as possible in the process of change. This means far more than simply saying, "Turn liabilities into assets." It means that every person always makes the best choice possible and, given a new and greater range of choice, will continue to do so. My role in helping change occur is that of a catalyst. I do as little as possible to facilitate, engaging the natural force and organizing principles of the clients' experience to do the rest.

Doing this, however, requires that I also have the sensory experience necessary to perceive and respond to the most miniscule changes in the client's behavior. You must have the ability to identify the structure of the process creating the presented problem and the indicators of change. Accepting all the messages a client offers presupposes being able to notice them. The client's predicates, skin color, voice tone, pupil dilation, muscle tonus and gestures provide a wealth of information and resources for achieving the desired changes. Such sensory experience will tell you that people change constantly from moment to moment anyway. As you develop your ability to make finer sensory distinctions, you can determine which channels of expression will guide you and a client to the resources needed to expand the range of choice and experience within her map.

Transpersonal Humanism

"The cure lies within." It is often difficult for therapists to apply this aphorism because the client's talents, skills and discarded dreams often seem so remote from the reality of his problem(s). The process of carrying out a hobby, however, might contain the same attitude that a client needs to accomplish a reasonable change in behavior toward one of his wife's foibles. Most individuals' resources are nearly boundless. Many clinicians have the capacity to co-create changes in clients that they cannot quite manage in their own lives. A man named Bill came to me in a workshop and asked for help to end a chronic "buzzing" in his ears. It began the day his family moved into a new house. As a number of people were helping with the move, Bill left the old house last and found that he had locked his keys in his car. He was temporarily stranded and somewhat upset. As the new house was not far the others managed to arrive and unpack the family belongings before Bill was able to "christen" his new home. From then on Bill's ears had rung. He had been medically tested for every conceivable and reasonable cause. The doctors finally told him that his problem was "psychological."

The resources Bill needed he already had. These included his ability to learn, construct visual pictures, temporarily distort his sense of time, and imagine feeling. I arranged to direct these resources toward his problem. He was able to reconstruct sensorily his experience of a past move—what he saw, heard, felt, and smelled—and use the memory to fill in the recent experience he had missed. Then, with my assistance, he proceeded to time-distort into the future and imagine having his present sense of satisfaction and completion return as often as he chose. When he completed this task he reported that the buzzing had stopped and it had yet to return at the time of this writing.

This symptom would have most likely defeated our attempts to "cure" it whether we "gave" Bill understanding, encouragement, love, or various experiences like crying, screaming, and talking to himself. This orientation allows clients to employ parts of themselves that they would have perhaps never consciously realized were the resources for the problem part. I do not have Bill's resources within me, but between the two of us we have both the means and the resources. This is not the type of humanism that fosters a subtle blaming of a client's "lack of readiness for change" or "investment in a problem;" in a two (or more) person system each person makes the best choice available as a co-creator. This is what I call "transpersonal humanism."

Now, the idea of a change taking place "within" a person is not very accurate. The experience of one individual influences the experience of anyone else present. I'm sure many of you have witnessed group therapy sessions wherein there is a rush to work with the leader after one person has resolved a conflict. In doing therapy, we sometimes get secondary personal benefits when our clients change. The sum is greater than the parts. The experience that two or more people can have together is more than that available to them separately. The patterns I will present that occur in effective personal change will also thus apply to changing experience between family members, groups, or multiple parts of a single individual.

Subjective experience is also far more than words can explain.

In a modeling or cybernetic approach we find it pointlessly limiting to explain what should or should not be or what caused what to happen. We find it far more useful and respectful to observe *how* experience and external behavior change and how to assist it in happening again successfully.

All of us involved in professional communication or therapy, are able to influence experience of our clients, notice the effect of our messages, and be influenced in turn. Therapist and client together access more than the sum of each divided. This is not so much a theoretical abstraction as an operational rule. The issue of responsibility in therapy and communication thus becomes very clear cut: each person will influence the other to varying degrees for a variety of outcomes. With the NLP model we are objectively interested in the process that brings about the outcome. *How* is depression induced and maintained? *What* sequence of representational systems is involved? *How* can we speak and move to facilitate change in the process and enable the client to reach a more desirable state?

Personality Model vs. Choice

There are numerous models of personality. They are, at times, useful maps to help chart and navigate through internal landscapes. But they are only maps. Each allows for certain options as it defines limits. Occasionally, the limits of a theory are hauntingly invisible until it is usurped by a new model. Parts of a theory remain in fashion until—according to the law of parsimony—new concepts are found to answer questions in a more compact and believable formula.

Richard Bandler was once asked to explain his "model of personality." His answer was very concise: "Choice." Instead of which ego function is being used by whom for what purpose, the focus is on *how many choices* a person has at a moment in time. Conscious or not, each choice helps or hinders a person's progress in specific ways. It is not necessary to categorize or label a client's experience when its structure follows uniform patterns. Nor must the client make way through the painful murky waters of childhood traumata for an unspecified length of time in order to change a specific aspect of his behavior. Experience and patterns of experience can be altered relatively quickly and painlessly when choice is the sole criteria. What choices clients are subsequently able to make in the structuring of their own experience will profoundly effect their entire lives.

Each of these aspects of clinical work—working at the level of process, respect for character, transpersonal humanism, and the value of choice—overlaps. When someone walks into my office my behavior could be described in the above ways all at once. While working to create change at the process level, I presuppose that there is a positive intent behind all of a person's behavior, thought, and feelings. The person is making the best choice possible under the circumstances and has all the resources he needs to change as well. It is my job as a clinician to have the sensitivity necessary to identify and be able to expand the client's limited sensory input, representation, processing, behavioral output, role enactment and social network. I also need the flexibility and willingness to utilize whatever behavior the client presents to that end.

With these clinical presuppositions in mind let's turn to a presentation of the core concepts of Neurolinguistic Programming.

Learnings

The journeyman not only shares from the wisdom and attitude that he has acquired and honed through his previous studies, he also learns to understand each lifestyle that he experiences. It is as if he sees through the eyes of those with whom he stays. He hears through their ears and becomes sensitive to the temperature and weather changes to which they are sensitive. He enjoys the smells of their foods, of the flowers, the fish, the sand and wind, just as each of them experiences those things. It's as if he learns to speak a new language, the language of each of the persons with whom he stays or journeys. He learns to survive in each of their climates just as they survive. To the extent that he does this well he seems to be one of them; he is accepted by them.

He lives and plays among them and he enriches his life as he enriches theirs. He learns their customs by learning their language and studying their particular idioms. He realizes how the same word has different meanings to different tribes, different areas of the globe. Different dialects begin to have a different emphasis for him. Soon, he is able to meet a fellow traveler on the road and identify his origin by simply noticing the adjustment he has made to his climate and his environment and listening to his dialect.

The more prepared the traveler has made himself, the more sensitive he is able to be when he experiences those that he encounters. Those that become the most sensitive have related that some people living in the very same town believe the world to be quite different. They have related the contrast between the herdsmen who raise their children in a very uniform manner as they were raised. Their grandparents, themselves and their children all notice the same shift in wind, the same color of grain, the same movement in the hills, the same sounds at night and they respond in a uniform way, sometimes with appropriate emotions and sometimes with what the traveler considers inappropriate emotions, but nonetheless uniform, as if the methodical care and careful discrimination of those things in their environment has been shared for generations and constitute a strong cultural fabric.

In contrast to this, the traveler speaks of those people in some towns where apparently the children have not been raised to notice and respond uniformly to the same things their parents do. Or perhaps the teachings were so inconsistent as the children grew up that they began to respond in a random fashion to similar events. Some children wouldn't notice the wind that other children responded to with relaxation. Some children would notice the breeze and would become frightened. Other children would hear the sound of coyotes and know that game was near. The sound of coyotes, to them, means confidence that their parents will bring the game home, that they would eat well for the next several days. Other children hear the sound of coyotes and they shiver and cower in the back of their huts.

Those travelers who have become the most sensitive have even speculated that each person they encounter on their journey has his own private world of perceptions and thoughts and beliefs. They make many explanations and many theories about the cultures in which those people live. Many make ethical judgments about the nature of the worlds in which each person privately constructs. But our journeyman is not interested in such speculations and such diversions. He gathers the learnings that he has and uses the sensitivity to respond appropriately to the attitude that he carries with him on his journey. As he does so, he begins to refine what it is that he is gathering for himself, what it is that he wants to learn, how he wants to grow, and what he wants to bring back should he ever return to the village from which he set out. And as he develops this goal more clearly, more strongly and more soundly, he also develops an increasing respectability and precision for his interactions with those fellow journeymen who, like himself, are going from town to town, from prairie to prairie, and from shore to shore.

CHAPTER II BASIC TOOLS AND CONCEPTS

The Four-Tuple

To simplify the discussion of consciousness and experience I want to employ a notation introduced by Bandler and Grinder and Delozier in *Patterns II*, specifically the notion of the four-tuple. The four-tuple is a set with four members. It is a way of representing a person's sensory experience at a moment in time. Its general form looks like: $<V, K, A, O>$. The capital letters are abbreviations for the major sensory channels: Visual, Kinesthetic, Auditory, and Olfactory/Gustatory. Since, as you shall see, it is necessary and useful to distinguish between experience that is internally generated—remembering or imagining a visual image sound, feeling, or smell—and sights, sounds, sensations, or smells that we receive from the external world, the superscripts e (external) and i (internal) are attached to the letters. So the experience of someone whose senses are tuned fully outward would look like: $<V^e, K^e, A^e, O^e>$. Another person fully attending to an internal event, oblivious of the immediate surroundings, would be represented with: $<V^i, K^i, A^i, O^i>$.

Most of us, consciously aware or not, are generally experiencing a "mixed state" in which some of our senses are outwardly attending and some of our experience is remembered or imagined. Each of us, to some extent, use our past experience to make sense of our present circumstances. The 4-tuple notation helps make explicit the psychoanalytic terms "transference" and "projection" which also allude to this; the patient is responding to what he sees, hears or feels internally to the exclusion of present external contact with the therapist. Represented visually via the four-tuple, the superscripts would be a mixture of both e and i. If you are looking at and smelling a lilac bush as you remember the sound of your

REPRESENTATIONAL SYSTEMS
THE FOUR-TUPLE

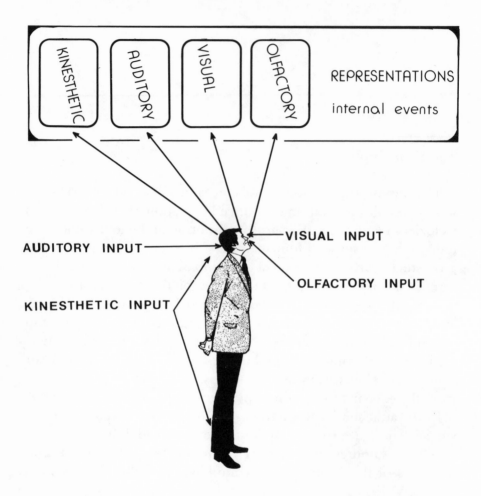

ACCESSING CUES

Up Right
Visual Constructed

Up Left
Visual Eidetic

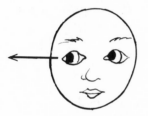

Horizontal Right
Auditory Constructions

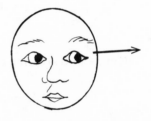

Horizontal Left
Auditory Tape Loops

Down Right
Kinesthetic

Down Left
Auditory Tonal

grandmother's voice and feel secure the four-tuple notation would look like: $<V^e,K^i,A^i,O^e>$.

The four tuple, then, is a way of visually noting the *form* of sensory experience. The content is another matter: the sound of Grandma's voice which brought back by the smell of lilacs, might also produce feelings of anxiety. The sight and smell of the flowers could also lead you to exclaim to yourself, "Those are beautiful!" and feel joyous. The four-tuple for all these subjectively different encounters would nonetheless look the same: $<V^e,K^i,A^i,O^e>$.

As you watch and listen to your clients there will be a vast body of distinctions that you can make for any experience they describe. The four-tuple is among the most elegant (simple and yet effective) ways to organize your thinking about activity in a client's sensory channels at a moment in time. You are naturally free to adapt the schema to fit your own observations and requirements.

Representational Systems Cont.

Husband: "If you can't see my point there's no need to go on talking."

Wife: "I feel like you're pushing me away."

Husband: "That's not what I see; I see you acting dense."

Wife: "I am so fed up with your cutting remarks! I always feel hurt."

From your glancing familarity with the way predicates reveal consciousness in the representational systems I am sure you can tell that the husband here is thinking in pictures and the wife in feelings. Although an obvious source of conflict here, neither of these modes of thinking is better in and of itself. They are just different.

Each person is considered to have a most highly valued representational system for each experience. As Bandler and Grinder state:

you may be able to close your eyes and see very clearly your closest friend but find it difficult to fully experience the smell of a rose. Or you may have found it easy to experience hearing a taxi horn, but found it very difficult to picture in your mind your closest friend. To some degree, each of us has, potentially, the

ability to create maps in each of the five representational systems. However, we tend to use one or more of these representational systems as a map more often than the others. We also tend
to have more distinctions available in this same representational
system to code our experience, which is to say that we more
highly value one or more of these representational systems. For
instance, those of you who have a highly valued visual representational system will have been able to close your eyes and vividly
"see" a red square which became green and then blue. Also, you
probably were able to make a very rich, clear picture of your
closest friend. It is likely that you assume that other people who
read this book will have this same experience. This is not true
in all cases. The representational systems that are highly valued
and highly developed in each of us will differ, either slightly or
dramatically. Many people can make only vague pictures and
some, no pictures at all. Some people must try for an extended
period of time before they are capable of making a vivid image,
and some can create a vivid image almost instantly. This wide
variation in the capability to create a visual representation is also
true of all the other representational systems.

Thus, each person's map or model of the world will differ both
from the world and from the maps and models created by other
people. Furthermore, each person will have a most highly valued
representational system which will differ from the most highly
valued representational system of some other person. From this
fact—namely, that person X has a most highly valued representational system that differs from that of person Y—we can pre-
dict that each will have a dramatically different experience when
faced with the "same" real world experience. (magic vol. II, p.
8–9).

So, for some, seeing is literally believing, for others, how things
sound is the key, and for others still, if something feels good it is
worth doing.*

This difference in representational system primacy partially accounts for notions like "talent" and "character" as well as the
ability to learn to cope effectively in certain types of situations. A

*In this culture, olfaction and taste tend to play lesser roles in our conscious
experience of reality.

person attempting to learn chemistry will have an easier time doing so if he is primarily visual rather than kinesthetic; having feelings about each equation one learned would likely be a slow and laborious process. Conversely, ballet will be learned more readily by an individual who can code and remember information kinesthetically. Composing music requires the ability to make extremely detailed auditory distinctions. Clients who come to us will often describe their difficulties with phrases like: "I can't see myself doing anything different; it doesn't fit my image" or "I just hear him telling me the same old story" or "I try to get a perspective on things but I still just feel depressed." Like anything else, relying heavily upon one representational system is a limitation as well as a resource; there are times when it is appropriate to see things clearly, to listen to oneself and get a handle on a problem. Obviously, the representational system used and the types of distinctions that can be made will profoundly affect the way an individual can cope with his environment throughout life. Changes in the use of, and distinctions within, each sensory processing channel will be part of the ongoing task at each point of his physical, psychological and social development.

In the course of growing up, responding to an environment and establishing behavioral programs, people learn to favor particular representational systems for particular events. The physiological factors that determine this include genetic inheritance, states of neuro-development, cell size, and migration distance within particular nerves (For a detailed description see, *NLP* volume I). In addition, environmental circumstances during a person's formative years also play an enormous role. Certain families train their children to make more frequent and elegant auditory distinctions in order to appreciate classical music or reading done out loud. This includes, in addition to the musical event or reading, an extended amount of discussion, explanation, movement of physical bodies, direction of social roles and sensory experience. A child will obviously be influenced by the primary representational systems of his parents and significant peers. If a fourteen year old, already at a certain "critical" stage of physiological development, is given piano lessons rather than a surfboard for Christmas, this will logically have implications that extend into his adult life. Assuming there's an ocean for this imaginary surfer, he may spend two or more years of his life making refined kinesthetic distinctions while the pianist spends his available time for long periods making refined auditory distinctions.

The four-tuple notation presupposes that there is activity in all the representational systems either internally and/or externally at a particular moment in time. When the husband on page 42 selected the visual predicates he used he did so because he was most aware of the visual element of his experience. Likewise, his wife was mainly aware of her feelings. If either of these individuals were questioned in detail about the rest of his/her sensory experience for the time during their argument, he/she would to some extent be able to recount sensory activity in all systems. We are taking in information and/or representing it to ourselves in all systems all of the time. However, in a particular context or, consistently, we will be aware of one system more than another.

This is easily verified in experience. Try the following exercise: sit down in a quiet place allow yourself to relax, and begin to pay attention to your ongoing flow of awareness. Don't try to control it, but rather just notice what happens.

This exercise was often used by Fritz Perls, who called it the Awareness Continuum. Typical responses to the experiment include an urge to terminate it quickly, becoming side-tracked in the content of a memory, and being able to only make one particular type of sensory distinction with any consistency. Out of this "sea of infinite possibility," you can only ever fathom a filtered stream. There is experimental evidence to suggest that the brain wave activity in an individual's primary representational system has a higher "signal to noise" ratio than the brain waves monitored for the other out-of-consciousness systems (NLP Vol. 1, 1980). For purposes here, it is enough to state that each individual will have a favored representational system at any given moment through which they present information to the world and of which they will be most conscious.

Listening to the predicates in a client's speech is just one reliable way to determine which representational system is dominant in his consciousness at a given time. There is also a vast amount of information being offered non-verbally as well. Breathing depth, skin color changes, speech tempo and tone hand gestures, and body postures are also consistently dependable indicators. In keeping with my strategy to present the most elegant number of steps, however, I want to offer you the class of non-verbal accessing cues that people in my seminars find easiest to learn and verify with their senses—that of eye scanning patterns. Bandler and Grinder and DeLozier first presented these in *Patterns:*

> . . . each of us has developed particular body movements which indicate to the astute observer which representational system we are using. Especially rich in significance are the eye scanning patterns which we have developed. Thus, for the student of hypnosis, predicates in the verbal system and eye scanning patterns in the nonverbal system offer quick and powerful ways of determining which of the potential meaning making resources —the representational systems—the client is using at a moment in time, and therefore how to respond creatively to the client. Consider, for example, how many times you have asked someone a question and he has paused, said: "Hummmmm, let's see" and accompanying this verbalization, he moves his eyes up and to the left. Movement of the eyes up and to the left stimulates (in right handed people) eidetic images located in the non dominant hemisphere. The neurological pathways that come from the left side of both eyes (left visual fields) are represented in the right cerebral hemisphere (non dominant). The eye scanning movements up and to the right conversely stimulate the left cerebral hemisphere and constructed images—that is, visual representations of things that the person has never seen before (see *Patterns,* volume I, page 182).

Developing your skill in detecting the client's most highly valued representational system will give you access to an extremely powerful utilization tool for effective hypnotic communication. There are two principal ways which I have found effective in teaching people in training seminars to refine their ability to detect representational systems.

(1) attending to accessing cues which may be detected visually. Specifically (for the right handed person):

accessing cue	*representational system indicated*
eyes up and to the left . . .	eidetic imagery
eyes up and to the right . . .	constructed imagery
eyes defocused in position. . .	imagery may be either eidetic or constructed
eyes down and to the left . . .	auditory internal

telephone postures. . .	auditory internal
eyes left or right, same level of gaze . . .	auditory internal
eyes down and to the right . . .	kinesthetics

These categories apply to normally organized right handers; for left handers they are often laterally reversed, i. e. eyes down right —internal auditory, eyes down left—kinesthetics and so on. The "happy face" diagram will apply to most of the people you meet. As always with rules there are exceptions: there are some right and left handers whose categories are reversed; occasionally an individual will store some memories through constructed rather than eidetic imagery (See transcript with Pam, Chapter 6, p. 132). Whenever you find an exception to these rules it will be a sign that you have trusted your own sensory experience over something you have read in a book and are to be congratulated.

Lead System

As you begin to listen to people's predicates and watch their accessing cues you will sometimes notice that they do not match. That is, when asked a question, someone will look up and to the left and begin his reply with "I *feel*. . . ." Another right handed individual might move his eyes level and to the left and speak in kinesthetic predicates also. What is happening is that these people are processing information through one system and expressing it consciously through another system. In NLP the former is called the "lead system" while we have been calling the latter the primary representational system. These may or may not differ for a client at any moment in time; when it does, the lead system will be apparent to you through accessing cues and the primary system will be echoed in the person's predicates. The interaction between the lead and primary representational system has been written about elsewhere as "synesthesia" or "fuzzy functioning":

Numerous child psychologists have made the point that children fail to differentiate themselves from the world around them. They have developed no mechanism either to delete incoming stimuli or even to tell the difference between stimuli originating in the outside world and those originating in their own bodies. The sensory stimuli from each of the input channels in the new

infant is represented kinesthetically. For example, if you make
a loud noise near a child, the child will cry, not only as a result
of the noise, but also by representing the noise as a body sensation. (The child, as well as many adults, will flinch.) The child's
major process of representation, then, is to take information
from all of his input channels and represent these sensory infor-
mations as body sensations. The child *sees* you smile and *feels*
good, the child *sees* you sneer and *feels* bad. A stranger smiles and
places his huge face in front of a baby; the baby feels frightened
and cries.

Thus, we define a fuzzy function as any modeling involving a
representational system and either an input channel or an output channel in which the input or output channel involved is in
a different modality from the representational system with which
it is being used. In traditional psychophysics, this term, *fuzzy
function*, is most closely translated by the term *synesthesia*. As we
will state throughout this section, fuzzy functions are not bad,
crazy or evil, and the outcome of what we consider effective
therapy is not the elimination of these functions, but rather the
realization that these functions can be the basis for much creative activity on the part of humans as well as being the basis for
much suffering and pain. The effective therapeutic outcome, in
our experience, is for the client to have a choice as to whether
he operates with *fuzzy* functions or with *unfuzzy* functions.

(Magic II, pg 100–101)

Differences in lead and primary representational systems will be
evident in many of the examples that follow—see, particularily, p.
85 with David, and the session with Joe later in this chapter. It will
be pertinent, as well, in the discussion of strategies in Chapter V.
The diagram on the next page is a visual representation of the
experience a client of mine had whenever he thought of divorcing
his wife of eight years. As he described how guilty he felt for
wanting to split up his marriage his eyes moved level and to the
left. He was leading auditorily, out of awareness, and only register-
ing the feeling of guilt. By utilizing the Overlap technique (deliberate synesthesia) he was able to come to hear the voice of his father
speaking in a harsh tone and claiming, as he often had, that "bro-
ken homes came from the men not tryin' hard enough." When Bob

FUZZY-FUNCTIONS: SYNESTHESIA
(CROSS-OVER MAPPING)

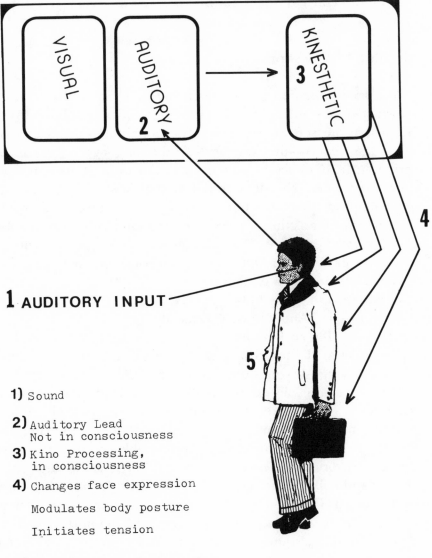

1 AUDITORY INPUT

1) Sound

2) Auditory Lead
Not in consciousness

3) Kino Processing,
in consciousness

4) Changes face expression

Modulates body posture

Initiates tension

5) Behavior initiated by the
"feeling" of the sound

realized that both the tone and the content of this message were
leading to his feelings of guilt, he was greatly relieved and was able
to begin to concentrate upon the more immediate problem of
taking steps to end his marriage. Bringing the activity in his lead
system into consciousness, in this case, led to greater freedom of
choice.

Meta-Model Questions

As all of us begin to generate language in childhood we come to
attach specific four-tuples or sets of four-tuples to specific words.
But just as our sensory representations of reality—our maps—are
not actual reality—the territory—so the language we use to describe our experience is only an approximation of our inner and
outer experience. The Meta-Model is a specific set of linguistic tools
and categories that rests upon the premise that words only have
meaning insofar as they are associated to internal representations
or sensory experience. Meta-Model questions are designed to
bridge the gap between language and sensory experience.
  Consider these two exchanges:
  Client 1: "I'm really hurt."
  Therapist 1: "About what specifically?"
  Client 2: "I'm really hurt."
  Therapist 2: "I know what *that's* like; how bad is it?" As a native
speaker of English you intuit that the two therapists, by the form
of their questions, are going to elicit two very different answers.
Therapist 1 is more likely to get a response that will lead to understanding what "hurt" means to the client and how the client has
arrived at that state. Therapist 2 will probably continue to assume
that his sensory experience of the word "hurt" is the same as the
client's and fail to fathom how the client's model of reality differs
from his own. The client's statement suggests as much as it actually
reveals; that is, he *deletes* both the source of the hurt and what it
specifically feels, sounds, smells, and looks like to hurt—potentially valuable information for the therapist and the client. By asking, "About what specifically?" the therapist helps the client to
retrieve a full representation of the dilemma, thereby taking the
first firm step toward changing it.
  The following chart briefly outlines five typical language transformations and the Meta-Model responses that can be used to elicit

the sensory experience associated with a client's words.

1. Deletion (material has been completely left out of the sentence).

Transformation	*Meta-Model Question*
"I'm inadequate."	To do what?
"I'm now able to cope."	With what? or With whom?
"The decision was reached."	By whom? or When? about what?
"My thinking is better."	About what? Better than what?
"I need help before blocking happens."	With what? Blocking of what? Happens to whom?

2. Referential Index deletion (a person, place or thing is introduced into the the sentence but not specified).

Transformation	*Meta-Model Question*
"Things get me down."	What things?
"I got a certain understanding."	Which one did you get?
"Something should be done about it."	What should be done about what?
"People get me down."	Who specifically?
"This one is the last."	Which one?

3. Unspecified Verbs (the verb is introduced but is not clarified).

Transformation	*Meta-Model Question*
"I can deal with it."	How specifically?
"He just won't love me."	Love you in what way?
"This is what I believe."	How do you believe, specifically?
"When he starts another conversation I'm compelled."	Starts how? Compelled how?
"I'm blocked."	How are you blocked?

4. Nominalizations, (words like "pride", "respect", "love", "confidence", "harmony", are introduced as nouns in the sen-

tence but they represent activity and process in the person's deeper understanding and not static nouns).

Transformation	Meta-Model Question
"There is no respect here."	Who is not respecting whom? Respecting in what way?
"She needs more strength."	Being strong in what way?
"Knowledge is most important."	Who's knowing what and in what way?
"Can you have thought without experience?"	Thinking how? Who experiencing what and in what way?

5. Modal Operators ("can'ts" and "musts" and the like. These words express limits on the nouns and verbs in the sentence and constitute limits on the model itself. These are therefore of higher order than are the first four transformations and operate upon the first four transformations).

Transformation	Meta-Model Question
"I can't do anything right."	What prevents you?
"You must go."	What might happen if I don't?
"People can't know."	What will happen if they do? What will prevent them?
"I can't think."	What prevents you?
"I can't hurt anyone's feelings."	What will happen if you do?

It should be obvious that the value of this form of questioning is in its exactness. There is a dependable and predictable logic to Meta-Model questions that insures you of sensory based answers. And by requesting all the information of the client you are relieved of having to search internally for your equivalent meanings. To translate a client's words into your own subjective experience, at best, results in valuable time and attention lost from the therapy session. At worst, the meaning you make of a client's experience may be wholly inaccurate. When you have sensory based information, you can easily identify a client's presenting limitations as well as the resources that he needs to evolve beyond those limits.

There are certain Meta-Model questions and transformations that are very important for therapists to know. I have chosen the preceeding five categories for their elemental role in mapping and representing experience. The full range of Meta-Model categories has been laid out elsewhere; if you want to become proficient in the basics of Neuro-Linguistic Programming, I strongly urge you to go read *The Structure of Magic*, Vol. I and use the study guide in the back of this book as you do. Here I want to list a few more of the most revealing transformations as a "head start:"

Lost Performatives: Statements that delete the authority behind some "should" or "must" statement. "People should know better."

Generalizations: Statements that indicate that a whole class of experience is being associated with the same meaning. "Potatoes taste terrible."

Universal Quantifiers: Indicators of the extent to which certain generalizations apply. "I'll never cry again!" "Everyone hates me."

Presuppositions: The elements in the statement that must have some existence for the statement to be true or valid. "I think unicorns ate the roses." This obviously presupposes unicorns exist, so do my roses, and that unicorns would eat such things as roses. "My wife tried to lie to me again." Presupposes a wife and that she has tried to lie to him in the past.

Causal Modeling: Making any cause-effect statement will link two or more situations in a cause-effect fashion. "As my girl friend talks to me I get happier and happier." "My family make me mad."

Mind Reading: A statement that indicates that the speaker was privy to the internal states of others. "I know what you are thinking." "You think I did it because I love Mildred."

Some linguistic transformations are of a different logical level than others. If someone says he "lives with loneliness," the change he needs to effect is categorically different from what is needed by a person who *"can't* feel anything *but* loneliness." In the first case the nominalization "loneliness" must begin to take on an active form such as "living alone" or "feeling lonely occasionally." In the second instance the Modal Operator "can't" must first be ques-

tioned and challenged to allow the person the possibility of having
any active feelings. The latter statement implies a a host of limitations, not just one. The sentence, "I will always be full of loneliness," is similar: the Universal Quantifier "always" is much like the
Modal Operator "can't" in that it restricts the conditions in which
feeling will occur. The chart below illustrates the difference in
these logical levels:

Presupposition
Causal Modeling
Mind Reading

operates upon

Universal Quantifiers
Generalizations
Lost Performatives
Modal Operators

operates upon

Deletions
Referential Index deletion
Unspecified Verbs
Nominalization

   Consider the extensive implications of the following statement:
"I can't find what I need to get love from any of these angry
wombats and its just making me crazy." Now, the speaker is in a
spot. First, he presupposes that wombats exist, then that they are
angry (mind reading), and worse, that they are making him crazy
(Casual Modeling). The bleak set of assumptions on this highest
logical level leads to further complications: at the next level we find
that there are not any (Universal Quantifier) wombats that are
other than angry and that the speaker can't (Modal Operator) find
what he needs to stop them. All of the wombats are the same, too
(Generalization). At the more mundane level, the statement implies that the speaker is having a rough time trying to find (Unspecified Verb) what the "something" is that he needs to get love
(Nominalization). All in all it is a real tough jam.

In helping this person we would best begin gathering some information by questioning at the highest logical level. If we ask him what he means by "love" or how specifically he is trying to get it, we are wasting our time. If we ask him what prevents him from finding what he needs, we might be on greener turf. We might also challenge the Universal Quantifier "any" or the generalizations about the nature of the wombats. But this would really be like trying to remove a door by chopping it down with a hatchet. By directing our questions first to logical level one—the Presuppositions, the Casual Modeling, and the Mind Reading—we begin to remove the hinge pins upon which the entire dilemma revolves. Smoothly and rapidly this opens wide, new possibilities for the speaker suggesting more alternatives to his than any of his previous choices.

Meta-Model Questions are fundamental to the basic framework of NLP. Of equal weight is the concept and process of "anchoring."

Anchoring

Stated simply, an anchor is any stimulus that evokes a consistent response pattern from a person. This can occur through any of the sensory channels as an internal or external representation. Natural language, by this definition, is a complex system of anchoring. To make sense of a given word, you must access past experience(s) and form a gestalt of sensory information—a four-tuple. In our earlier example, the word "lilac" is anchored to the sight and smell of the flower as well as Grandma's voice and the feelings of security. If I change the stimulus to "dead lilacs," the combination of these two words will evoke a completely different set of representations.

Similarly, anchors occur through all the sensory channels in a potentially infinite number of ways. The facial expressions and gestures of your friends, the sight of a crucifix, a Star of David, a flag, a billboard, an internal image of your childhood home and family, a matchbook from a hotel where you once vacationed—all are visual anchors that produce sensory-rich associations along the other parameters of the four-tuple. Auditory anchors may include music—think of couples who say "they are playing our song"—external sounds like fingernails scraping across a blackboard, radio jingles, voice tones, catch phrases and internal activity like hearing "tape loops" of old parental injunctions, mantras, and talking to yourself. A woman I knew who was raised in a very small town still, years later, associated the sound of an ambulance siren with the possible death of someone she knew personally. Kinesthetic anchors could take the form of touches, the texture of cool sheets, chronic postures and feeling states—think of how many clients you have worked with who are habituated to suffering—postures, the feeling of fullness after a large meal and so forth. Olfactory anchors are often extremely powerful. Practically everyone has had childhood memories brought back vividly from the smell of a flower, fresh cut grass, pumpkin pie, the musty fragrance of old books, etc. The possibilities are endless.

Anchors also vary across cultures. In this country, the averted eye contact of a passing woman means something entirely different than the same behavior means in Lebanon. Anchors are stimuli that are paired with a highly predictable set of responses. These pairings are usually relative and often quite idiosyncratic; the way in which meaning is made frequently makes no sense to the rational mind. Nevertheless, the phenomenon is universal in human behavior.

In workshops, I have asked professionals to pair up and perform the following exercise: sitting face to face they are to take turns establishing kinesthetic anchors (a touch) for both a highly-valued positive experience and an anxiety producing one. As one person watches his partner's face intensely express the positive experience, he firmly touches a spot on the partner's knee. A few moments later after the negative experience has been recalled and the subject's face muscles, skin color, breathing, etc., have changed expression this is anchored with a touch on the other knee. The participants are then instructed to go back and touch the two knees in precisely the same spots sequentially and discover what happens. They are often amazed by the fact that their meaningless touches reproduce the facial expressions associated to the two experiences and that the subjects report a parallel change internally.

The process of anchoring is deliberately designed to associate a stimulus to a particular experience. Clients who come to us in pain and dissatisfaction have, somewhere in their personal history, the ability to imagine exactly the resources they need to allievate their sufferings. Anchoring, whether through touch, visible gesture, voice tone or a combination of stimuli, is a way to access and reinduce these resources so that they can be brought to bear upon problems. The intensity of the anchor will depend upon how intensely an experience is recalled or recreated by a client and your timing in pairing a stimulus to it. The concept is, of course, very much like the notion of Stimulus-Response conditioning but there is a difference: anchors do not require constant reinforcement in order to be effective. If all the sensory elements of an experience are accessed and your timing is good, the anchor you introduce will "take" in a single trial.

How and where to anchor are vitally important. You want to capture the intensity of an experience as well as how it looks, feels, sounds, and smells to the client. If you anchor kinesthetically, care should be taken to reproduce the touch in precisely the same spot with the exact pressure you initially applied. Where you touch a particular client will make a difference too: a touch on the knee or shoulder might be less effective than a spot on the arm or the back of the hand where people are less frequently touched. With some clients touching is not appropriate at all; in such cases your best manuever would be to restrict your use of all anchors to the visual and/or auditory channels. Pairing a gesture that is visible to the client with a voice tone shift is often extremely effective; further, if you ask a client for a specific word to describe his problem and one to sum up the resources he needs to deal with it, these too will constitute auditory anchors. When you wanted to help the client retrieve the experience, you might verbally return to the established label for it as you lower your voice and open your left palm (a cultural anchor for asking). The fact that a portion of what you are doing will be out of the client's consciousness is to therapeutic advantage. Many of the naturally occurring anchors we respond to daily are out of our awareness—which is part of what makes them so powerful. In general, the more sensory channels through which you can anchor the better; this is called "redundancy" and is considered the best way to insure your work.

I had a client who agreed to be hypnotized during the course of our interviews. I asked him to recall the last time he was in a deep trance (retrieving resources). As he did, slight changes in his facial muscles and skin color were apparent, his breathing deepened and he seemed more relaxed. The words "deep trance" were enough of an anchor in themselves to induce a light trance. Since the language system can be thought of a series of anchors, people in effect, *do what they say.* If you ask a client extensive sensory grounded questions about the last time he felt "confident," he will begin in degrees to look and act more confident as he answers you. So any resource that a client needs can be induced by you the therapist whenever appropriate. In fact, your words and gestures are always anchors eliciting various conscious and unconscious experiences in your clients.

The unconscious nature of many anchors can occasionally cause complications in therapy. As every professional knows, there are times when some aspect of a client's behavior or verbal narration will set off associations from the therapist's own life and personal history. This is the classical countertransference phenomenon. One can appreciate how small a role is played by consciousness and current intent or motive in the countertransference drama. This special class of anchors is discussed later as a calibrated response. Clinicians also often inadvertently anchor their client's pain and limitations. If, while you listen to a client's presenting dilemma, you are nodding, interspersing his complaints with the words "I understand," spoken in a hushed tone and, perhaps, let's just say, patting his shoulder, what happens at the end of the session when you say in a low tone, with your hand again on the same spot, "I understand there have been some changes today," nodding as you do? You will very likely find the client experiencing the problem again. No matter how good your work is, it can always be undone. The concept and technique of anchoring is a way to formalize such behavior so that, as therapists, we can avoid these non-verbal complications as well as utilizing all of our own available behavior to aim at getting desirable outcomes for our clients. As with anything else, learning this technique will be a bit difficult at first. Then, as you come to master it consciously, it will soon drop out of your awareness and become automatic.

Anchoring is an important key in doing family therapy, too. If two people are together for even a short span of time, they will have developed a large number of naturalistic anchors that influence each other's experience both within and out of awareness. Leslie Cameron-Bandler's book, *They Lived Happily Ever After,* is rich with detailed description of anchoring in the context of family work. The job of the change agent is to identify these anchors and either change their experiential significance or use them in another beneficial context. How you can begin to do this will become increasingly obvious through the next chapter and the presentation of the Change Patterns.

Pacing

Pacing is the essence of what is needed to establish rapport (Charny, 1966). It involves meeting the client at his model of the world and establishing a conscious and, more importantly, unconscious affinity with him. There are as many ways to do this as your sensory experience will permit; to the extent that you can match another person's verbal and non-verbal behavior, you will be pacing his experience. In essence, this means that a therapist makes himself into a biofeedback mechanism, a mirror for the client. It is another of the most fundamental and powerful techniques highlighted by NLP for influencing behavior.

The concept of pacing, like that of anchoring, is universal. Friends pace each other naturally; they have rapport of some sort, they understand each other, have a little or a lot "in common," they speak the same language. If you meet a stranger in a social situation the first thing you do is cast for some commonality. You may find nothing to discuss but the weather or you may discover that he shares the same home town, or college, or profession, in which case you will begin to see, hear, or feel some connection with him. This could lead to further mutual interests and experiences and a deepening sense of rapport. I once got on to an airplane ill with the flu and sat next to a man who was also sick. He looked at me, saw that I was sick and apparently deduced that I, too, had run in a marathon held earlier that day. He began talking to me about how much he had enjoyed the race and I was interested to hear about it from a participant's perspective. He talked for quite some time assuming a like experience because of our mutual physical condition. When I mentioned that I had not been in the race, the man went silent and ignored me for the rest of the flight! I'm sure that you can think of innumerable instances of pacing in your own life; any emphatic connection, deep or superficial, with another human being involves pacing.

In therapy, establishing rapport with your client is, of course, critical and the following model offers a way to do this smoothly and quickly. In workshops around the country, trainers have asked participants to pair up and spend some time matching all of the behavior that one partner presents. When the partner nods her head, the other follows; when she moves her left arm the other partner mimics the movement; they inhale and exhale together and even wind up blinking at the same time. This type of matching has two significant elements to it: the first is the feedback loop established. Only with such precise responses could partner A adjust her behavioral output in any meaningful way. The second component to the exercise is the subjective sense of rapport that the participants report. It is especially distinct since the partners rarely know each other before the exercise.

You can pace a client by matching his body posture, breathing, voice tone and tempo, predicates and syntax, gross or minute muscle movements eye blinks, and so on. If you have enough sensory experience you will have a myriad of choices limited only by your own flexibility of behavior. For the sake of beginning to learn this skill for yourself I would like to suggest that you begin with something simple and take it one step at a time. Begin by matching the client's rate of breathing, then practice matching the angle of his head and then his posture. Since you have already begun to listen to and match the predicates of your clients, you will be pacing in two channels—more can follow as quickly as is appropriate for you.

The kind of matching being learned in the exercise above is direct. As with anchoring, many therapists match unconsciously with sometimes unproductive results. How often, for instance, have you spent a day seeing clients who are in pain and frustrated with their lives only to go home yourself feeling burdened with the residue of all that suffering? If you match and pace someone who is deeply distressed or afflicted with a physical problem, you may end up with some regrettable side effects. Another choice is to pace indirectly—"cross-over" matching. Instead of trying to match breathing along with an asthmatic you might pace by raising and lowering your thumb; you could tap your foot whenever a client blinked, move your hand when he shifted his head and so on. You can match in the same channel through which the behavior is expressed or through any "cross-over" channel. The main thing to remember is to be consistent.

Leading

Once an effective pace has been established, you can gracefully begin to lead the client into new experience. The dynamic of pacing and leading is pivotal to every change pattern and therapeutic operation presented in this book. Having matched the client at his model of the world, for the first effective maneuver in therapy, the therapist then changes the pace; if enough rapport has been established, the client will follow.

Try this for yourself: spend some time breathing along with another person until you think you have established rapport with him; then try alerting the depth of your breathing. If the two of you have been breathing high in the chest, begin to inhale more deeply; if your mutual breathing has been deep, make it shallower. If you have matched the person well enough, his breathing will alter in depth along with yours. If this does not happen the first time, go back to matching him and later try it again.

There are many examples of this dynamic in daily life. Consider a family saying "Grace" before a meal: everyone adopts the same posture and folds his hands during the ritual. Once the blessing is spoken, heads raise in unison and the family members may wait for someone to first pick up his silverware and commence eating. In dancing with someone, a pace must first be established before one partner or the other begins to guide the momentum. Martial Arts such as Judo and Akido are founded on the principle that meeting force with more force is not the only desirable alternative. Students are, instead, taught to blend with the aggression of their attackers and then use their incoming energy to thwart the attack.

Dr. Milton H. Erickson, the world's leading medical hypnotist, is a master at such matching, pacing and leading. He utilizes the presenting behavior of the client, no matter how superficially problematic, to take the client in the direction of a solution. Here is an example with a ten year old boy:

> A mother called me and told me about her ten-year-old son who wet the bed every night. The parents had done everything they could to stop him. They dragged him in to see me—literally. Father had him by one hand and mother by the other, and the boy was dragging his feet. They laid him face down in my

office. I shoved the parents out and closed the door. The boy was
yelling.

When the boy paused to catch his breath, I said, "That's a
goddam hell of a way to do. I don't like it a damn bit." It
surprised him that I would say this. He hesitated while taking
that breath, and I told him he might as well go ahead and yell
again. He let out a yell, and when he paused to take a breath,
I let out a yell. He turned to look at me, and I said, "It's my
turn." Then I said, "Now it's your turn," so he yelled again. I
yelled again, and then said it was his turn again. Then I said,
"Now, we can go right on taking turns, but that will get awfully
tiresome. I'd rather take my turn by sitting down in that chair.
There's a vacant one over there." (Erickson in Haley, 1973, p.
199)

Having paced the boy's hostile state well enough to begin to play
a game with him, Erickson then led him into more manageable
behavior and began to address the problem of the bedwetting.
Another extreme example was a woman who came to Erickson on
the verge of suicide because of a variety of problems. Erickson
listened to her complaints and *agreed* that only suicide could end
her chronic depression. He then casually suggested that, since she
was about to end her life, she had nothing to lose by dressing up,
going out and having one last good time. She agreed, went out, as
prescribed and changed her mind about the suicide. A short time
later, she was systematically led and assisted by Erickson to make
changes related to her problems.

This dynamic will be implicit in virtually every example I present.

A therapist might, for instance, be matching a client who was
representing a difficult problem kinesthetically. At an appropriate
moment, with enough rapport built, the therapist may pace and
lead the client from the kinesthetic channel to visual by remarking,
"I certainly know how you *feel* about being unable to *get a handle*
on things, but has there ever been a time when you had a different
perspective and were able to see things clearly?" The client is then
led into accessing visually and contacting possible resources. "I
understand that you can't *see* yourself as confident, but hasn't there
been a time in the past when you did *feel* that way?" The client here

is matched at the visual channel and led into accessing the resources available kinesthetically. As I said there will be many instances of pacing and leading in the case examples and transcripts I will be presenting. Whenever possible I will specify how the dynamic is being used. The process pattern of Overlap consists entirely of pacing, leading and anchoring.

Overlap

Overlapping is a technique for retrieving personal resources and creating new experiences for clients. The client's conscious attention is guided from the representational system it is in to awareness in another channel. This is often done with a guided-fantasy type narration that begins with description of experience in the client's favorite system and gradually overlaps: "As you *see* yourself acting confident from this *perspective,* noticing your posture and the expression on your face, perhaps the reactions others around you have, *seeing* them really *clearly,* I wonder as you *watch* yourself talking, how soon you will be able to *hear* what you are *saying* and the *tone* of your *voice* . . . .". The client might then be led into feelings by being asked to step into the picture and feel what it would be like to be confident.

A client of mine named Paula called me at home. At first, she was crying so hard that she could not speak. When I asked her what had happened she said that she had been raped. Her kinesthetic experience at that moment was so strong that she was unable to function past calling me on the phone. I told her that I was sitting down comfortably and that she could listen comfortably to the sound of my voice. When she acknowledged through her sobbing that she was seated and listening, I proceeded to assist her in overlapping from every kinesthetic sensation she was having to visual representations of those feelings. I asked her to see the room in which the rape took place, see herself in it, see her position on the bed, see the bruises on her arms and legs and how he must have been holding her to produce them, etc. Everything that she could remember feeling, I had her picture. After about five or six minutes of overlapping, Paula's voice suddenly changed. She said she could almost see the whole thing and she didn't "feel so all over the place now." A couple of minutes later, she reported that she could think about it calmly and thought that she would talk to the man—who was her former "boyfriend"—and find out if he knew that she had felt raped. She speculated on some other avenues to pursue and then we terminated the call. Having been overlapped out of her overwhelming and debilitating feelings, she now had a choice in how she represented the incident to herself. That choice led her to find other resources in turn.

Case Examples—Pacing and Leading

I worked with a child abuse family recently that had been sent over by a local agency. The father of the family virtually screamed at me in a staccato voice that I needed to teach his sixteen year old daughter to have some respect for both him and the family. In responding to this man initially I was quick to match his predominately visual predicates and load my reply with words like "learn," "respect," "right now!" In addition, though, I also delivered the words at the same volume and staccato tempo he was using. When I talked *with* him I talked *like* him. I was careful not to overdo it as I wanted to avoid suspicion of parodying him. When I talked to the other members of the family, I similarily entered their models of reality. With the father, however, I forcefully agreed that he had something he wanted his daughter to learn.

Having matched and paced him that far, I then began to lead the discussion. I told him that it was urgent that she learn respect so that she could see his interest in her. He agreed. I went on quickly to point out that his interest is one of the ways that he shows her he loves her. He agreed. I added that he was so concerned that he had even come down to this office with the family to get the message across. He agreed. "And the message," I said forcefully, "is that you love her and you want her to know it!" He again agreed. I then said, "so go ahead and tell her how you love her." When he found himself puzzled and speechless I offered to help him learn to express that to her. He accepted my offer largely because I spoke his language right down to the accent.

Another time I worked with a man and wife who had previously been seen at an Illinois agency for six visits. In that time, the social worker had struggled fruitlessly to get an agreement about what they would work on in the therapy sessions. The couple had recently participated in some sexual partner-swapping and presented themselves at the agency a short time later for marital counseling. The husband served as the spokesman and said that he wanted to have his wife learn to give him more affection and share her sexual fantasies with him. The worker had been unable to get the man to state any changes that he wanted to make in himself. All she could say about Joe with any certainty was that he "rapes his wife morning, noon, and night." The wife wanted to change the situation, but had yet to deal with her husband successfully.

When I saw them, she was only willing to speak when spoken to and he was offering one theme. He said, "I want her to learn to not terrorize me. She terrorizes me verbally and makes me scared." Joe was about five feet ten inches tall and his wife was about five feet one. He was very muscular; his body had a fine tonus so that his muscles had definition on his arms and neck. He spoke through his teeth without opening his mouth to fully form the words and his lips stayed tightly pressed against his teeth. His breathing was plainly audible because he inhaled and exhaled through his teeth as he spoke. His breathing was in his upper chest and rapid. He looked directly at me and his wife whenever he spoke. He sat in the chair facing me with his legs stretched out and crossed at the ankles. He alternated between crossing his arms over his chest and putting his hands behind his head.

In talking with the staff I discovered that they felt intimidated; they thought Joe was trying to scare them. This mind reading led to an exchange called the "calibrated communication loop" (see chapter 4 for more detail). When he tightened his mouth and breathed loudly the staff interpreted and labeled this behavior into terms which included "violent" and "resistant." They calibrated or measured their communication with him based on their assumption and the feelings of intimidation that were retrieved and anchored to it. So, Joe had more requisite variety than the staff; he could very easily control their responses to him. Thus, they had gone nowhere. Further, the more they treated him as untrustworthy, the more he experienced the staff as being against him. These sorts of communication loops are called "self-fulfilling prophecies" elsewhere. Suffice it to say, the social worker had failed to establish a pace: when I saw Joe and his wife, there was talk of terminating therapy.

So my first goal was to establish rapport. I stretched out my legs and crossed them at the ankles. I began breathing with him, to speak at his speed and tempo, using his words when I could gracefully do so. My blinking became the same as his, my face muscles tightened, particularily my cheeks and forehead, so that they moved very little as I spoke. My breathing was also as loud as his, though not to the degree that I seemed to be mocking him. After speaking, I paused as he did and when he moved his arm or head angle, I did the same (again, only to a degree). After a few minutes, I had rapport and attention from Joe and I began to ask questions to which he listened intently.

Gathering Information

Initially, there are two basic pieces of information I am after:

1. What is the current state of the client?
2. What is the desired state for the client?

The client will offer this information directly or indirectly to me. By detecting accessing cues, listening for predicates and challenging any distorted, generalized or incomplete statements with Response-Specifying Meta-Model Questions, I can very quickly learn of the problem's structure and how associations could be different at the level of process.

When I asked Joe what he wanted from the session, he made the following statement: "I want her to learn to stop terrorizing me; she makes me scared." As he said this he looked up and to the right—visual construction. I now know that he is leading visually—a constructed picture with content not yet known to me —and representing kinesthetically with words like "terrorizing" and "scared."

I chose to ask specific Meta-Model Questions in response to his statements which contained "violations" from the highest logical level I presented earlier. Specifically, "she *makes* me scared" implies Mind Reading and contains Casual Modeling *("makes")*. The presupposition to the whole notion is that *she* makes him and he does not make her. I could have directed my questioning to any of these. Note, too, that "terrorize" is an Unspecified Verb. *How* exactly she manages to terrorize might also be useful information to gather. These are choices.

We have two other categories of inquiry that often follow:

1. Have you ever in the past achieved the desired state? When and how?
2. What prevents you from doing so now?

These questions are, in effect, Meta-Model Questions since they are "about" his model. Asked with the appropriate representational system predicates and non-verbals, they will retrieve resources that can be anchored and utilized.

Given Joe and his wife's behavior together, I had good reason to suspect that his presenting statements were rather idiosyncratic to his model of the rest of the relationship. Just looking at them I knew that his meaning of the word "terrorize" was different from mine. Since I knew that the presupposition in his presenting statements would also have to be represented in his constructed image (See Chapter 4), I moved to indirectly question the presupposition in his picture using the causal-moding violation he used— "makes."

"In other words," I said, "you can't see yourself," I gestured up and to his right, *"making* her respond to you the way she should to the man you are?"

Joe immediately moved his eyes up-right. He searched his picture and answered, "No, I only see her."

S: "What do you see in your mind's eye?"
J: "I see Harriet (his wife)."
S: "Do you see yourself with her or do you just see her?"
J: "No! I just see her."
S: "Can you find a picture you remember of yourself and put the two of you both in the picture?"
J: "I'll try," (voice tone changes to a softer variety). (Joe moves his eyes over to the upper left one time and then back) "O.K., I can see us both. You know I've never done that before!"
S: "I wonder if you can see what you are doing to get her responses?"
J: "No, not yet."

This is why Joe presents the problem as Harriet having to change
her behavior: he literally can't see his own.

> S: "I would like to have you watch and see if the scene will
> clear up so that you can see how to make her respond the
> way you would like to have a woman respond."
> J: "O.K."

Since Joe can not see himself in the picture with Harriet and his
behavior toward her is initiated by constructed pictures, this then
constitutes a severe limitation. If he can't *see* himself being nice to
her, then he is not going to choose to act that way consciously.

Case Example—Retrieving Resources Through Overlap

Joe sat across from me quietly, eyes up-right, for about three
minutes. He then looked at me directly and said, "I'm getting
scared looking at myself this way." He was again "see-feeling" (See
Synethesia, page 49 to grasp what I mean), leading visually and
representing kinesthetically. I responded:

> S: "What would you like to feel when you look at yourself with
> Harriet?"
> J: "Relaxed and confident."
> S: "Do you have any pictures about times when you were
> relaxed and confident in the way you wish to be right now?"
> J: (Looking up and to the left) "Well, there are times with my
> friends when I have felt that way and I liked it then and I
> felt confident." (Still speaking through his teeth and
> breathing in shallow audible gasps.)
> S: "Locate one of those times that you saw your acquaintances
> and let me know when you have it."
> S: "O.K., Now see yourself in that scene and see yourself
> feeling relaxed."
> J: "I can see it."
> S: "Now, step into the picture and have the feelings that you
> see him having in the picture."
> J: "Yeah. I've got them . . . and they feel good."
> S: "Good, now keep them constant or intensify them and
> watch the picture of yourself with Harriet." (gestures to
> Joe's upper right.)

J: "It's hard." (Looking up-to-the-right.)

S: "Well, then take your time and also watch the Joe in the picture change as you feel the relaxation and comfort."

So: I have a direct report from Joe that he needs the resource of feeling relaxed and confident to go on picturing himself with Harriet. I then asked him to search with his lead system for what he needed. He found the picture with no trouble and I then had him overlap from the picture into the good feelings—visual to kinesthetic. "Now, step into the picture and *have* the feelings . . ." Note that this is the reverse of the kinesthetic-to-visual overlap that I used with Paula above. It makes no formal difference which "direction" you have a client overlap; you can do it through any combination of sensory channels. In Joe's case, going from pictures to feelings was easy—he does it every time he gets scared. I simply used the same pattern to get him to a resource. He now has an expanded picture of himself and Harriet as well as a way to let it continue expanding in comfort. This he can use toward developing the behavior he wants or needs to have with his wife.

At this point, by the way, Joe had demonstrated a very high degree of participation relative to what the staff told me to expect from him. I attribute this to the matching and pacing I did. I spoke his language. I entered his world and was interested in his behavior with Harriet and his image of himself as a man. I gave him my attention rather than my interpretations; when he said he was scared I did not diagnose him as "resistant". I helped him immediately access the feeling that he would rather have. I believe that this sort of behavior on the part of a therapist is what determines how cooperative a client is and whether he makes the desired changes. Why would people *be* in therapy if they were "resistant" to change? I take the fact that someone has come into my office as a statement that some part of them, at least, wants to behave differently. I also take it as a challenge to be maximally flexible in my own behavior and help them get what they want.

Case Example—Anchoring

Joe was sitting "relaxed and confident." I do not know the actual subjective content of these feelings, just that the words are anchors for the four-tuples that he needs to go on while

watching him and Harriet in his mind's eye. I moved to give
Joe a way to control the coming and going of the feelings:

> S: "Joe, when the feelings are sufficiently intense and you are
> satisfied that they are, then I want to suggest that you hold
> your wrist like this (demonstrating how to hold the wrist of
> the left arm with the right hand) and sort of anchor them
> to this spot."
>
> J: (moves his hands in the manner suggested) "O.K., Yeah, I
> can do it. That's really different."
>
> S: "Do you mean that you didn't know you could do that kind
> of thing to use your memories for your own betterment?"
>
> J: "I never knew it." (Here Joe looks back up into the visual
> construction that he had been examining.)

Once this anchor was established I left him in complete control
of it and proceeded:

> S: "Have you been able to picture yourself getting the behav-
> ior you want from your wife?"
>
> J: "Yeah, she is there with me and I'm (breathing loudly)
> sitting on the couch touching her neck and rubbing her skin
> on her shoulder and down her back."
>
> S: "Now you can see how you effect her response to you."
>
> J: "She is responding like Olive Oyl."
>
> S: "What do you mean by Olive Oyl? How specifically is she
> responding?"
>
> J: "You know, Olive Oyl in the Popeye cartoon! She is cling-
> ing to me and making me feel like a man the way Olive Oyl
> does to Popeye."

We now know that his visual ideal for her behavior is modeled
on the Popeye cartoon. No wonder he has trouble! At this point,
either Harriet is going to have to act like Olive Oyl or Joe must
learn to be able and willing to cast her in a different role. More
importantly, Joe must be able to represent to himself visually how
he would look as he encourages and elicits new responses from
her.

The easiest choice for bringing this about is to continue using
anchoring to introduce new behavioral options into the picture
just as we had accessed the pleasant feelings. Here I depart from
the transcript as what followed was a lengthy search for other

possible behavior that would influence Harriet in new ways. It turned out that he had seen and even used actions that supported the emotional, occupational and recreational pursuits of Harriet and other women in his life. Using the resources of his own past behavior and memories of men he respected, Joe was able to generate a number of new options. Every time he did we checked with Harriet to find out if she would be satisfied. Then I double-checked with Joe to discover whether he wanted to enhance his ability to encourage and support Harriet in these new ways. When the answers were "yes" we proceeded to make sure that Joe could *see* himself performing differently and that he looked comfortable in the picture. Thus, the new images, feelings, and verbal descriptions are anchored to Joe's picture of himself and Harriet. In the future, when Joe refers to his previously "terrifying" image of Harriet, he will instead have pleasant feelings and new ways of approaching her.

Joe left the session with the ability to use different voice tones, facial expressions and body gestures in certain situations with Harriet. He also had generated for himself some entirely new ways of relating to a woman that were not sexual nor even physical in nature. He also gained increased ability to use his own conscious (visual constructed) thinking process. He thanked me for my time and we parted with mutual respect.

Future Pacing

The true test of any successful change work is whether the new learnings and choices created in therapy generalize to the "real life" contexts in which the client needs them. Otherwise, no matter how well a session goes, the client's behavioral gains will be anchored to his experience of being in your office and perhaps the sight of your face and the sound of your voice. To "future pace" is to bridge this gap, to anchor in the choices so that they are associated with representations of anticipated events.

There are several ways to accomplish this. One choice is to anchor the new choices to the stimulus that originally triggered the problematic behavior. I did this with Joe: his original visual representation of Harriet triggered a new series of images of both of them with pleasant feelings. In the future, this sequence will occur as automatically as the original one did. In the reframing paradigm

(p. 115), the "part"—i.e. stimulus pattern—that is responsible for the problematic behavior is asked to "take responsibility" for implementing the new behavior created in therapy. This, too, is anchoring. Another way to future pace is contextually: the therapist asks, "When will you first know in some future time and place that you need this resource? What will you first see, hear or feel?" The client's possible new reaction(s) are then rehearsed for that future context. This rehearsing serves to associate the resources at an unconscious level and, since, both fantasized and actual experience share the same neural pathways in the brain, one is as effective as the other for changing behavior. Also, it is very effective to use any naturally occurring anchors as triggers for the new choices. For example, if a man folds his hands together and laces his fingers whenever he feels helpless, then anchoring the new behavior to that habitual gesture will constitute an effective therapeutic maneuver.

Whenever possible, I also recommend that you test your work. That is, if the client's presenting problem is that she feels frightened when anyone points his index finger at her and frowns, I would advise you to do it at the end of the session and watch her reaction carefully. If another client has worked on being more assertive, you might do well to try bullying him and find out whether the changes you have worked on making have taken root. Likewise, work on a snake phobia could be tested with a rubber snake. Silly as this might sound, the value will be apparent to you the moment you become that active. By structuring a situation so that a client has to respond to the stimulus he originally found problematic, you will elicit very direct feedback that will tell you whether your work has succeeded or that there is more to be done. If the latter is the case, you can then simply proceed with the next therapeutic option.

If someone wants to cross a river and you know that there is a bridge several miles north, it would be helpful of you to remind that person that he has good strong legs, money for the toll, and that he has crossed bridges before. What he also needs is directions to the bridge so that he can see where it is and hear the sound of the water passing beneath him as he steps firmly over it. Only then can he continue on his way. Future pacing is the best way for you to insure that the resources that your clients shore up during a session span across into their daily living. In my opinion, it is among the most important steps in all successful therapy.

This chart is presented as an aid to further organizing your intuitions about how and when to use some of these powerful tools while working with clients.

	Establish Rapport	Gathering Data	Accessing Resources	Programming Behavior and Building Experience
Pacing	Channel per Channel	Continue Pace	Continue Pace	Continue Pace
Matching Rep. Systems	Match Predicates	Data is gathered best by using the approp. Lead & Rep. Systems	Use Lead & Rep. System	Each Rep. System will have valuable resources
Overlapping	X	Overlap for full representations	Used to get full representations	Used in future pace
Meta-Model Questions	X	To get sensory based answers. Used to identify the limiting form of the exp.	Helps specify what resource will be made of in desired state	X
Anchoring	Anchor the rapport. Select your words to pace		Used to build small changes into needed resources.	Used to associate both 4-tuple components and behaviors

Summary

The concepts and basic operations offered in this chapter are meant to help you organize your thinking about the structure of subjective experience and how to *approach* changing it in your clients. We all build internal representations of the world that rule our subjective experience and what we communicate to each other. Precisely how a client structures his reality and the problems he brings into your office can be revealed to you through your sensory experience of accessing cues, sensory based predicates, naturally occurring anchors in their behavior. Using Meta-Model questions and response-specifying questions will also elicit sensory grounded descriptions of your client's map and help you to challenge its limits as well. Possibilities exist in the land of sensory experience.

The definition of communication bears repeating: we communicate when we influence each other's experience. As a therapist you can't *not* influence your client despite any intention to avoid being "manipulative" or "interfering with the process." Your client will always be responding, in some way, to your words, voice tone and tempo, gestures, posture, breathing, facial expressions, etc. Once you have learned to use the tools of pacing and anchoring, you will have a means to do what you do already in a systematic deliberate way that will enhance your therapeutic acumen and facilitate consistently powerful results. The major factors in your success are a) how much sensory experience you are able to bring to your clients, b) how flexible you can become at adapting your own behavior to meet the client at his model of the world, and c) the specific patterns you utilize to facilitate therapeutic outcomes you are after on your client's behalf.

With these basic tools and concepts we are now prepared to explore how experience comes to be structured in the first place and the problematic forms it can take. First, though, I want to urge you to begin to test the techniques and observations I have offered. Discover and verify for yourself how useful and powerful the knowledge of eye scanning patterns, sensory based predicates, Meta-Model questions, anchoring, analog matching and pacing can actually be.

Memories

The journeyman of whom we are thinking was always eager to speak of those places to which he had traveled. He kept a journal and that journal read as a logbook of the learnings and perceptions that he had in his travels. In one town he speaks of a group which doesn't fit any particular mold. As members of the tribe they become so specialized that one would hardly think that they were from the same land at all. There were blacksmiths, midwives, shamen, and lookouts. There were storytellers and minstrels. The blacksmiths never paid attention to the windchimes. They never heard the rustling of the leaves that the minstrels used to spin their tunes. The lookouts were not interested in the tales told by the storytellers; they never heard those tales except for on those occasions that they used them for enjoyment. And yet the storytellers made their livelihood by gathering the tales of different gods, different personages. Likewise, the lives of the minstrels and storytellers did not require that they attend to the specific needs of others like the midwives did. The shaman, on the other hand, seemed to play an entirely different role in the culture, unlike that of the blacksmiths or the minstrels. They noticed things both arcane and profound. You could depend upon the shaman to have noticed the sparkling diamonds in the water, the rhythmical cycle of the tides and the sun and the moon. They began to regulate their lives by these rhythmical cycles and when they spoke of these to the blacksmiths, the blacksmiths shrugged their shoulders and walked away because the only rhythmical cycle the blacksmith was interested in was that of the bellows, and of his arm which lifted the hammer and shaped the material of his trade.

And as the traveler told of this story, he made special note that the people who seem to have very little in common in this society nonetheless stayed together, each person performing what seemed to be an integral part of the society's needs. The music and art and stories and tools, even the beliefs, were similar even though they were expressed differently by the various families and the different tribes within the community system. Somehow, specific needs and changes and pressures reflected by each individual or each family were able to be used as a guideline for the members through the rites of passage that they took as they went from childhood to adolescence, from adolescence to manhood and from adulthood into their respective roles as elders. And finally the elders died, and when they did they had managed to pass on their special trade to those who had followed them. And there was an ever present following for each of the persons.

It baffled the traveler how dissimilar that society was from the one he had lived in only a week before where all the herdsmen and all the herdsmen's children and all the elders knew of similar sounds in the wind and similar colors of the grain. And the journeyman told of the story but made no special conclusions about which was better or worse nor which was more appropriate for whom. He simply told the story of his various travels with a special interest and shared the special abilities he had gained to live among such diverse peoples. "Come to know their special ways," is all that he would say. "Each has his own value. Each knows best."

III MAPPING AND INCONGRUITY

Central to our learning to recognize and apply process patterns in the clinical setting is what I call the "Construction Postulate." It states that each person selectively perceives and creates his subjective reality. Though constantly subject to new input and revision, this created world is *the* reality in which we live. We construct "external reality" from the learned perceptual distinctions we make with our five senses. We may at times shift our focus, reach for new possibilities, or sound out directions that were unheard of; what will have changed is not the actual world, but rather, our sensory mapping of it.

You may have sometime seen the delightful reaction of children discovering snow for the first time. Until a child has learned, through visual, kinesthetic and, perhaps, gustatory sensing, what snow is, the word will carry no charge. Once snow is encountered sensorily the child will still not know what it *really* is; he has the unprecedented opportunity to make snow any number of things. This meaning is partially influenced by the child's family and culture—Eskimo language of Greenland has over seventy words for snow. First, though, snow must be sensed somehow and that sensing must be sufficiently intense to produce signal and be coded neurologically.

There are constraints imposed upon us by our neurological make up and our individual sensory "biases" that limit what classes of phenomena we can perceive. Telescopes, microscopes, and some audio equipment serve to translate sensory remote realities into the type of signal we can recognize. Without their aid we would know very little about the existence of super-novas, viruses, microbes, infra-red light, radio waves, and so on. Such equipment extends our senses, giving us maps of territories we would have barely supposed to exist.

Once a primary experience occurs, formal distinctions will be established and stored within each sensory system. We all take for granted the contours of rooms, automobiles, and other people, for instance. Forming these sensory patterns is similiar to making die-casting molds. Consider the face of a friend who had a beard and later shaved it. If you are male and have ever done this, you know that some of your aquaintances, at first, did not recognize you, while others looked you over at length wondering what was different. People who lose limbs often report being able to still feel them. Once a perceptual mold has been cast, a representation is formed that will shape future perception. Unless changed and updated, it will be as much a limiter of experience as a guide.

The marriage of language to sensory experience brings on a new dimension to this process. Language learning in children occurs when brain and muscle development reach a certain critical level. The child then attaches sensory equivalents to the first nouns and verbs offered by his parents. Among families and cultures, particular words will get paired with similiar events. By the group's standards, the teaching process is the most effective when individuals learn to anchor shared perceptual distinctions to given words. Though the content of the word/experience will always vary slightly, the distinctions will otherwise tend to be uniform to the extent that a *type* of distinction is shared (David Gordon, 1978, pp.103–142).

So "Snow", to those raised in one family is primarily a kinesthetic experience; the shared perceptions are of a similiar temperature, texture, and the feelings of all related physical activities. In another family, the word might be associated with the sound of heavy boots swishing and crunching, between a muffled silence. In still another group, snow would be distinguished for how beautifully it blankets a landscape, the crystalline structure of its flakes, etc.

Reality Postulates

Down through the ages debates have raged over the extent to which human beings control their own fate, create their reality and guide their own destiny. It is certainly obvious to all of us by now that we selectively perceive and make meaning of only a fraction of the sensory data available to us. Psychology, both clinical and experimental, has employed various metaphors to explain this process. Regardless of which theoretical angle you view as the most accurate, the postulates below are consistent with the model of therapy and human experience that *Practical Magic* offers and I'm indebted to a similar taxonomy proposed by George Kelly (1963).

Postulates

a. People build internal replications, maps, simulations, or representations of events. Construction Postulate:

b. Experience and behavior are channelized by the way people construe events. People operate out of their maps and not on the world of sensory experience. Experience Postulate:

c. Individuals differ in the simulations, or constructions they create of similar events. Variance Postulate:

d. People evolve ordinal relationships, that is, a structure or a pattern, between the contents of their internal representations. Organization Postulate:

e. Each person may operate a finite number of polarity patterns. Dichotomy Postulate:

f. A person may employ a number of sub-systems which are incompatible with each other (incongruity). Fragmentation Postulate:

g. People make the best choice available to them at any given time. Choice Postulate:

h. The system with the greatest range of options or choice will be the controlling element (Principle of Requisite Variety). Variety Postulate:

i. A person's construction is convenient for a specific range of events. Range Postulate:

j. Novel experience may create variance within the *content* of the mapping: Changes in the ordering of experience will create variance in the *process* of mapping. Dimension Postulate:

k. Changes in understanding and choice will be limited by the range of events which are experienced. Modulation Postulate:

l. The extent to which people have similar mappings they have similar psychological processes and similar subjective experience. Commonality Postulate:

m. The extent to which a person construes the structure of

another person's experience and operates within it, they experience a consensus reality. Sociality Postulate:

Visual Syntax

Once the Meta-Model transformations are learned, it becomes quickly apparent that our verbal reports of experience are packaged according to specific syntactic forms. Even listening to your friends will reveal that they have only a few discrete patterns. As we have said, people experiencing stress and personal limitations will be found to have an even more impoverished repertoire, especially when they try to talk about the problem area.

Remember our earlier expanded definition of syntax. It is convenient to borrow from the NLP model and use the word in reference to the sensory form of experience as well as the structure of grammar. Subjective experience has a form and order that can be detected through language. The selection of words is obviously able to operate beyond the jurisdiction of the conscious mind; otherwise talking would be an impossibly slow task. Listening to your client's selection of words will reveal not only which representational system(s) they are processing their experience through, but also how exactly the representations are formed. Just as the auditory channel—dealing with language—can be questioned with Meta-Model questions so, too, can the visual and kinesthetic systems be specified and enriched by following the same laws of form and transformation.

The difference between the experience attached to the words "relaxing" and "relaxation" is not just a linguistic one. The use of a verb to describe experience implies movement, action, an ongoing change. The nominalization "relaxation" suggests a thing, a static state. The nature of the feeling states implied by the two words is very different. Many people find highly active sports relaxing, but they are not in a state of relaxation when playing. The same distinction is applicable in these contrasting sets of statements: "I want more love in my life"—"I intend to do more loving;" "I can't get rid of this depression"—"I've been depressing myself all week." The verb usage includes the possibility of choice and change while the nominalized form intuitively expresses a helplessness.

The difference between representing the same experience actively or passively is a difference in what we shall call "chunking" (George Miller, 1956). It has been well established that conscious attention is limited to a specific number of bits or chunks of information at any point in time. How these chunks are formed will influence a person's ability to cope. If a client consistently represents his experience in nominalizations, it is safe to assume that his internal representations take on the same form, and are chunked as nominalizations (non-changing experience). In my experience people who organize their perceptions in nominalizations do not have as much flexibility in their behavior. Being able to determine how a client chunks his experience will tell you a great deal about how much range he has in responding.

For instance, I recommend that the next time you hear a client talk in nominalizations about his internal picture, you assume the picture to be one of frozen action. If someone chunks visual data in nominalizations he may fail to notice change and action in his visual field. If a man describes his childhood environment as one in which he "didn't see any love," he will probably be unable to "see love" in the present. Until he learns to represent differently, he will continue to see a frozen pictoral memory and miss any ongoing changing data in the present as well.

Examples of Deletion in the visual channel are common. Picture the last time you were in an airport. As you reexamine the memory you may realize that you only have visual recall for the people in the airport and not the lobby signs or the gift shop. Of all there was to see, you represented only a fraction of it to yourself. Deleting visually may be a limit or resource depending upon what is deleted. Some of us fail to delete the appropriate material in certain circumstances and the net result is that we are plagued by useless or distressing pictures. Others of us delete so frequently that we literally overlook options we could utilize for enriching our lives.

Referential Indexing done visually means simply picturing the *things* one sees. Go back to the airport again: did your visual recall include people moving through the lobby or just people in the lobby? Do you recall planes taking off or just planes in and of themselves? If you were asked to comment freely on the memory would you emphasize *things* or *processes*? Shifts in referential Indexing means being able to move things around visually, from picturing various combinations of living room furniture to putting yourself in someone else's body and modeling his complex behavior.

Distortion in visual perception is apparent when a careful translation of certain words is sought. Looking at her secretary's face, a boss might see the minor muscle movements in the lips, cheeks, jaw and chin area and describe the movements with the word "frown." The word might not apply at all to another observer's experience.

Applying the *form* of the words a client uses to describe his existence to the pictures, feelings, and sounds that make up subjective experience will help you to determine the limitations that those representations contain. The more rapidly and precisely you can identify a client's presenting limits, the more efficiently you can work to expand them.

Mapping and Incongruity

Incongruent experience can be thought of as a four-tuple comprised of mis-matched chunks of content. The visual, auditory, kinesthetic, and olfactory elements of a given act or memory are inconsistent. For instance, again, when someone reports feeling "depression," the nominalized kinesthetic chunk remains constant despite changing visual and auditory input he experiences. If this person goes to a rock concert, he will maintain the negative feeling even though the band sounded good and the show was nicely lit. The person might later report the concert to have been "wonderful" with little or no excitement in his voice and a listless shrug of the shoulders. His unchanging feeling affects both the experience and his attempt to communicate it. To the observer, the several channels of communication will not present the same message. This is called "simultaneous incongruity."

The other form of incongruity is called sequential incongruity. The Fragmentation Postulate states that an individual may employ a number of sub-maps that are incompatible. Sequential incongruity arises when, say, two events in the same context are mapped congruently but the content of the mappings are radically different. So a child goes to school for the first time and finds her classes "fun" yet when she returns the next day, she is bullied on the playground and scolded unreasonably by the bus driver. These two four-tuples are now anchored to the word "school" among other things; they are both congruent in and of themselves and wholly incongruent with each other. If this child is subsequently asked how she likes school, her face might initially light up at the word and then show signs of fear.

Whether incongruence occurs simultaneously or sequentially it must be regarded as an accurate and sincere representation *for an individual.* People do the best they can, given their experience and how it is mapped and chunked. If a client tells us that he wants to get better and he shakes his head "no" at the same time, we are faced with incongruent communication. It is too facile to hold one part of the communication as "the real message" and ignore any others.

Both messages are to be considered valid and real; they simply mean that experience in the client's history has been mapped and chunked incongruently.

Case Example

In front of observers I worked with a couple. The man said: "Sure, I love her. I told her I do." As he spoke, he slowly shifted his eyes left to right horizontally, then defocused them up and to his left, and made a fist with his left hand. He shook his head in the manner usually taken to mean "no." His wife said, "I guess I believe him." Her face muscles went flat and the color left her cheeks. Her shoulders slowly raised in a shrug and her voice tone was monotonous. Of the observers, about half believed his verbal statement and half did not. Others thought that she was not convinced while others still had theories about her non-commital response.

From his accessing cues we can surmise that he is conscious through his auditory representational system. He recalls hearing himself say what he is now repeating: that he loves her. This is consistent with his horizonal eye movements from left to right. As we shall see and hear later in the chapter, activity on the dominant side of the body coincides with the use of the primary representational system. The husband's right hand remained in his lap as he accessed auditorily. It follows that activity in the least conscious representational system will be accompanied by expression from the less dominant side of the body. In fact, just as the client defocuses his eyes and directs them up to his left, he begins to make a fist and shake his head "no." Upon inquiry, he was not only able to realize that he was recalling what he had said to her, but that he had, "in the back of my mind," a picture of a domestic quarrel from several months back. In the picture his wife was striking their daughter. He had witnessed the incident and still associated to it when thinking of his wife in the present.

He was feeling strong objections to her past action at the present point when he shook his head; that is, the visual representation was triggering strong negative kinesthetic sensations out of consciousness. As he was usually aware of only auditory information, this visual memory became a strong anchor that led to an incongruence between his words and nonverbal behavior.

Polarity

It is our Internal Representations (IR) that comprise our version of reality and dictate our External Behavior (EB). It should be apparent by now that our maps of reality, though shared in varying degrees, are ultimately highly personal and idiosyncratic. No one else completely shares your way of making meaning, the associations and anchors that have developed over the course of your personal history. When you talk to another individual, you have no final assurance that the pictures, words, and feelings that you intend to communicate will be accurately received. You can, of course, always *assume* that the message you projected is the one being received, but this amounts to little more than making IR's about your own representations.

Sometimes people will hear words, feel a touch, or see a gesture and respond to the logical *opposite* of what was intended. This is a Polarity Reversal. It is a kind of automatic distortion best suggested by colloquial labels like "being contrary" or "stubborn." Person A says to person B, "I like your new hairstyle," and person B thinks, "He's being sarcastic;" A hypnotist suggests to a subject that he is beginning to relax and the latter tenses; Roomate A asks Roommate B to take out the garbage and B says "OK," but then can't bring himself to do it. Polarity Responses are the behavioral dynamic at work in most instances of therapeutic "resistance." They also govern behavior labeled rebellion, subversion, and various forms of conflict within and between people. They are the constant in most political activity. When polarity reversal patterns are identified they can be easily predicted.

The way you respond to a Polarity Reversal depends upon your goals in communicating. If you want rapport with a person, you must respect the polarity and pace it. A friend of mine has a small daughter at a familiar phase of child development: If her parents tell her to take a bath she says "No!"; if they suggest that she go to her room, she goes anywhere but her room. The parents put up with this behavior for some time before they hit upon the idea of telling Sara to "Go anywhere except the bathroom," when they wanted her to bathe. Similarily, I was once introduced to a man who was described as "violently anti-social." As I extended my hand to him I said, "Go to hell, how are you?" The hostile expression on his face gave way to a light smile as he replied, "Bug off, pretty well, thanks."

In both of these examples the pattern of polarity was paced in order to deliver the intended message. A Polarity Reversal, of course, attempts to allow for two possible reactions. It has often been noted that the acts of conforming and rebelling are formally similiar since both presuppose that the actor is being involuntarily controlled. The content may differ radically, but a person is not "free" to rebel or comply unless he has been given a context in which to do it. Thus, a "resistant client" is potentially very cooperative if the therapist is willing to pace and creatively utilize polarity patterns.

The structure of Polarity Reversals can be explained with the distinctions of 1) External Stimulus, followed by 2) IR, followed by 3) the EB. If an individual has a visual representation of a smiling face and the picture is associated to a pleasant kinesthetic experience, it is likely that when the person sees a similiar smile on someone's face that the pleasant feeling will be triggered. The External Stimulus would thus activate the IR—positive K—and lead to the EB of smiling back.

Suppose, however, that you grew up in an atmosphere where kinesthetic pain always followed a smile. A client of mine named David was frequently physically abused as a child. As far as he could recall, his father only smiled when he struck David. While growing up he also had a number of experiences outside of home that contradicted the original meaning he had attached to smiling. Since people smiled at David daily without hitting him, he was left with two congruent maps for the same behavior and an incongruence in his own behavior that was most noticeable in

his voice tone and facial muscles. When David was smiled at, he
would attempt to return the gesture and produce motor behavior
consistent with the memories he had of people away from home.
But outside of his awareness he was also reacting to the other set
of memories by wincing. His face would develop a partial smile
on the left side and a sort of cringe on the right. His physical
experience at these times was very familiar to him and labeled by
him as "chronic tension." I think this tension is more usefully
modeled as the outcome of two incompatible memories driving
mis-matched motor operations. The muscle reactions produced
by this conflict was so severe that his voice tone quavered whenever he spoke to someone smiling.

This example is quite extreme, but such Simultaneous Incongruence is not uncommon. David's IR's totally dominate his External Behavior. Of course, his EB will be received by others and
translated into their system of meaning. The EB that David puts
out will lead to other Internal Representations that will mediate
the responses people have to him. The IR's others make to understand David's incongruence may also be out of *their* conscious
control. In fact, David tended to confuse people who were unfamiliar with his background. This confusion was a tremendous handicap in that he elicited it without choice or control; socially, David
was often avoided or treated unfavorably.

Lateralization

It has been my pleasure to demonstrate in training seminars
another set of sensory based distinctions that are, like the eye-
scanning patterns and predicates, easily verified in experience. I
have come to expect a certain amazement from participants when
they realize that the movements and gestures on the right and left
hand sides of the body reveal so much about the sensory structure
of a person's experience. The term "lateralization" refers to the
splitting of tasks between the two hemispheres of the brain (Gazzaniga, 1967) and, naturally, this activity is expressed somatically.
The following observations should be double-checked with your
sensory experience and, like all generalizations, will periodically
not hold true. In any such case I would urge you to act on what
your senses reveal.

In general, the primary representational system will initiate

LATERALIZATION

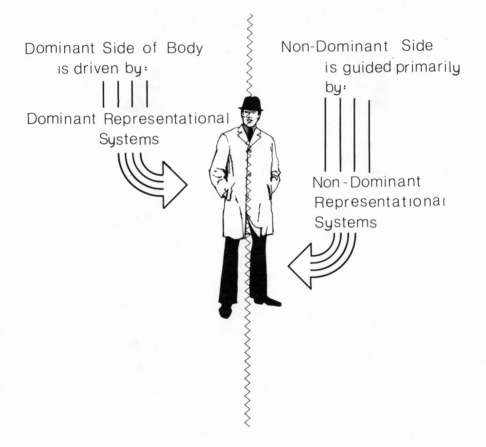

LATERALIZATION EXAMPLES

A right-handed person
who is primarily aware
of visual experience.

A right-handed person
who is primarily aware
of auditory experience.

A right-handed person
who is primarily conscious
of kinesthetic experience.

A left-handed person
who is primarily conscious
of visual experience.

motor behavior in the "handed" side of the body. The movement
in the less dominant side of the body will be dictated by activity in
the less conscious representational systems. A right-handed person who thinks most often in pictures, then, will more often express movement in the right side of the body when he is accessing
and representing visually. In parallel fashion, the left side will be
the most expressive when this person is generating auditory and
kinesthetic activity. Another person who is left handed and represents experience mainly auditorily will more frequently gesture
with the left side of her body. When she is accessing visually or
kinesthetically, the primary movement will be from her right side.
Another normally organized right-hander who mainly thinks in
feelings will gesture with his right hand when doing so and when
accessing pictures or words will express through his left side and
so on.

This means that incongruently mapped experience will be expressed simultaneously or sequentially in the motor behavior of
the two sides of the body. A client of mine named Jane, for instance, usually moved both her hands as she spoke. In one session,
the topic turned to situations in which she was indecisive. At one
point, she (a right hander) looked up-right (visual construction)
and moved her right hand as she said, "I thought I would really
like to see Marty again." Then she proceeded to place her right
hand in her lap and lifted her left hand palm up, as she looked
down-left (internal dialogue). Accompanying this she said: "But,
on the other hand, I tell myself that something is missing." This
type of incongruence is a common phenomenon and, as you will
begin to notice, is just as commonly expressed in the two sides of
the body concurrent with the dominant and non-dominant representational systems used by a person.

Somatic Difficulties

There are a number of theories concerned with incongruence
expressed through the body. Usually these theories presuppose
that the body is the primary "cause" of difficulties in character,
thought, action, and social behavior. The body is sometimes lik-
ened to a hydraulic pump and incongruence is compared to
blocked discharge or the inability of the body/pump to take in
fresh water or to discharge its current storage (Lowen 1958). This

is an interesting and occasionally useful metaphor, but I find it much more fruitful to approach the body as a system of representation. Make no judgment on how it ought to work, but rather attend to how, specifically, a person expresses himself somatically.

Someone using the hydraulic pump metaphor would diagnose David's incongruence (p. 85) as a type of blocked discharge. Effecting a cure would no doubt entail inducing in David some form of emotional catharsis so that the discharge could flow freely. Even then, of course, the therapist could not guarantee that David's presenting problem would be resolved, though certainly some measure of change, however imprecise, will have taken place.

I find it far more graceful and far more enjoyable to work toward changing the form of incongruent representations. In David's case, I helped him to develop a congruent representation for the behavior of smiling.

This can be done quickly and painlessly and the change would then be reflected somatically. No catharsis is necessary.

So: which patterns result in somatic difficulties? There are two major ones that I can identify and both involve synesthesia. The first occurs when there is a chronic unconscious stimulus in the lead system that is represented kinesthetically. There may be a trigger in the external environment that continually stimulates the lead representation which in turn produces negative feelings. I had a client who could not hear the word "marriage" without coming upon remembered pictures of his unhappy first affair. At that time it was a chronic problem, as he wanted to get married to someone. The somatic outcome of his remembered pictures was a chronic tensing of his mouth, forehead and shoulders that occasionally brought on severe headaches. The individual visual or auditory representations, that lead to somatic problems are also usually chunked in "large" pieces (See page 79). In other words, the remembered picture or words are of past circumstances that were painful or difficult. It stands to reason that, over time, this type of pattern could produce extreme reactions in the body even to the point of restricting muscle groups and altering the posture—what is called "character armor" (Reich, 1945).

The other pattern that leads to somatic discomfort occurs when there are two representations that result in feelings and the two are incongruent. That is, there is synesthesia from the auditory-to-kinesthetic channel and the visual-to-kinesthetic systems. A client in this case, might picture sexual relations with someone and feel excited while hearing a tape loop of a Priest's admonishments on the subject that inspire the feeling of dread. If this experience is habituated over time the incongruence will be manifested in the body. Again, this somatic expression could be approached as "blocked discharge" or "armor" or "repressed sexual energy" and, perhaps, altered in some way. I would submit, however, that there are much speedier and more elegant ways to change the form of the client's problem. The techniques for doing this will be presented in the next chapter.

Calibrated Communication

Many therapeutic disciplines have noticed and assigned labels to the phenomenon that can be called calibrated communication. Terms like "game" (Berne, 1964), "Life scripts (Perls 1973; Berne 1972)," and "self-fulfilling prophecies," are attempts to describe what happens when communication between two people gets redundant and inevitably leads to the same unpleasant outcome.

Have you ever had the experience of getting into a verbal exchange with an intimate and sensed, almost the moment you first spoke, that you had been through the exchange before? Nearly the same words were traded, perhaps in the same tonality, the pattern is fixed and the exchange proceeds almost compulsively down the same track to a familiar dead end. Or, perhaps, the content is different, but you know that in the end you and the other person are going to be stuck in fixed positions toward each other; the topic could be making dinner or international politics, but the pattern and the outcome will be a familiar one. This pattern is called a calibrated communication loop.

One way to explain how this can happen is by saying that the communicators are arranging their perceptions so that large portions of their experience during the exchange are filled with their own representations. In other words, the participants are mostly closed to ongoing sensory feedback. Its like talking to yourself; when your own representations are (mis)taken for data about the external environment, you are operating on automatic-pilot and not even checking the instruments. Even if I already know how to find the post office, I cannot ignore the stop lights, rights of way, and other cars while driving there, without getting into a wreck.

Socially, calibrated loops are often perceived as repetitive arguments or disagreements. It should be noted, though, that loops do
not always take the form of arguments; the participants' subjective
experience may still be one of "deja vu" however, and they will
have very little contact with anything other than their own internal
representations during the exchange.

Calibrated communication is often a special case of what I have
called elsewhere operating out of a "mixed state" of consciousness. Some of the communicator's senses are tuned externally and
the rest are concentrating, consciously or not, upon internal representations. Another factor to add to mixed communication to yield
calibration is anchoring. In any exchange, especially between people who are intimate, the sender and the receiver will be anchoring
each other in a myriad of ways. There is data being received in each
sensory channel and each stimulus will trigger representations
that, in themselves, are anchored to past memories that may or
may not be represented in consciousness! The subsequent responses a person might have would be a conglomerate of conscious design and whatever representations are being accessed out
of awareness. This set of circumstances will, naturally, affect the
person's subjective experience as well as their output—which, in
turn, can be responded to with the same complex variables. This
chart simplifies the overlapping steps to this process:

Messages sent
    Messages perceived
        Representations triggered and meanings derived
            Complex generalizations (related meanings to other
parts of receiver's model)
                Calibrated response limitations (Bandler, Grinder &
Satir, 1976, p. 98).

The following diagram will serve to represent visually more than
the auditory portion of a calibrated exchange:

Here, person A makes a statement to person B and the latter
responds consciously to only the words. While this occurs, person
B is, however, also being influenced by A's voice tone and tempo
in at least one of two ways. B may already have certain responses
that are anchored to past experience of listening to A's voice, or
B, upon hearing A's tone and tempo, may associate to other past
experiences from his personal history. If B's anchored association

MULTI-CHANNEL COMMUNICATIONS
MIXED COMMUNICATION

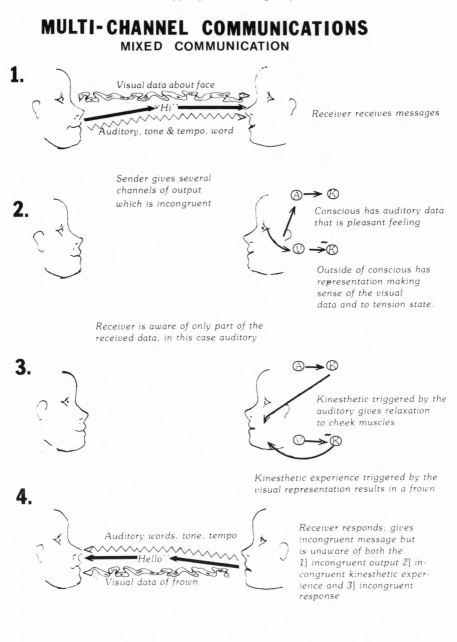

1.

Visual data about face

"Hi"

Auditory, tone & tempo. word

Receiver receives messages

2.

Sender gives several
channels of output
which is incongruent

Ⓐ→Ⓚ

Conscious has auditory data
that is pleasant feeling

Ⓥ→̃Ⓚ

Outside of conscious has
representation making
sense of the visual
data and to tension state.

Receiver is aware of only part of the
received data. in this case auditory

3.

Ⓐ→Ⓚ

Kinesthetic triggered by the
auditory gives relaxation
to cheek muscles

Ⓥ→̃Ⓚ

Kinesthetic experience triggered by the
visual representation results in a frown

4.

Auditory words. tone. tempo

"Hello"

Visual data of frown

Receiver responds: gives
incongruent message but
is unaware of both the
1] incongruent output 2] incongruent kinesthetic experience and 3] incongruent
response

INTERNAL RESPONSE-- EXTERNAL BEHAVIOR

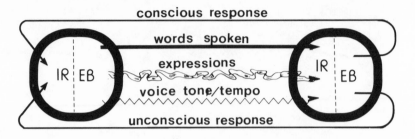

for A's voice is a pleasant one, the two of them will have a good time talking. If the tone and tempo are anchored to a painful experience, the conversation may deteriorate no matter what A's words attempt to convey. The only way she can alter this is to notice the responses she elicits from B and then alter her behavior until she gets a different reaction. It is impossible not to influence someone's experience while talking to him; it is only possible to have sensory experience and vary your output accordingly.

Given that multiple channel processing, anchoring, and mixed states all given structure to communication, the complexity of it can begin to seem staggering. The nice thing about problems in communication is that they are highly patterned and, therefore, redundant. Once a calibrated loop is identified, the process will reliably occur over and over again as a person lives out life. Each person will be making the best choices possible under the circumstances, but their range of behavior will be severely hampered by such patterns.

In families, of course, calibrations go on for years, the patterns being learned, practiced, and reinforced continuously. The ongoing relationship can pass along whole categories of limitations to the offspring that can make it difficult to adapt to the world outside the family. Children often go on translating new information and experiences into the syntax of the family calibrations. A teenage girl named Judy came to me with a problem. She tended to date boys her age who, sooner or later, would end up physically abusing her. Even from a distance we can recognize a repetitive pattern. Upon further inquiry I found out that she had learned programs for being very argumentative with men from her father. For months he had been seeing her with make-up on at home and reacting by telling her that she was going to get in trouble with the boys she dated. Upon hearing this Judy would challenge her father's judgment and he would respond by describing the various activities that he suspected a "slut" like herself would probably engage in. So much for the pattern with the father. Judy was clever enough to have acquired some other ways to approach men. Wearing make-up was one try, acting flirtatious was another.

Some of the boys she had dated had not offered the "blaming" behavior of her father but she had been unable to find a way to relate to them. The boys she wound up dating steadily did demonstrate this attitude toward her to varying degrees. Consistent with her background with Dad, Judy was "getting attention" in the most automated and unconscious way she knew; she often flirted and could easily be induced to argue with her dates. Typically, then, she would go out on dates and try to get close to a boy in the best way she knew how—by acting flirtatious. However, this usually elicited some kind of sexual advances from the boys, at which point Judy, apprehensive and believing herself to be out of choices, would abruptly stop flirting. Since she was sensitive enough to choose to go out with boys who had limitations like her father's, they would generally react by blaming her for being a "tease." For Judy, this meant that they were even more like her father and she would then fall back on the tactic that worked the best with him: arguing. Thus, the tension would escalate and occasionally Judy would be physically abused.

I do not think it is adequate to conclude that she was "masochistic" or secretly wanted to get slapped and beaten. She congruently told me that she wanted to date and be able to enjoy herself. The calibrated loops that she learned with her family simply allow her very few choices. She is stuck with a repetitive struggle that yields hurt feelings and occludes learning other, more satisfying programs for courtship. In working to alter her map and her experience, I helped her to open the calibration, question her linguistic Meta-Model violations (generalizations and mind reading), and then associate and anchor in new experiences that led to her developing more effective behavior for encountering men.

Family Communication

As all the metaphors of psychotherapy recognize, the family is the first and most powerful socializing institution. It lays the foundation for intrapersonal and interpersonal relationship, learning skills and abilities, moral values, etc. The family's foremost function is to define reality and the child's relationship to it—essentially to teach a child what is and is not possible. The family also teaches sensory distinctions: what representational system(s) to favor over others, how to chunk and store information, synesthesias, sequences of representational systems (strategies), and response patterns of various sorts. Many influential anchors are established early on in a child's development that will limit and enrich his experience years after he has flown from the nest. And the bulk of this teaching is done out of awareness or unconsciously.

John Grinder once said that the family is primarily a hypnotic relationship. Sigmund Freud made a very similar statement years before (Freud 1922). For most people, the family relationship lasts longer than that with any other socializing institution. Not only does the family initially associate and anchor in programs, establish options, limits, and sensory distinctions, but these learnings are future-paced as well and associated with representations of anticipated future events. To encourage a child consciously or otherwise, to feel and act limited in the future is, operationally, the same as post-hypnotic suggestion (p. 182). It is customarily known that using hypnosis, one can program behavior to begin at certain times in specific contexts. In families, children are programmed for common sensical behavior—washing hands before eating, watching for cars on the street, etc—in addition to patterns that are idiosyncratic to the group. The latter category might include *compulsive* hand washing as well as making repetitive self-derogating statements, developing poor eyesight, believing that life is one long hardship, and so on.

The family, then, influences the structure of its members' unconscious experience in at least five ways: by assigning representational systems and the types of distinctions that can be made within them; 2. by directing a child to what is and is not supposed possible; 3. by teaching and reinforcing calibrated communication; 4. by establishing associations to anticipated future events (future pacing) idiosyncratic anchors for various content-bound experiences;

and 5. by establishing and encouraging certain sequences of sensory processing (strategies). The last point will be made more obvious through the discussion in Chapter 5.

Knowing the prerequisites and fundamentals of how experience is formed and structured and how incongruence operates as a process, let's turn to a presentation of the Change Patterns which are highly effective techniques for changing experience and uniting incongruities.

Wisdom

The traveler's journal tells of those kinds of aid that he gave to the various persons and those kinds of learnings that he took. He spoke of his own learnings, his ability to close his eyes and see those enticing colors and those shapes and special textures and illuminations that had dazzled his mind in the city, and those landscapes and spacious areas that had brought him serenity when he was in the open plains. He wrote about his ability to sing the tunes he had taken from the minstrels and his ability to remember the conversations that had taken place between the tradespersons as they went about their daily business. He was able to share, even in the writing of the journal, the same excitement he shared when he spoke, the same enthusiasm and the same touching drama that he had acquired along his journey. And likewise, he spoke and wrote of those things that seemed to be of the most help to those he encountered.

He spoke of one man who had a family of eight children. He was the sole provider for the family and their hungry cries pressured the man to go out and seek food and employment day and night until he was practically starving himself and worn thin. But his strong bones and muscles had a continual drive to feed his family. When the traveler encountered him, he suggested that the cries of the children, especially those that were old enough, could instead become a signal to themselves that they, too, could gather food and berries. Soon the man learned to use the cries of the children as a way to delegate authority to them so that six of this family of nine were out, in a harmonious fashion, gathering berries gathering wool, finding remnants of wood and copper that could be used to build lean-tos and houses. The journeyman was proud that this delegation of authority he had shared with this huge family was something that he had brought from his previous travels in the big cities where delegation of authority was something understood by all the craftsmen who had apprentices to help them.

He wrote of a man who had been the city's newest member in a small tribe and how in talking to the man, the traveler had suggested that the he go onto a high cliff and look back at the city below. From that perspective, he instructed the novice to imagine that he was a teacher explaining to those in the city below him, who were, of course, far from earshot, just what it was that each of them did and just how it was that he fit in to the city, and to explain to each of them how he wanted to change his role from newcomer to that of judge or blacksmith or minstrel. He left the man to decide for himself and only shared this special task that he had learned from the Indians and taken to the city.

And for another person, a young woman who believed that she was pursued by the shadow of death, the traveler had been able to open her eyes to the sunrises that greeted her each morning. His journal tells, in detail, how he sat with the young woman at the appropriate time each day and spoke to her of the sunrises at the very instant that she began to fear the oncoming shadow of death. Within a very short period of time the woman came to find the sunrises for herself. He had taught her a special language he had learned from the plainsmen, a special observation of the sunrise they use every morning and every evening when they speak of the rising moon.

And the traveler's journal speaks of how the hungry family became respected guides for others in the community who were hungry and how the newcomer had indeed become a blacksmith, respected by all in the town and how the young woman pursued by death had married and looked forward to having children with a similar bright future as hers. The journeyman told of many other tales that had changed both the experiences of those whom he had passed and his own life.

IV CHANGE PATTERNS

At the risk of making the axiom unforgettable through repetition, it is not possible to communicate without influencing behavior—producing some measure of change. In the interest of creating salient change, most of the techniques I am about to present are essential and indigenous to every form of therapy.

Some established therapies employ one or another pattern implicitly and some use several, as we shall see in the last chapter. The goal of this chapter is to make explicit the formal steps of these powerful techniques so that you can easily begin to learn and apply them in your work.

At training seminars I have often used the metaphor of three juggling balls. Learning to juggle them all at once is a nearly impossible task, certain to end in frustration. Beginning with one ball, however, is easy. The student could start by simply throwing one ball into the air and catching it, first with one hand, then with the other. Nothing fancy is required or helpful. Once that maneuver is mastered, it is only a small step further to learning to toss the balls from hand to hand in both directions. Soon the third ball can be added and the student is juggling like a pro. Learning is a matter of breaking the task down into small enough chunks and then building upon them in a systematic fashion. Once the basic steps of the Change Patterns have been easily understood, you can build upon them until you can aim for more complex and precise outcomes with your clients.

Collapsing Anchors

To collapse anchors is to change the influence that a non-integrated and often painful experience has upon a person. To imagine how a non-integrated experience might be formed, suppose, humorously, that a group of, say, killer bees burst into your living room intending to wreak havoc. From beginning to end the attack will be mapped by you. Your subjective experience will probably be one of an overwhelmingly unpleasant blur of activity. When it is all over, you will have a single chunk representation for an incident that lasted perhaps an hour. It is sort of swallowed whole.

It would be different if, when the bees broke in, you were able to just push a button and put the entire scene on "hold" and go on about your daily business. When you returned to the scene, you would have associated the break-in with meeting some friends for lunch. Just a bunch of killer bees in the middle of the day. The savage behavior of the bees would then be mapped intermittent to the pleasant interlude of lunch and gossip. If, after each subsequent flurry with the bees, you were again able to hit the hold button attend to your stings and search for insecticide, the attack would ultimately come to be associated with your ability to take care of yourself and find solutions to problems.

The second circumstance is not as traumatic as the first in that there is a different level of chunking to the experience. While the former is gulped down in one unpleasant chunk, the latter is mapped in bite-sized pieces more easily digested and stored for future use. The chunks may be said to be "smaller."* Therefore, the "bigger" a chunk, the more likely it is, as a memory, to impede a search for resources and solutions for many situations. Kinesthetically, of course, the subjective difference between these two degrees of chunking is obvious; the fear and pain would be considerably less debilitating if the experience is chunked in smaller proportions. The object of collapsing anchors is to alter and specifically, reduce chunks of the content of a difficult memory in the same naturalistic way that is occurring in "nature:" social situations or therapeutic change.

Case Example

Mentioned in the introduction was a young woman who had difficulty having a sexual relationship with her husband. Within the first twenty minutes of the session she had identified her father's voice and saw a picture of him that she remembered from childhood:

*The reader is reminded that this is only a way of talking about it.

S: "Jackie, how is it that you manage to get scared."
J: "Well, (eyes down and to the left) I don't know, I just suddenly (eyes up and to the right) get scared."
S: "What did you just see when you looked up?"
J: "Nothing, I didn't see anything . . . (eyes defocus) oh, yes, I do I see my father (eyes up right, cheeks flatten, voice tone raises) holding me on his lap."
S: "Do you hear anything with this picture?"
J: (pauses, then eyes go down left) "I can hear him (begins to cry) scaring me about how girls can get into trouble."
S: "I want you to notice closely and tell me if you get the sound of him speaking before or after you get the picture."
J: "I . . . think . . . I hear the words first. You know, (changes voice tone) I never realized that before, but that's what happens."

Jackie has been searching through these remembered words and pictures for the solution to her current sexual problems. She repeatedly comes upon a four-tuple containing the sight of her father holding her, the sound of his voice, and the kinesthetic experience of fear—in other words, an oversized chunk, a memory so "large" that it blocks and disrupts her attempts to organize her present resources for an exciting sexual life. The intensity of this feeling greatly inhibits her associations to many other things she does know about sexual conduct.

We can comfortably draw this conclusion from both what Jackie tells us in words and her accessing cues. Listening to her voice, I hear her tone rise, her tempo slow and her timbre switch whenever she accesses visually. In plain terms, she sounds scared.

The information Jackie got from her father did not get associated with and supported by other relevant resources in her history. She cannot solve her problem as she might make a complex career decision because when she attempts to engage cognitive, emotional, physical, and social resources, memories and experience, this four-tuple chunk pops to the surface. As John Grinder has said, it is as if the four-tuples were a deck of cards and one of them is over-sized; when you flip through the deck the big one always pops into prominence.

To collapse anchors is simply to arrange for two or more four-tuples to come together at once. The more mutually incompatible they are, the more they reduce one another. This, in effect, creates a new four-tuple comprised of the first two and anchored to the original stimulus (the memory of Father). The experience with the most structural integrity will prevail. Since the goal is to expand the limits of the original four-tuple, the particular new elements that you introduce will be important. The "positive" four-tuple(s) must have intensity and strength enough to counter the negativity of the original experience. The latter must retain more of its integrity than the former four-tuple.

I asked Jackie to locate a visual memory to which she associates comfort and with which she *felt* very comfortable. I then asked her to concentrate on the detail of the picture while she felt comfort all through her body. As she watched the new image and described to me many of her specific body sensations, I associated or anchored the experience by a touch on her hand. Then I asked her to go back to the memory of her father. When she signaled me that she had, I touched off—"fired"—the anchor for the pleasant picture and feelings. This pairing put two diverse sets of stimuli in the same place at the same time. Given the limits of consciousness, the collapse produces an experiential overload. When the two experiences come together neither can be taken; instead a new one is formed. The new one will be most like the more intense of the two original experiences. In fact the more-intense experience may not seem significantly altered—but the less-intense experience will seem to destructure.

Clients often report feeling confused and Jackie's immediate reaction was that her picture of her father began to shrink. Responses will vary from person to person. Pictures may become darker, more vague, recede into a distance, etc. Jackie had also found the sound of puppies barking to use as most dissimilar to the sound of her father's voice. When I collapsed those auditory anchors she said that the voice had gone completely mute. The creative alterations that occur in the auditory and kinesthetic channels are, of course, just as diverse as those of the visual.

After that four-tuple was reduced and re-mapped, Jackie was able to "think clearly" and reasonably about her sexuality, her father's early warnings, and her husband. The face muscle and voice tone changes that had occurred earlier were absent. She no longer looked or sounded scared. Treatment was concluded after inquiry revealed that she was well informed and satisfactory skilled in the related social and sexual experiences she wished to share with her husband.

There is nothing new or uncommon about collapsing anchors except the formalizing of the process. If you are feeling depressed and a friend reminds you of your achievements, conflicting elements of your experience will be brought together and may form a new state of mind. If a child comes home from school discouraged about a test she has to take on the following day, a parent may take her by the hand and remind her that she has been confident before and will be again. The two visual, kinesthetic, and auditory portions of incompatible four-tuples will become paired and re-chunked into a new combination. Collapsing anchors is implicit in many successful therapeutic interventions (Chapter 7). Here we present the explicit steps:

Collasping Anchors Paradigm

1. Retrieve the unwanted experience. Get a sensory description of it that includes all the elements of the four-tuple. Anchor it.
2. Retrieve the necessary resources making certain that they are as intense as the problem four-tuple. Anchor them.
3. Have the client return to the problem state. Fire off both anchors at once. Hold them until sensory experience or feedback from the client tells you the integration has taken place.

Phobias

If Jackie's response to her father's frightening behavior had developed into a life long apprehension around men with red hair and led to feeling fear each time she heard a voice tone that approximated her Dad's, then merely collapsing anchors on the original experience would not be enough. A phobia is a "no-choice" response of fear to an internal representation that is externally triggered. A snake phobia, or a red-hair phobia, for instance, will usually have the following sensory structure: Visual External-seeing the snake—Visual Eidetic Internal-picture of a snake—Kinesthetic Internal-feeling afraid.

$$Ve \rightarrow Vi \rightarrow Ki$$

What distinguishes a phobia from a single painful experience like Jackie had is that with phobia, the K^i (fear) has come to be associated with a *set* of visual and/or auditory signals. The fear can be triggered by not only a live snake but also a garden hose, a picture of a snake, a sudden hissing sound, etc. It is quite likely the response has a long history as well. In other words, there is a number of four-tuples to de-structure all of which contain the K i element of fear.

Collapsing anchors on the phobia will only work if we take into account how the fear has generalized. If we bring in the necessary resources to deal with only the client's fear of the garden hose, then we leave the other anchors, with their long histories, intact. So we must collapse anchors on the phobia in such a way that the results expand across time through various contexts. Changing the phobic response means incorporating the same pattern of generalization that went into creating it.

Phobia Transcript

S: "What would you like to change?"

B: "I have a phobia about some sexual activity because (face reddens and neck muscles tense) I was almost raped when I was very young—six" (forced swallow)

S: "Do you care to say which sexual activity you are fearful of?"

B: (tensing jaw) "Any kind of oral sex." (moves eyes up and to the right and shakes head back and forth slowly). "My husband and I both have tried to overcome it but I'm just too afraid. Trying it ruins everything and just turns me off completely" (eyes become moist and she swallows in a forced manner).

S: "O.K. Before we begin, I want you to picture a time when you were very relaxed and serene—perhaps as a child, as you were then, or any one of a number of times when you never even questioned your safety and security."

B: "O.K. (eyes down left, then up right) I feel that way now."

(head nods up and down slowly. Her jaw relaxes and her face becomes less reddened. She looks calmed and composed.)

S: (places his right hand on her left shoulder) "Feeling this kind of security now, you have an opportunity to really think about what kind of joy and happiness you want to bring from the past as a resource. Go inside and find several experiences you'd like to have in oral and all other sexual activity. You might . . ."

B: (Nods her head up and down slowly as her eyes move from down-left to up right.)

S: "You might have different names for them such as "excitement," "trust," "warmth," "love," "joy." Have you identified a few either by name (B nods her head up and down slowly) or by experience directly?"

B: (smiling and blushing slightly) "Yeah, I remember some real good times."

S: (anchoring with a touch on her elbow) "We'll come back to this later. Now I'd like you to recall the very last time that you had anxiety about any sexual activity. And nod your head "yes" when you remember it. (takes her hand and positions his fingers to anchor her negative experience by pressure on her index finger knuckle).

B: (Nods "yes.") "O.K."

S: (Squeezes knuckles) "Now I want you to do two things at once. Give me a head nod and a verbal for each memory you have. In other words when you *think back, B,* to the next to last time you felt this (squeezes knuckle) anxiety or scare and when you remember where you were nod "yes" and give some reference for it (like, on Main Street, 1978, in college, or so on). Do you understand my direction?"

B: "Yeah." (pause, nods head.) "It was at the lake."

S: *"The lake.* O.K. Now search for another time which occurred before that.

B: (She was motionless for a few seconds. Then her neck tenses and she makes a grimace with her mouth.) "O.K. This one was in San Francisco."

S: "San Francisco. O.K. now find one before that."

B: "O.K. (face is now showing much muscular lassitude and is reddened). This one is on our honeymoon."

S: "Honeymoon. O.K. Another one?"

B: "Yeah, college."

S: "O.K. college. Now go to the original incident. (turning to group: "You only need to have a few, say five, of these, to insure that generalization of change will permeate the range of traumas through which this negative kinesthetic experience has generalized")

B: Nods head.

S: "O.K. you have the original one, too."

B: "Yes" (swallowing hard and looking only at the floor).

S: "Now turning to the group like this is a disruption of her ongoing experience. (to B) Turning to you and speaking about the group causes you to switch your mood so we call it a 'pattern disruption.' "

B: (Looks at therapist and tilts head to the left).

S: "Now *B.* I want you to use your intuitive judgment and identify some of the experiences you believe will be resources for this change. You have already found *these* (touching her elbow at previous spot) resources of happiness and joy. Let me suggest that we add some security experiences and perhaps you can name some others. What do you want to experience during oral-sexual activities."

B: "O.K. I guess I would like to feel sexy."

S: (Humorously) "Oh, yeah, that's a good one!"

B: (Laughing) "And safe . . . protected . . . I guess it's I'd like to feel like I can control myself."

S: "Right. First look for a memory of being in control in the way you mean."

B: (Looks up to the right) "O.K. I've got one."

S: "Now make it very clear or bright."

B: (Nods head up and down)

S: "Now I want you to step into the picture and have all the feelings that go with it. And do you hear the sounds or what you had said to yourself at those times?"

B: "O.K. I feel all that."

S: "Now (squeezes the anchor on the elbow) find a picture or the feeling of being sexy . . . and the smells and sounds . . ."

B: (Pauses for a few moments with a smile.) "Yeah, I've got it" (chuckle).

S: (Squeezes anchor) "Now I'd like you to judge if you think these resources are sufficient to be more powerful than the scares and (pause) are they sufficient for you to feel the way you'd like to feel?"

B: (Motionless then begins to shake head up and down) "Yeah, I think so (smiling)."

S: "O.K. then I want you to listen carefully and follow my direction. (Holding the anchor on the elbow) Go to the experience you called 'the lake' and nod your head when you are certain that you can have *these* (squeezes anchor) resources in that situation."

B: (Motionless, eyes up to the right, pauses, exhales, begins to nod head, then looks at therapist and smiles) "O.K."

S: "Now go to the situation you called honeymoon and nod your head when you are convinced that you can have these resources in that situation."

B: (Repeats behavior, pauses longer, nods head).

S: "Good. Now I want you to go to the situation of college and . . ."

B: Starts nodding head.

S: "Let me know when you are sure that you can have these resources in that situation."

B: "I've got it already, yeah."

S: "O.K. let's go to what you think is the original scene and nod your head when you are sure you can have these experiences in that situation. Take all the time you need."

B: (Tenses, gets somewhat strained tension as her lips, forehead and brow tighten. Her legs jerk involuntarily and then she begins to relax and smile slowly.)

S: "Is there anything else you needed then . . ."

B: (Nodding head) "I've got it. I feel good, yeah" (Begins to giggle, then smiles warmly).

S: "Are you certain?"

B: (Congruently) "Uh huh."

S: "O.K. (to group) If she were not able to overcome the intensity of the original scene, we would simply stop and build more resources (Group nods and complies).

B: (Looking around at group, relaxed.)

S: "Now *B,* I think it would be appropriate for you to imagine a future situation very soon or in the next days when you want to have these resources again . . . (to group) and this constitutes a test of our results in an acceptable way . . . (group laughs) . . . in fantasy. (To *B*) And verify that you can have these resources available to you."

B: (Smiling and looking up to the right. Nodding head.) "O.K. yeah I can."

S: "Is this experience complete or do you need more resources of some type we've left out?"

B: "No it's fine."

S: "O.K. Imagine another future time as well and we'll be done."

B: "O.K. I'm done. Thanks."

During this group in Indiana several folks changed dog phobias, height phobias, claustrophobia and others. I had many of them test the results from elevators and high places for our own satisfaction. But with *B* it was two weeks later when she and her husband wrote me a letter saying, "Thanks, everything is straightened out." The openness and risk that *B* took in the group was very moving and powerful. I expect that the willingness she displayed is partially a result of a change method which was content-free and extremely non-judgmental, logical, and systematic. A contact was made during this writing (a year and a half later) and things were still fine with them.

The Phobia Paradigm

1. Retrieve the fearful experience.
2. Anchor it.
3. Hold the anchor constant and search chronologically through memories of the problem from current to earliest.
4. Interrupt this four-tuple you have built.
5. Retrieve the resources that are needed for the change (incompatible four-tuples, etc.).
6. Anchor the resources.
7. Return chronologically through the history keeping the resources constant from the current to the most recent phobia four-tuple.
8. Anchor the change options to representations associated to stimuli likely to be encountered in the future (future pace).

Dissociation

Dissociation is a way to alter the relationship of the co-anchored elements in a given four-tuple. If, as in a phobia, a client has a four-tuple in which the visual and/or auditory components lead to an unpleasant K, the pattern to engage is that of dissociation. This situation is different from a phobia in that the recurrent K has not generalized to a variety of stimuli. While collapsing anchors pairs diverse experience so that it comes together to form a new four-tuple, dissociation divides the co-anchored elements so that they remain "intact" but influence each other very differently. Visually we can display this change as:

(V,A,K,O) Dissociation pattern to (V//A//K//O)

In the latter dissociated four-tuple, each piece of sensory content has been held back from influencing the others.

Dissociation is called for when an experience (although not a phobia) is of such intense pain that collapsing anchors will force an undesirable kinesthetic consciousness. The memory of a loved one's face may consistently evoke sadness, but the client may also be able to over-ride the response by thinking of something else. To dissociate this experience, the therapist would first match, pace, and associate an anchor for comfort and various other resources, and then encourage the client to watch a scene unfold as though he were watching movies at a theatre. Watching a scene occur over there "while sitting in comfort here" allows a non-integrated experience to be examined with a minimum of discomfort. Had you endured the above "imaginary" attack of the killer bees and were still haunted by the memory, a therapist could have you replay the scene in perfect safety. In the example of overlap with Paula (p. 63), the next step toward assisting her in fully integrating her experience would have been dissociation. The technique is extremely effective for dealing with experiences that are remembered or imagined in large "chunks." These include not only traumatic experiences such as rape, physical assault, etc., but also anticipatory fears. As the client sits anchored in comfort, he can watch "the worst" happen without pain. The net result at the process level is a change in the possible associations the client can make in the face of this previously overwhelming experience. It is often desirable to retrieve, associate, and anchor other needed experiences and motor patterns to this dissociated memory and that simply requires additional care and work.

Case Example:

Dorothy came to me having been labeled "permanently age-regressed." She had been seeing a therapist who had encouraged her condition with the rationale that he was training her as a parent might have. She was eventually sent to me because the "reparent-ing" had not taken and Dorothy was a 28 year old child, and the therapist moved out of the state. The client was very bewildered and her new therapist was at a loss to handle this overly dependent and extremely "manipulative" young woman.

I worked with Dorothy for two hours. At the onset she informed me that she was not in control of herself. A part of her that she considered to be five years old was directing the show. She said the five-year old was very good at getting people to take care of her, though sometimes the tactics did not work. In that contingency, she would make herself physically sick and thereby coerce some-one into taking care of her. She was frank, verbal and candid about the entire drama.

Watching her eye scanning patterns as she spoke, I saw that whenever she referred to feeling helpless her eyes went up and to the left—visual memory. I asked her to look up and tell me what she saw. She immediately identified a scene with her parents that occurred when she was five years old. Since I knew that her mem-ory of this incident was associated with her current state of help-lessness, I moved first to anchor the resources she would need to re-encounter it.

I asked Dorothy to separate the part of her that was five from the part of her that was older, mature, and competent. I presupposed the latter part's existence in the phrasing of my question and she was able to make sense of the words and contact the qualities I asked for. If she had been unable find maturity and competence, I would have asked her to imagine them. When anchoring re-sources, I find fantasy often does just as well as actual experience. As she accessed the qualities, I anchored them with a touch on the arm.

We had accomplished steps #1 and #2 (see paradigm) at this

point. Dorothy was then instructed to *see* and *hear* only the five year old part (*over there* on the floor), living *over there* as she once did when *she was* young.

It is very important that the client be able to sense or project the visual and auditory components of a disturbing experience so that it happens "out there" and not where they are sitting. The K element of their experience will, of course, be the feelings of security that you have anchored "here." You will not only assist the initial dissociation but can continue to maintain it with the words you select. Through the emphasis embedded in your continuing instructions—"Go on watching her have those feelings there while you sit here in comfort"—you will guide the clients toward a deeper involvement in the fantasy they have constructed. Step #3 was complete when Dorothy signalled that she could keep her feelings of security constant while she watched that old situation unfold across the room.

I next had Dorothy imagine the mature adult part of her drifting out of her body to watch the scene with her parents(Step #4). She did this, easily nodding when she could see herself as little girl and adult. As I signaled the anchor for competence, I asked her to keep the comfort constant and review in words and pictures only "what happened to that girl back then." She watched briefly and reported that her parents were fighting, occasionally turning to hit the little girl, and that the latter wanted to have the feeling of being securely held.

At this point I let the client's response be sufficient reason to depart from the dissociation paradigm to aid her in more strongly connecting the two parts of herself. I suggested that as an adult she had recently experienced the feeling of being held innumerable times with her last therapist. She agreed. I asked her to retrieve some of this feeling. When she signalled with a nod that she had done so, I told her to open up a nonverbal channel of communication with the image of the little girl. I then asked the little girl part if the feeling of being held was what she lacked "back there." Dorothy reported that the little girl's head nodded "yes."

Still departing from the simple dissociation paradigm, I instructed Dorothy to concentrate on the fact that she had all the resources within herself now and that she could use them whenever the little girl needed. She agreed and the little girl nodded. I then asked if the little girl would be willing to trade with the grown woman: since both parties agreed that the grown woman was more equipped to "direct the show" (Dorothy's present existence), would the little girl be willing to give up her control in return for the sense of security when ever she wanted it? The image nodded to Dorothy; both parties agreed. I returned to the dissociation. This tangent into retrieving and trading resources required fifteen minutes.

I asked her to bring back into herself the little girl (Step #6) and to "tell her that you'll love her and care for her." Dorothy did this with a smile and her posture immediately changed to reflect confidence. She stayed immersed in this feeling for a few moments and then brought back her other part that had been hovering in the room "watching and learning" (Step #7). I suggested that her "new learnings" find expression in the next few days, weeks, and months to come and that her new ability to care for herself could be applied to specific areas of her life—education, employment, socially, recreationally and so on. This constituted the future-pace association to representations of anticipated future events.

Prior to this dissociation, each time Dorothy would form the picture of her parents fighting she would feel helpless. With the experience dissociated she can still produce the picture, but it no longer automatically yields the negative feelings. Also helplessness felt in any context will not in turn trigger the memory of parents fighting. All the other co-anchored components in the four-tuple are detached in a similar way.

The day following our session Dorothy took her second therapist out to lunch. This therapist had earlier told me that Dorothy had been so withdrawn in recent months that she had not left her house except to go to therapy. She was now driving, dining, and socializing. Other changes needed to transpire in Dorothy's family and social system to help reinforce and anticipate more mature behavior from her. Her therapist was advised to address these subjects and Dorothy stayed in therapy for a time. I was in contact with her for several months and the initial changes not only remained, but generalized to many areas of her life.

Dissociation Paradigm

1. Retrieve an experience of security in the here and now.
2. Anchor it.
3. Keep the security constant and *see and hear only* that disturb-ing experience *over there.*
4. Let a part of yourself float out over there and just watch and learn.
5. Rerun the experience that you wish to dissociate while holding constant the new kinesthetic "security." Allow the client all the time that's necessary to complete the re-run of the incident.
6. Re-integrate the kinesthetic part (from step 5).
7. Re-integrate the visual observing part (from step 4).
8. Anchor the change to stimuli that is likely to occur in the future (future pace).

Reframing

Make those problem parts resources! I can not think of many psychotherapies that would disagree with this principle either in spirit or practice. In the Psychoanalytic model it translates as the therapeutic use of the ego defensive-adaptive mechanisms, and it is shot through more recent renditions of personality, capturing the essence of the "Human Potential Movement."

Anyone who has wittnessed, heard, or read the work of Virginia Satir, Fritz Perls, or Milton Erickson is amazed at their skill in transforming problems into assets. To turn a client's negative be-havior, thoughts, or feelings into resources does not involve im-posing something from the outside nor is anything removed. The function of the problem part is simply altered and employed on the clients' greater behalf to get them what they want more effectively. You may think reframing is the product of genius, but the proce-dure can be outlined step by step and easily incorporated into your repertoire. The outline that follows is taught in many training seminars:

Reframing Paradigm

1. Identify the problem part—this could be a habit, chronic feeling, any thing from undesirable external behavior to a disease to a mood. Anchor it.
2. Establish a channel of communication with that part— again, remember that any response can be considered communication. Words are often less reliable than a foot twitch, a change in skin color or an internal image.
3. Identify and separate the part's positive intent from the manner in which it tries to fulfill that intent (the undesirable behavior). Anchor the intent. We have found it appropriately and enduringly useful to presuppose a positive intent behind all behavior no matter how logically remote it may seem. To assume anything other than a positive intent is to create another intent.
4. Retrieve a set of four-tuples for "creativity" and anchor it.
5. Have the client create three ways to satisfy the positive intent without engaging in the problem behavior. To assist this you may associate the anchors established in steps #3 and 4.
6. Get the original part to "take responsibility" for implementing new behaviors. This insures that the new ways are associated and anchored to the stimulus or representation that occured at the onset of the undesirable behavior.
7. Ecological check—ask whether there is any other part that objects to the changes. If so then cycle back to step two and begin again. These may be "parts" of the person or other people who are "parts" within his family or social system.

Case Examples

Diane was married and 34 years old when she came for therapy. She sought help because she was chronically angry at her husband for what she termed his "whimpy" behavior. Although she had given up a conscious attempt to change her husband she was still frequently angry. She did not like the way she felt and she thought she sounded "bitchy" most of the time. She wanted to feel and sound less abrasive.

She first identified a tension in her abdomen as the first signal that her anger was engaging. I asked her to "go inside herself" and ask this tension what it was trying to do on her behalf. She thought for a moment—eyes down-right, then down-left, then again down-right—looked up at me and said that it was trying to get her love and support from her husband. I asked her to decide consciously whether she believed this to be a positive intention. She congruently said, "Yes."

I then asked her to retrieve creativity in the following way: "Go inside and recall a number of times, past or present, when you have been particularily creative, for instance, while raising children in today's society, when you have had to learn and use creatively a large number of communication skills to cope effectively and other times in which you behaved confidently and gracefully in spite of potentially trying circumstances!" Note the number of presuppositions in this statement. My phrasing serves two purposes; first, it constitutes a non-specific pace of Diane's background and second, it induces nominalizations likely to be associated to the very resources that Diane needs to cope with her problem. This use of language, particularily nominalizations and presuppositions, to evoke experience in clients will be carefully detailed in Chapter XII. Diane's response was to go on congruently nodding as I spoke. I anchored the creativity.

Holding the anchor firm, I asked her to develop three creative ways that would fully satisfy the positive intention besides the original behavior. I specified that the new ways should be "at least as effective if not more" than getting chronically angry. I suggested she take all the time she needed. If clients take more than a few minutes, I also suggest that they break the new ways down into smaller more manageable chunks for now.

Diane soon said, "OK, I have three. Do you want to know what they are?" I inform my clients that it is usually all right with me to listen and discuss them if they think it is important. Otherwise, I need not know exactly what they are; it is enough to know that new behaviors have been created and that they meet the criteria we have established.

When she had the new possibilities, I told her to "go back to tension in your abdomen and ask it if it is willing to take responsibility for using these new choices." This question in effect anchors the presenting problem of tension to an entirely new set of choices designed to work for the same outcome; it associates the two anchors. Diane said "it" was willing.

To check for congruence with the new arrangement, I asked Diane if there were any other parts that objected to the changes. With a warm smile she shook her head and replied, "I don't have any objections, I like the changes." If there had been any incongruence—a minute head nod for instance—we could have also structured that part through the reframing outline. The part would also be assumed to have a positive intent behind its objection and we would have designed three ways to satisfy it, etc.

Since Diane was congruent with the changes, I moved to "future pace." I asked her to imagine situations in the next few days and weeks in which she could implement her new behavior and to rehearse her responses mentally. Future pacing is, again, insurance that the client will expand what they have learned to situations outside of your office. It gets the new choices to where they are needed.

Reframing also creates change for many somatic problems. One of my clients had been pained daily for five years by canker sores. She had submitted to innumerable medical tests but nothing could be isolated as the cause of the malady. Given the depth and history of the behavior, I decided to offer her a chance to change the experience that creates the sores. Reframing was the logical choice.

Sallie could clearly identify the signal that preceded her awareness of the pain in her mouth, but could not fathom a positive intention behind the sores. Since reframing works with only the formal expression of behavior, it is not necessary or even preferable to know the content of a problem. I asked that Sallie have the part communicate "yes" by making the pain in her mouth increase. She thought the request was unusual and a little silly, but she asked the part to intensify the soreness and "it" did. I then asked the part to discover the positive intent behind its behavior and to signal with more soreness when it knew. It was not to make the intent known to Sallie's conscious mind. When a moment later the signal came, Sallie was startled and delighted.

We proceeded through the reframing outline systematically while the part signalled to confirm our work at each step. Sallie completed the entire exercise without objection and without a conscious clue to what had been causing the sores or what the new

	creating resources	changing behavior	changing representations	changing a strong undesirable feeling
Anchoring	use for both building pieces of four-tuples and for full four-tuples	basic tool to use for building and adding programs	basic tool changes representation	basic tool by adding to it
Collapsing anchors	X	re-chunks the contents of the four-tuple useful for re-chunking trauma memories	can rechunk in any rep. system changes representation by competing with it	will work to the extent that the desired feeling is stronger than the undesirable one changes representation by competing with it
Phobia Paradigm	X	Use for Phobias Changes Avoidance	generalizes above change to several similar situations	use this pattern for Phobias
Dissociation	Some experience may become a resource after an unpleasant K is dissociated	X	disconnects the overlaps between rep. systems	use for reducing the discomfort the client's representation contains
Reframing	Only reframe an objector which interferes with the desired goal of creating a resource	Works with situations where there are too many four-tuples attached to use collapsing anchors	can reframe any rep. system. Will work for pictures and sounds and words and feelings It changes content of a rep. by anchoring it to a *set* of 4-tuples	will work as well for strong feelings therapist and client together must generate some options and often a strong feeling state will influence the success of this goal. It changes content of a rep. by anchoring it to a *set* of 4-tuples

resources might be. All she knew was that she got the "yes" signal at every step of the way. She called me three days later to report that the sores and pain had vanished for the first time in five years. The change stayed firm for the duration of my fifteen month follow up.

The four techniques I have presented can be thought of as ways to rearrange four-tuples—that is, experience—and the attached verbal labels. They predictably produce profound change in clients and occupy a special place among the change patterns that Bandler and Grinder have extracted from psychotherapy. As always, the foremost criteria for deciding which pattern to employ will be based upon the clients' presenting problem versus their desired state. The following chart will organize and guide your judgment of which of these powerful techniques will be the most appropriate therapeutic response in a given context.

A Quest

As the traveler continued on his journey, his storehouse of attitudes, knowledge and wisdom began to take shape. The personal truth which he sought became an increasingly important force which pulled him onward as if his body were pulled by some force outside of himself. Others took it to be ambition while others took it to be a simple wanderlust, but his journal tells of his seeking for the truth. He became a "Siddhartha" on his journey, setting out to find that person who knows the truth or those persons who can guide him in the proper direction. He talked with the shaman, listened to the minstrels, learned the crafts of the tradesmen and the blacksmith, he acquired the serenity of those who live in the forest as well as the methodical peacefulness of those who are herdsmen. And yet each of these people spoke that the truth lay elsewhere, that he would find it in another city in the lands beyond.

He asked careful questions of each person on his journey. Not only did he find that their answers were different, but that also the ways they went about their answering were different. At first he became confused, irritated and frustrated, thinking perhaps he was never going to find the person who seemed to know the truth. Those in the tribes and towns that he considered the wisest and the most skillful were those of whom he asked the most questions. He paid careful attention to what they did and how they did it. Some people claimed to know the truth. They told him that he was to take a pilgrimage to the fork in the river, to sleep there comfortably, to wait until a vision occurred to him and when his vision occurred, he would hear a voice and that voice would tell him the truth. He took the man's advice. He journeyed to the river, slept, waited, and visions did appear to him and voices did speak to him. But these voices urged him to move on and to seek the truth elsewhere. Another wise person that he met encouraged him to

make great lists, to draw pictures from those lists, to make blueprints of the projects that he sought and to tell others about those
blueprints, to take all the ambition and courage that he had and
make all those blueprints become realities to find the truth. He
tried that on several occasions and found that he could build both
small huts and large buildings. He could organize town meetings
and keep track of cattle. But as the months passed he began to
suspect that there was more to truth than just this and asked
elsewhere to find a complete truth.

Several people were seeking the truth in a nearby town and he
journeyed to that town to find answers they could provide for him.
One particular group of individuals sat quietly and cleared their
minds, trying to find the truth through quietly doing nothing in a
methodical, systematic and tedious fashion. He tried to do nothing
for a good period of time and still the thoughts crept into his mind
that this was only a partial and temporary truth. The truth lay
elsewhere. He remembered the vision and the voice that urged him
on and he found still another community where they did a similar
practice, filling a cave and chanting endlessly into the night, claiming that they had the truth and that they would be guided. But
when he left their community he felt as he had when he entered
their community—that they had not the entire truth but only a very
small chalice shining in the sun.

CHAPTER V STRATEGIES

Once students in training seminars become adept at recognizing lead systems (via eye scanning patterns) and primary representational systems they typically report that the people they have been observing seem and sound like they process information through a whole sequence of representational systems and not just one or two. I usually compliment them on their ability to sense that human beings often generate their subjective experience through both simple and elaborate chains of representational systems. In NLP (NLP Vol. 1, Dilts, et al, 1980.) these sequences are referred to as "strategies."

Consider these examples:

(eyes up-right) It looks like a good job to me and (eyes down-left) I've been telling myself for years that I wanted it, but now that its happening (eyes down-right), I feel a little queasy.

(eyes down-left) It sounds to me like she would rather run off (eyes up-right) with some pretty face than (eyes down-right) make a solid committment.

(eyes up-left) It just doesn't fit my image (eyes down-left) to say that to him, but sometimes (eyes down-right) I get so angry I could slug him! (eyes up-left) But then I look at him and think (eyes down-left) well, you could do worse, and (eyes down-right) then, I don't know why, but I get kind of sad.

In the first instance the person is thinking over a job possibility by a) making a constructed picture, then b) talking to himself about it, and c) getting a feeling. In the next statement, the speaker is processing information by a) talking to himself, b) making a constructed picture, and c) thinking in feelings. The third monologue begins with a remembered image, followed by internal dialogue, that results in feelings and the sequence starting over.

Try the following exercise: get in a comfortable quiet place, close your eyes and remember back to the last time you were in a supermarket. Notice through which of the major representational systems you accessed the memory. Did you lead visually, seeing the food on the shelves or the cashier in the check out line? Did the sounds made by the shoppers and the cash register come back to you first? Or did you recall, perhaps, the temperature in the store, the act of squeezing fruit to sense whether it was ripe, your emotional state as you shopped that day? Whichever channel you first retrieved the memory through is very probably the system you lead with most of the time. It is also the first step in one of your favorite strategies for making meaning of the world. If you go back to the memory and try to reaccess it through one of the two other channels first, you will likely experience some difficulty. Try this for different memories. Generally people rely upon a particular lead system, and can retrieve memories most fluently in that system. And just as the name "lead system" suggests, the first channel which you employ to make meaning will be followed by a sequence of other sense systems that will recur quite predictably.

Obviously, detecting a strategy is a more sophisticated sensory feat than determining just lead and primary representational systems. I strongly suggest that you take the time further to enhance your skill at making these sensory distinctions, however. The operations available with a knowledge of strategies can yield the most pervasive and generative changes imaginable. People in training seminars often like to experiment with the process once it has been introduced. I suggest you sit down with a friend sometime soon and practice: Ask some general questions of them about how they make decisions, what it is like when they are creative, how they know when they have learned something, how they choose a restaurant to dine at, how are they motivated to perform a task, and so on. Make sure that your questions are phrased to allow the maximum possible response and do not direct the person into a particular sensory system. Many people find it helpful to also have a notebook handy to write down the order of steps in the sequences they observe.

These chains of sensory systems make up the structure of an individual's subjective experience at the time he is speaking. Strategies are a sort of syntactic "bottom-line;" the way in which

people organize and manage the vast array of input that is continually being received through the senses. As students begin to more
easily be able to discern strategies, they usually discover that the
chains are recursive and that each individual has only a few selected sequences through which he generates his experience.

There are countless therapeutic implications to the concept of
strategies. Once you have noticed that people generally have a very
small repertoire of sensory sequences, it will also be obvious to you
that most of the steps in the sequences are out of the user's consciousness. The fact is neither good or bad. Generally, the more
habitual and unconscious a behavior becomes, the more we can say
we have fully learned and incorporated it. This is a tremendous
asset since most of our daily behavior—driving a car, conversing
with friends, dialing telephones—is functionally unconscious. The
same is true of more skilled behavior. Once you have learned to
play a musical instrument, for instance, the sequence of steps
involved in doing so drops out of awareness and you are able to
learn subtler distinctions. The fact is also a limitation, however, if
the strategy out of consciousness happens to be one which results
in tension and pain in its current context. An individual may be
continuously processing current information through a chain that
has a step involving memories of painful failure. This strategy will
be operating just as unconsciously as the one at work while driving
a car, but the individual will be controlled *by it* rather than having
the automatic behavior at his service.

A therapist, faced with a client who had a pain-inducing strategy,
would want to work towards making the strategy's outcome a matter of choice. As you will see in the transcript on page 132, bringing the troublesome step of the chain into the client's conscious
awareness is not especially necessary. Having the client confront
the content of the painful memories is not a necessary alternative
nor is it the only choice. We can also very easily and comfortably
alter the steps in the chain so that the outcome is completely
different.

The fact that individuals usually have just a few strategies for
organizing their behavior also implies that a wide variety of tasks
and circumstances are met with formally similar responses. The
Range Postulate states that people's internal constructions are
convenient for a specific range of events. Someone could have an
ideal strategy for writing poetry—lots of internal dialogue and
visceral feeling—that would be very poorly suited for learning to

ride a horse or painting pictures. Likewise, as we all know, a person could grow up in an environment that he experienced as hostile, develop a certain strategy that was very appropriate for that time and place, and continue to use it well into adult life. In other words, strategies that are convenient for a range of events often get used for contexts and tasks that demand other responses. As always, I assume that people make the best choice possible. The logical outcome of being limited to a handful of ways to approach the constantly changing external world is, however, a habitual set of boundaries to perception and behavior.

The way strategies work is analogous to cooking. The sequence of representational systems can be thought of as the steps in a recipe. A strategy, like a recipe, is a means to an outcome—namely, getting nourishment in a way that is palatable and delicious. Recipes, like strategies, must be followed in sequence; if you add an ingredient too early or too late in a recipe, you may wind up with an unsavory outcome. So, too, each of the steps in a strategy is associated and anchored to the one before it.

Whether we want to cook tempura, a roast, an omelette, spaghetti, or crepes, we need to know the recipe. Some dishes have several possible recipes—multiple means to the same outcome. Others can be prepared in only one way. After learning a recipe it becomes unconscious, just like a strategy. A client who comes to you for help is like someone who has learned to cook a few basic dishes really well but misplaced his cookbook. He may even believe that the book is no longer somewhere in his house but, rather, lost forever. As is natural, he would like to try as many new dishes as possible, but has the resources for cooking only a few. He may even have trouble with the recipes he knows; perhaps he learned to cook every thing very well-done to accommodate the tastes of his family but now gets complaints. He might try to prepare new dishes with the recipes he knows well with frustrating results. Applying highly valued strategies for inappropriate tasks is like using a proven recipe for crepes to try and fix meat loaf.

The therapist facing this man has several options. She can help him first, perhaps, to learn to adapt his existing recipes to present circumstances—i.e., teach him to cook what he knows according to his own and other's current tastes rather than serving everything well-done. This is like altering a pain-producing step in an existing strategy. Another choice for the therapist is to teach the man some new recipes; she may know many that he has not tried but would

probably enjoy. Best of all, of course, would be for the therapist
to help the man to retrieve his lost cookbook or take the steps
necessary to buy a new one. This will allow the man to expand his
repertoire of recipes far beyond the range of what the therapist
could teach him and eventually enable him to become a gourmet
cook in his own right. This last level is generative change.

The following case example will make clear to you how a strategy convenient for one set of circumstances can be dysfunctional
in another. Notice that I have slightly expanded the four-tuple
notation: in addition to the superscripts that tell you whether an
experience is internally or externally generated, I have added a
subscript that notes whether an internal experience is newly
created or remembered. A remembered visual image is thus:
V_r^i where the i means internally generated experience and the r
stands for remembered. If the image is constructed the notation
looks like: V_c^i .

Case Example

Ted was 42 years old, once divorced, and a highly respected
business executive for a large department store chain located in
New York City. His presenting problem was concern over an ongoing dating relationship he had with a woman. The relationship
was satisfying in a number of ways, so many that the possibility of
marriage had arisen on several occasions. Ted's trouble was that
whenever he thought of marriage he immediately felt "stubborn."

As he described the situation to me, his eyes scanned consistently through the following pattern: up and to the left, then down
and to the left, up-left again, up and to the right, before finally
looking down and to the right. Noted linearly, this sequence looks
like:

$$External \rightarrow V_r^i \rightarrow A^i \rightarrow V_r^i \rightarrow V_c^i \rightarrow K^i$$

From his accessing cues, we can surmise that Ted reviews a
picture from his past, then talks to himself, returns to a remembered picture, then constructs a new picture and proceeds to have
feelings.

So far we know that Ted is leading visually. The content of the
various representations is unknown. I only know that whenever I

asked him to think of marriage the sequence was the same. When he looked up-right the first time, he tensed his mouth and brow and shook his head slightly from left to right. By the time he accessed kinesthetically, he reported feeling stubbornly opposed to the prospect of marriage. He could not say "why" but he definitely said he was opposed to it.

Essentially, Ted has no choice in the matter. When he searches his internal visual field, he finds some representation that triggers the negative feeling. Though he is conscious of his feelings, they are biased by the wholly unconscious steps that have come before. Every time he thought about marriage he would cycle through the same sequence to the same outcome.

I asked him to go through the strategy slowly and tell me what happens when he thinks about marriage with his girl friend. As he moved his eyes through the sequence he came up with the following: he first sees his girl-friend looking at him (V_r^i), then he hears her asking him again if he is interested in marriage (A^i), next he sees her again much the same as she looked in the first remembered image (V_r^i)—a sort of comparison check. He then makes a constructed visual image that is accompanied by his head shaking "no" and which depicts Ted sitting in his apartment alone. This is followed by the final step, the feeling of stubbornness toward the idea of marriage. As Ted quite literally reported, "I just can't *see* myself living with a woman."

The word "can't" is a Modal Operator. Consistent with our earlier discussion of visual syntax (Chapter 3), the visual representation is formed congruent with the linguistic description. He can't see her living with him because she's not in the picture he sees. At some point, a therapist would want to challenge this Meta-Model "violation" and work towards expanding Ted's ability to broaden his own horizon. The use of the Modal Operator constitutes a severe limitation and Ted will be unable to respond to any of his girlfriend's suggestions until he can see the two of them in the picture.

I moved to retrieve resources by asking Ted about the last time he had made a successful business decision. As he recalled it, his eyes moved up-left, then down left, up-left again, up-right and finally down-right. The same sequence!

This turns out to be a very fine strategy for doing business. Ted was very successful and doing business well required that he be rational, quick to see the facts, and able to talk things over objectively *before* feeling out the best decision. Thus, placing feelings last in his strategy was a good choice since personal feelings are sometimes inappropriate in the relatively impersonal business of the marketplace. By putting feelings last, he still has the resource they constitute available and yet is not slowed down when evaluating information first. So this strategy was useful to produce desirable outcomes for Ted in the business arena. For the range of interpersonal relationships it was not so convenient and for the specific task of making a satisfying decision about whether or not to marry his girlfriend, it was just about useless.

The strategy was dysfunctional for two reasons. The first, as already noted, is that the constructed visual step was governed by a Modal Operator—i.e., he could only see himself alone. The second reason is that the kinesthetic experience is the fifth step, which is very late in strategy. If you and I are intimates and I ask you how you feel about me, I'm going to be puzzled if you take eight or ten minutes to answer the question. Once more: strategies that are superb for one context are troublesome in another. The demands that life makes on us constantly change. Having only one way to make every decision is like going through all the steps involved in making a casserole when what you want to eat is ham and eggs.

It is also not enough to say that Ted was an "unfeeling" person who was "invested" in having problems in his relationship. Ted came to the session with concern for his girlfriend and apparent good will; he sincerely said he would like to change. He simply had a strategy, operating out of consciousness, that he had allowed to generalize to contexts where it was useless.

In the end I helped Ted to develop a new strategy for making interpersonal decisions that had several kinesthetic steps occurring early in the sequence. I then anchored in this new strategy so that it automatically occurred in the contexts where it was appropriate. The "how to's" of this operation will be explicit in the transcripts that follow.

By now you have had the opportunity to see, hear, and feel the effectiveness of matching predicates and pacing the representational systems of your clients. An even more powerful step is to pace sensory experience as it is sequenced in strategies, that is, matching representational system predicates in the spontaneous order that they are offered. For example: "I *see* what you mean and, *talking* about it really *feels* right". The strategy runs:

$$External \rightarrow V^i \rightarrow A^i \rightarrow K^i$$

Since the predicates reveal the organizing strategy of that person at the particular moment in time, a response that is packaged in the same sensory order—see to hear to feel—will constitute a profound and largely unconscious pace.

Your response might thus run, "It *looks* as if our *discussing* your problems will really help you *get a grasp* on them." If a client comes to you for the first time wanting help, her accessing cues and speech patterns revealing the above strategy ($V \rightarrow A \rightarrow K$), you could package all of your verbal output to accommodate the sequence she is using: "I'll be glad to *see* you *show* up regularily for interviews. We can *discuss* your goals and *feel* our way onto *solid* ground that will help you make the changes you want." If the client has been adequately matched and paced non-verbally, your sequencing of information to fit her strategy will work like a key slipping into the tumblers of a lock, opening up a greater sense of trust and rapport.

Obviously, matching a strategy is also more sophisticated an operation than simply matching the predicates of the client's primary representational system.

However, once you are able to look at eye-scanning patterns and listen to your client's speech, you will feel comfortable enough to approach this new level of gathering information. If you had a client who continually ran through the $V \rightarrow A \rightarrow K$ sequence, matching his words in the visual channel would be pacing only one third of of his experience. Many strategies have four, five, and six steps and no one you will meet will be likely limited to just one sequence. But pacing and packaging your output to match strategy sequences will enable you to develop an even deeper rapport with clients.

Another effective way to package information using strategies is to present what you have to communicate in the reverse order of a person's sequence. In the example above the order is $V \rightarrow A \rightarrow K$. The reverse would then be $K \rightarrow A \rightarrow V$. The therapist might then say, "As you are feeling *depressed* I wonder if you would go inside and *ask* yourself if there was ever a time when things *looked* bright for you." The client will very likely be able to follow this chain of reasoning because it is her own sequence played through back-wards. Having "thought back" through your steps, she will end up at her own first step (V) and can proceed through her own most comfortable strategy to answer the question. This enables you to pace and retrieve resources at the same time.

Reversing strategies is a very good way to motivate people, whether in therapy, education, business, or elsewhere. If two peo-ple with reversed strategies are interacting they will be constantly motivating each other. If person A's strategy is $V \rightarrow A \rightarrow K$ and per-son B's sequence is $K \rightarrow A \rightarrow V$, then B will be constantly presenting information that will end with a visual step. In other words, B will pause on A's *first* step, thereby initiating A's strategy. When A has cycled through her sequence she will stop at B's first step. The more A can do, the more he will trigger the beginning of B's process which in turn will set off A again, and so on. It is a great way for people to motivate each other. To reverse someone's strategy might be analogous to turning the crank on a wind-up toy and setting it loose.

Perhaps the most common way that strategies get exchanged is randomly. I may package information through a strategy that is very comfortable to me and turns out to be totally alien to listen-ers. If my strategy is the $V \rightarrow A \rightarrow K$ loop and the someone I am talking to is ordering information through the sequence $V \rightarrow K \rightarrow A$, she could only follow my first two steps with any ease. The visual link would pace her own strategy and probably lead her into the kinesthetic step. She would probably ask me to repeat myself though, so that she could listen again for the auditory link. This can get more complicated with strategies that run up to six steps in length; the same representational systems can be sequenced in any possible combination with repetitive steps as well. The "shot-gun" approach to packaging information, of course, typifies most communication and explains why harmony and understanding be-tween people is so often rare.

In general it can be expected that:

1. pacing the strategy produces the minimal steps necessary for intimacy.
2. reversing the strategy results in motivation for the learning or learning for the motivation given.

3. randomly sorting information with respect to order needed will result in mis-communication of various kinds (interesting, boring, painful, delightful, etc.).

So one of the requirements for rapport and intimacy is matching or pacing a person's strategy sequences. As you will soon begin to notice, this already happens unconsciously in close relationships. In this discussion, of course, I am not limiting matching and pacing to the verbal channel. There will also be a sequence of eye scans and other accessing cues that will correspond with the chain of predicates. When you get proficient at identifying strategies and have practiced matching the words, you can then move on to matching the sequence of accompanying non-verbal cues such as breathing, gesture, posture, expression, etc. The result of your efforts will be expressed in phrases like, "We have our heads together," "he has similiar views," and "We are sounding boards for each other."

Strategy Operations

Strategies make possible the following operations at the level of process:

1. Matching at a structural level.
2. Packaging responses so that they fit the requirements of a strategy.
3. Teaching entirely new strategies.
4. Changing existing strategies.
5. Broadening the effectiveness of existing strategies.

There are a few outstanding purposes for which strategy changing is invaluable:

1. For choice: Since greater choice is the ultimate goal of any treatment, any client response that is automatically set off by external stimulus is partially or completely outside of their conscious control and can become a matter of choice. To teach a client a new strategy is to help provide a set of new choices. Given opportunity, he may sometimes want to behave in the original manner; it is up to the client to determine at a conscious and unconscious level. I presup-

pose that everyone in some way knows what is best for him and makes the best available (for him) choice at any given moment.

2. To eliminate negative feeling states. The outcome of certain strategies is repeatedly to yield unpleasant feelings. Any sequence for processing information that does this ought to be questioned. Alternate ways to fulfill the same ends can be found and new strategies can replace the painful ones.

3. Increase of skill and ease of learning: A sequence change is called for when the operating strategy is obsolete for the task at hand. If the chain operating in trying to learn geometry places feeling first before visualizing, it will be considerably less successful than one which begins with a visual step and puts words second. You might best learn to dance by feeling first and sing by listening before feeling, etc.

The employment of a strategy is an automatic program quite beyond the conscious control of the client. Sequence change does occasionally happen quite by serendipity. Like the other change patterns I have presented, changing a strategy requires a high degree of openness in using your sensory channels to make fine distinctions. As always, there is abundant information you can glean from the client's face color changes, pupil dilation, movement of the orbicularis oculi, the oris, zygomatic and risorius muscles of the face, changes in respiration, posture, muscle tone in the face and neck, and eye scan patterns. These distinctions and others will give you immediate and reliable feedback as to how your non-verbal syntax is affecting the client's subjective experience. You will perceive milli-second long behavior as a client runs through sensory chains involving problem solving, recall, motivation, etc.

Case Example

I treated a 40 year old woman who was in much pain because of her husband's recent decision to divorce her. Pam was an accomplished professional in the working world but she "fell apart" whenever she thought of living alone. As she was interested in changing this negative feeling I first wanted to note the order of her accessing cues.

Therapist: "How are you planning to solve the problems that you'll be encountering?"

Pam: (eyes down-left) "I don't know. I just start to think about it (eyes down-left) and then I fall apart (eyes down-right)."

Her cheeks lose their tone, her eyes fill with water, and her mouth and chin muscles begin to quiver in a way typical of someone about to cry. The order of her experience ran: External auditory → Auditory internal → kinesthetic. Subsequent questioning revealed that she went through the exact same sequence time after time. She had not known, but became aware of her internal dialogue when I mentioned it. She was generating a strong set of negative feelings off of words out of awareness. The quivering of her mouth and chin as well as the muscle movement in her cheeks and diaphragm constitute the "body armoring" set off by her unconscious internal activity. I do not consider physical tension to be resistance but rather an obvious and logical result of the strategy and an elegant communication of process level information.

Therapist: "I wonder if you can think back to the last problem you solved at work, and when you have identified it, nod your head."

Pam: (eyes down-left and then up-right) Nods "OK."

After her auditory internal re-asking of the question, Pam's eyes moved to make a visual construction. Auditory external → A^i → V^i_c. Her skin darkened and a degree of muscle tonus returned to her cheeks. Her mouth relaxed and her chest lifted with deepened breathing. She looked more alert and might be judged to be "confident."

My request was carefully worded to avoid directing her into any particular sensory system; when I formed my syntax I made it purposefully vague to allow the maximum possible responses from Pam. The conversational postulate, "I am wondering if . . ." is open ended and not a command, "think back" is unspecific as to *how* she might remember. Like some exceptions to the rule, Pam stores a portion of her memory in visual constructions. I presuppose the existence of several solved problems with the word "last", and the nominalization "problem" engages a complex sensory task that led to a satisfying resolution. Having asked her to recall an event I now ask her to relive it.

Therapist: "When you (deepens voice tone) *reimagine that process* you went through, re-create it right here so that I can understand."

Pam: (eyes down-left) "I'm a nurse, and they brought this man to me (eyes up-left) and said I'd have to give him a shot. Then, I told them (eyes down-left) they ought to take him immediately to surgery (eyes up-left). And they did and it saved his life (eyes down-right)."

Pam's process for solving problems was: external $\to A^i \to V^i_r \to A^i \to V^i_r \to K^i$ and this could be shortened to:

$$\text{External} \to A^i \to V^i_r \to K^i$$

Therapist: "How do you know you solved it?"

Pam: (eyes up-right) "I just remember." (She asks in a questioning tone.)

Therapist: "Yes, but how do you know *you* made that decision?"

Pam: (eyes down-right) "I just felt it!"

Here I double-check my intuition that a kinesthetic internal feeling is the final step in her problem solving strategy. When she says she remembers, she again accesses visual construction; when she states congruently, "I just felt it!" she repeats her eye movement down to the right. The entire sequence, then, starts with Pam hearing her own voice within asking for a solution and generating pictures at each point of decision in the action. She repeats the $A^i \to V^i_r$ loop until all challenges are met at which time she has a positive feeling.

Now a comparison of the sequence in which she is unable to cope and the chain at play when she succeeds reveals an additional visual step in the latter.

Unsuccessful: $\text{External} \to A^i \to K\text{unpleasant}$

Successful: $\text{External} \to A^i \to V^i_r \to K\text{pleasant}$

The next step in treatment is to discover how the unsuccessful sequence can be changed. Note again that Pam stores visual memory through both constructed and eidetic images. Let me encourage you to expect exceptions to rules and to act upon your sensory experience whenever your perceptions contradict what you have been told. Taking her successful strategy on its own terms I went on to determine whether it was functional in coping with living alone.

Therapist: "When I ask you this next question I want you to do the following: as soon as my hand moves up, focus on it and follow it up and to the left with your eyes. Then move them down to the right like this (demonstrates)."

By this I can be certain that she will put whatever question I ask through the successful sequence. Pam and I rehearse the instructions. Since she has never encountered me before this session she is unprepared to understand fully the procedure and curiously follows my directions.

Therapist: "Now (moves hand out), I want you to consider how to solve the problem of being alone in your house (moves hand up to his right, her left) next Easter."

Pam: (Focuses on his hand and moves eyes down-left. Then in response to his hand movement she moves her eyes up-left and accesses eidetic imagery, then her eyes move down-right and she manifests the same cheek, mouth, and chin movements as before and begins weeping.)

It is now apparent that her original attempt at problem solving used this sequence:

$$A^i \rightarrow V^i_r \rightarrow K^i(\text{unpleasant})$$

The change (deletion) to the $A^i \rightarrow K^i$ loop reflects a good choice, in so much as Pam feels the full effects of crying when she sees the visual eidetic image.

Since eidetic imagery can only be composed of things actually seen, we can now infer that her strategy is not very productive for learning entirely new tasks. Pam had earlier told me that she had never learned to swim because she could not *picture* it as enjoyable. She was not motivated to undertake any new activities unless she first felt the necessity and then only if she could refer to some scene in her past. She could then successfully learn what was required to reduce her discomfort. In short, her strategy was useless for dealing with the new circumstances presented by her impending divorce. The second obvious conclusion we can draw is that the act of searching remembered images to resolve the issue of being alone produces strong unpleasant feelings in Pam. The content of the remembered image is not of major importance but I will present it in the interest of being comprehensive.

Therapist: "What do you see when you look up to the left?"

Pam: "Nothing."

Therapist: (directing her to access up and to her left) "Move your eyes up there and become aware of anything you are looking at . . ."

Pam: (eyes up-left) "Oh . . . , I think . . . (eyes down-right and cries). I remember when I was ten or eleven and dad was gone and mom had to work. I lived (eyes up-left) in Toledo and I just remember (eyes down-right) being so alone (cries again)."

Therapist: "Are you aware of making a picture when you look up there?"

Pam: "No, I wasn't, but maybe . . . yeah, I guess I see that house in Toledo (drying her tears)."

So the picture Pam makes is of a traumatic scene from her childhood. As it has been triggered unconsciously, she has some difficulty bringing it into awareness. The content of the picture is nonetheless what induces her crying. When she tries to solve her current dilemma the memory of that early event interferes. She is trying to draw upon only the resources she had at age eleven and they are no more help now than they were then. So she has come to bypass the picture of Toledo to reduce the pain, instead using this abbreviated sequence:

$$\text{External} \rightarrow (A^i \rightarrow K^i)$$

This loop, unfortunately, leaves her even fewer ways to deal with being alone and making plans.

An analysis of this early scene would not better equip you to change Pam's strategy. Conventional insight therapy would press for her to explore her vision at the level of content. Pam might be helped to change her emotional and somatic response to the childhood scene or, perhaps, the content of her internal dialogue. Some approaches would opt to add on new behavioral programs even though the current strategy already cannot support her attempts to cope successfully.

Specifically:

1. conventional Bioenergetics (Lowen, 1975) would change the unpleasant K to a pleasant K while analyzing the content of the V^i.
2. conventional Gestalt (Perls, 1969) would change unpleasant K to pleasant K.
3. orthodox Transactional Analysis (Berne, 1961, pp. 139–187) would change the content of the auditory internal and would also dissociate to facilitate changing the content of the K to pleasant.
4. Rational Emotive therapy (Ellis, 1971) would initially change the content of the A.
5. Behavior Modification would attempt to attach behavior programs (Skinner, 1971) to the existing internal representations (Lazarus, 1976) without changing to a strategy that might be better suited to support and organize the new behaviors.

Each of these approaches would involve time and engage Pam in differing degree of pain. This is especially true of Gestalt Therapy and Bioenergetics. They would leave the structure of her strategy as it was and change the psychological function of one or another of the steps. Since Pam's strategy excludes the possibility of making future plans, keeping it intact and changing the painful content would leave her no better off. She would still be unable to make critical personal decisions even though the state would be less unpleasant. A therapist could also work to uncover the injunctions and other childhood events that shaped Pam's early experience. One could trace and probably find limiting patterns that were a part of her family life. But if all the necessary nonverbal information for a sequence change is being presented to the therapist, what would be the purpose?

Since Pam's somatic behavior is a response to the content of internal pictures and words, over time the strategy will have logically shaped her physique and even altered her biochemistry. Changing the sequence will alter any somatic by-products as well as other associated content issues. The operation renders academic the analysis of such things as scripting, body armor, and personal history.

Designing a New Strategy

The first task was to select a sequence to install in place of Pam's original one. This can be done totally arbitrarily, with sequences known to work with other clients, or by deciding what step(s) the problem strategy lacks. Pam's chain does not include a constructed visual step, so it would be wise to include one. Constructing images of things that have never happened works well in planning and problem solving. We decided to modify the existing chain:

$$\text{External} \to A^i \to V_r^i \to K^i$$

by installing both a visual construction and a pleasant kinesthetic step:

$$\text{External} \to A^i \to V_c^i \to K^i \to V_r^i$$

The new chain must function as automatically as the old one did: each link must trigger the next. To install the VV_r^i link I used the basic operation of anchoring.

> Therapist: "Pam, I want you to move your eyes up and to the right. When you have done that, make a picture of the last problem you solved or last time you overcame a challenge."
>
> Pam: (moves eyes up-right, then nods her head) "OK."
>
> Therapist: (touches her elbow in a specific manner just as she nods) "Now, each time I touch you like this move your eyes up and to the right and make that picture. We'll do this until it becomes automatic for you."

Pam and I rehearse this for 3–4 minutes. This is the usual length of time for such an associated response to form. I am having her return to the constructed picture that she easily and spontaneously made earlier in the session. Having established this anchor, all I now need do is make sure that Pam has pleasant feelings to follow the picture. This is a simple matter since she already connotes a feeling of confidence with this particular image.

Therapist: "Now when I touch your elbow and you move your eyes up and to the right, follow this experience by moving your eyes down to the right. As you do this, register the feeling of confidence and excitement that you have. Can you do this now?"

Pam: "I think so (moves eyes in the designated manner)."

Therapist: "What you think about really is not important at this point. All that I'm interested in is that you make these movements in an automatic manner whenever I touch your elbow. Let's practice."

Pam: "Like this?" (moves eyes in the designated manner).

Now we practice this movement several times to insure that she has the two steps associated. On several attempts she smiles or laughs. The new sequence will not yield the eidetic image of Toledo because the V_r^i step will follow the positive kinesthetic cue.

Installation of the New Strategy

After another six attempts Pam can run through the entire sequence very rapidly and "without thinking." The next move is to install these new links after the internal dialogue but prior to the visual eidetic steps in her original chain. This is very easy; the major factor is timing.

Therapist: "Now, I want you to (shifts voice tone down as done previously when using embedded commands) proceed to consider solving some of the problems about being alone."

The voice tone shift is an already established anchor for the embedded command to "consider solving problems." Without the anchoring, Pam would quite automatically revert to her original dysfunctional strategy.

Pam: (eyes down-left - her auditory rewording step) . . .

Therapist: (touches her elbow in the manner previously anchored to the new experience chain sequence.)

Pam: (eyes up to the right, down to the right, up to the left) "Well, ha, which problem?"

Therapist: (touches her elbow anchor) . . .

Pam: (eyes up to the right, down to the right, up to the left) "I can get an apartment and pay the rent. I've already shopped around" (smiles and tilts head to the left).

Firing off the anchor on her elbow interrupts her old strategy with the new one. The process is repeated coupled with questions relating to her present problem. I gradually make the questions more difficult in content as I continue to "fire" the anchor after her auditory internal step. I continue until the process becomes automatic as she deals with the no longer troublesome prospect of living alone. To repeat for clarity, the strategy now runs:

$$\text{External} \rightarrow A^i \rightarrow V^i_c \rightarrow K^i \rightarrow V^i_r \rightarrow \text{outcome}$$

The astute reader will observe that Pam will be able to connect her original strategy to the final step in the new one—visual eidetic. She can now repeat the $A \rightarrow V$ loop with ease. If she goes from the V to the A, as she used to, she will now spontaneously cycle through visual construct and the positive feeling before returning to the eidetic step. Not only can she avoid the regressive collapse and pain, but she can also construct pictures of possible solutions to further future problems. The questions I asked her enhanced this process and will also permit her to generalize the memory of previous successes to the constructed image of new ones.

The final phase of installation is to check whether the new chain operates fully unconsciously and without the external anchor. I continued to ask Pam about her plans and lifted my hand from her elbow. The new sequence continued faster than before. At the end of the session it was happening in milli-seconds, just as the original did. Pam, as others, stated that she was no longer conscious of doing anything deliberately. My series of questions amounted to a future-pace as well. Let me reiterate that the "acid test" of all effective therapy is whether the client can take what he has learned and use it outside of the office.

The session with Pam lasted one hour. When she entered the office she would collapse into tears at the slightest thought of being alone. As she left, Pam was responding to detailed questions about her new life and truly enjoying the new skill. She could not tell when the new sequence was working, but she did know that she could answer difficult questions and was not crying. The treatment did not involve any deep analysis or dredging of childhood traumata. In conventional terminology, her ego was strengthened, her impulses controlled, her ability to "reality test" improved, and she was generally more spontaneous.

It has been over two years since I worked with Pam. She reported that she had one or two bad days (of crying) but, in sum, was amazed that change could happen so rapidly and make her life so much easier. She thinks of herself as very much the same person. The process through which her subjective experience passes is, however, organized in an entirely new manner, allowing a multitude of choices.

Suffering is Unnecessary!

The kinesthetic element of subjective experience is thought to be the "most real" by some people (Hart, Corriere, Binder, 1975). Pain is commonly thought to be inevitable, necessary for growth, change, happiness, etc. Emotions are unpredictable, occurring without warning or choice. Some people grimly vow to live with pain, others maintain that expressing pain is the only way to get over it.

It should be obvious to you, by now, that the study of strategies offers a whole new way of getting a handle on the issue. The transcript with Pam might suggest that an individual does not have to suffer to cope.

Pain can be usefully modelled as a by-product of certain strategies. Some chains operate to gather unpleasant feelings consistently.

For instance, another client of mine structured much of her perception in five steps; she would see how she wanted her life to be (V^i_c), make a picture of how it is (V^i_r), feel depressed (K^i), tell herself that "things are hopeless" (A^i), and feel more depressed. She continued this as a loop, on and on, applying the sequence to a number of decisions such as whether to change jobs, living quarters, save money, etc. Working with her, I changed the process to run: See what she wanted, tell herself she can get it, picture the steps necessary, take action, and feel good. No matter what content she processes through this new strategy—break up with lover, future plans of any sort—she was able to plan out and arrive at feeling good about whatever she did. Altering her strategy took very little time and the effects were wide-ranging. The main difference, of course, was that she was no longer chronically depressed.

Changing a commonly used strategy can also alter a person's experience of chronic physical pain. I once treated an 84 year old woman who was in great pain from a stroke. Neurosurgery had not helped and neither did drugs stop the pain. She had grown totally dependent upon her daughter and her sphere of physical movement was limited to her bed, her wheelchair, and the bathroom. The constant pain was anchored to everything she knew. She also had several calibrated communication loops going with those around her. They would talk with her about her condition and Betty would invariably end up saying, "I'll never get over the pain." She said this often when I first met her. She had alienated all of her friends, felt alone and depressed.

My co-therapist and I worked with Betty over several sessions, systematically retrieving and creating resources and anchoring them, breaking her calibrated loops, and altering her verbal representation of her state. Specifically, we had her de-nominalize the word "pain" and begin to first, represent her kinesthetic experience actively and then note that sometimes her feelings were more or less intense rather than constant over time.

The most significant maneuver we made, however, was to change Betty's strategy for processing the proprioceptive experience she called "pain." Her report of being in constant pain was consistent with the sequence we saw her using repeatedly: she would lead kinesthetically, then make pictures of her other painful circumstances from her past. The pictures would often be interspersed with internal dialogue. The final step, though, was invariably auditory: the refrain of "I'll never get over the pain" that people around her were reacting to. My co-therapist and I changed the order of her sequence and anchored in the options of leading visually and auditorily, internally or externally, and of allowing the different ordering to result in feelings other than "pain." Betty had otherwise come to the pain first and it was unchanging.

Betty is now walking, talking, and able to generate pleasant feelings for herself. Changing her strategy and associating it to her resources provided transformations in her behavior that her family and aquaintances have deemed "remarkable." When feelings are approached as the result of interplay between representational systems, they can be changed. This holds true for "physical" pain as well as emotional disturbances. The proprioceptive data that Betty received from her body is now processed differently by her and, therefore, no longer means what it did. She later thanked me, expressed relief (rather than pain), and said, "I'm so glad my possibilities are no longer limited."

Conscious Mind Strategies

Sometimes teaching a person to use a strategy consciously will yield exciting results. I recently worked with a young man sixteen years old. Tom was in trouble with the courts for breaking and entering a business. His Probation Officer had referred him to a local mental health clinic because Tom seemed to be unusually shy and unresponsive.

At the clinic he was seen somewhere between twenty and twenty-five times and all he would ever say when spoken to was "Yes," "No," and "I don't know." The staff had discussed his case and decided that he was, in actuality, "resistant." They took up giving him commands and challenges that were the reverse of what they wanted from him—"I bet you couldn't even get a girl friend if you wanted to." Regardless of their tactics and random behavior the boy continued to respond with, "I don't know." The staff had succeeded in making some changes in Tom's family that had pleased both the family and the court. The agency called me to consult with Tom, however, because he was about to be expelled from school for truancy.

As I talked with Tom, I was initially impressed with how successfully he managed to say, "I don't know." He seemed to be expert at using this strategy to get a number of outcomes. But he also seemed limited to that sole response. Whenever I addressed him he would defocus his eyes and move them up-left. He followed this visual eidetic lead with a kinesthetic access, his eyes remaining defocused and looking away down right. He would end the sequence with "I don't know," as he shifted his eyes to an auditory access down left.

So his existing strategy for knowing that he didn't know was:

$$\text{External} \to V\,{}^{i}_{r} \to K^{i} \to A^{i} \to \text{"I don't know" (A)}$$

The auditory accessing and speaking came after the kinesthetic step so I suspected that the way he understood spoken words and formulated his usual reply was influenced by whatever feeling he consistently had.

The sentence, "I don't know," offers only a subject and an unspecified verb. The rest of the statement is deleted: (don't know what?) From his syntax I conclude that he is deleting the kinesthetic element of his experience.

> S: "What are you involved with the court about?"
> T: "B and E's," (eye scan pattern is the same).
> S: "How do you feel about this whole thing?"
> T: ($V\,{}^{i}_{r} \to K^{i} \to A^{i} \to$) "I don't know."
> S: "You look as if you've been paying some dues."
> T: "Yeah. I have." (same eye movement).

Apparently my second question was a good pace. The request for his feelings about the court case was designed to discover how he chunked his feelings. I wanted to know if they are chunked in small enough pieces that he can discuss his feelings in some way.

> S: "How long do you expect this to go on before you've paid all the dues you have to pay?"
> T: "I don't know" (same eye scan pattern).
> S: "Do you do as well as you want to in school?"
> T: "No" (same eye scan pattern).
> S: "What do you need to do better in school?"
> T: "I don't know" (same eye scan pattern).
> S: "Well, I know. And I would like to teach you another way to think so that you can look at people and feel comfortable and talk. Would that be all right with you?"
> T: "Yeah!" (same eye scan pattern and voice tone is higher and voice tempo faster).
> S: "Can you talk in words inside your head and see pictures in your mind's eye and remember feelings?"
> T: "Yeah."
> S: "O.K., I want you to try doing this: can you look at someone and instead of having a feeling next only talk inside your head about it?"

T: He looks at me and makes eye contact for several seconds and then smiles.

S: "You did it successfully?"

T: "Yeah" (still looking away).

S: "Now I want you to try making a picture like a double exposure, over the top of the people you talk about. Make a picture of what you think you might like to do with the person and then have a feeling about that."

T: Looking at the others in the room for the first time he makes eye contact, smiles and continues looking for some time.

S: "Could you do that? Now move your eyes down here (down to his right) and check that what you're thinking feels good to you."

T: "Yeah, I'd like to go bowling with him," referring to a psychologist that was in the room.

At that point Tom was talking *to* me. He was making eye contact and even offering information that I had not requested. To the workers in the clinic Tom had, for months, only seemed able to avoid socializing. The strategy I was teaching him ran thus:

$$\text{External} \rightarrow V^e \rightarrow A^i \rightarrow V^{\,i}_{\,c} \rightarrow K^i$$

The strategy was not being installed to operate automatically as the one of Pam's.

I offered it to Tom to initiate consciously—a "conscious mind strategy."

I asked Tom to run through the new sequence with everyone in the room. As he did so he began joking with those present, his overall countenance lightened, and he was very enjoyable to be with. I questioned him about his trouble with school. He said that he was in a special class and was especially having trouble with math. He wanted to learn math so that when he grew up he could work for the same company as his father.

In addition to speaking directly to the staff, this was the first time Tom had ever revealed his thoughts about school, his father, and his future plans. I was so heartened by his rapid changes that I thought it worthwhile to take him through some math problems using the new strategy. After the second problem he was able to get them all correct. I complimented him on being a quick learner and having a very fast mind. We then proceeded with some change

work related to his behavior at home and his need for more response from his father. I said good-bye to Tom having sincerely
enjoyed him as a client.

When the staff regrouped to watch a video tape of the session,
I was told that Tom was in a special class at school for those
considered to have learning disabilities. I think, from this session,
that you can already begin to imagine the applications that strategies might have in the educational process. They further suggest
new ways to interpret and change behavior that has traditionally
been labelled and accepted as "slow learning." Teaching Tom a
more efficient way to learn worked well . . . In following up I found
that he is doing much better at math, frequently socializes and no
longer skips school. I can only assume that he continued to use the
new strategy.

Further Implications

I am especially excited about the levels of specificity the science
of strategies makes possible. We are now, for instance, in a position to discuss exactly how poorly functioning parents raise similar
children; how the family "trance" is carried on over generations.
We could also research the possibility that certain habitual experience chains may inevitably result in particular types of somatic and
psychological difficulties. As I said, the tool of strategies also has
far-reaching applications in educational processes. Children who
have been traditionally labeled as limited in some way are often
found to have strategies that are simply cumbersome and inappropriate for learning. Problems with reading, social adjustments, and
learning particular skills can be comfortably solved with a creative
use of strategies.

It will be very exciting indeed when there are completed an-
thologies that will present the most effective matrix of thinking and
behaving sequences to use as successful geniuses have done prac-
ticing law, doing ballet, mathematics, physics, teaching, business,
etc. Finding the most appropriate sequence of representational
systems for learning and performing specific tasks and skills will be
the major thrust of future generations of social, behavioral and
heuristic scientists.

I want to close this chapter by coaxing you to begin to imagine
the evolutionary changes that are possible for humans with the

aquisition of efficient strategies. It is perhaps the first time in history that we are able to detail the thinking process in such an empirical manner. We can now identify the form and order of sensory representation needed to learn and perform successfully any task practiced by any member of the species.

Learning someone else's strategies will not produce a clone or lessen a person's individuality. Our personal history and essence make us all enduringly different. We cannot duplicate thumbprints with these tools. We can, however, reproduce the organization of experience so explicitly that any one can acquire another's skill at performing a task as well as even his "talent" for it. Those of us involved in the study of strategies have not been able to find limits to their application. . . .

The Oracle

The pounding of his heartbeat moved him ever onward to another city where he had heard that others lived in peace and serenity, where he had heard that someone could tell him of the whole truth, that there was a great oracle he could follow whose wisdom would bring him entire truth. He moved onward. As the traveler recalled and wrote in his journal, he paid attention to the tiniest of sounds and smallest of movements of the eyes, faces and behaviors of others as they went about their tasks in villages and huts and caves. He did not find all of the truth there. He learned, as he was instructed, to pay attention to temperature changes, to hear the wind blowing, to feel the softness of the fruit, to know its color and to pick it when ripe. He had learned to see the game and hear its cry, to grab his bow and like the best of hunters, he observed the pace of the game, noticing its behavior, listening quietly in the woods, watching for small movements, alert to the tiniest sound of the game. On the shores he was alert to the slightest change in humidity and temperature. He watched the fog move in and the movement of the clouds. He learned to gauge his safety by the behavior of the fish which he was seeking to catch. He recalled the skill of those who had taught him all these trades; the tribesmen who had become skillful had taught him to insure his plenteous food supply. The teachings had been tailored so that comprehension was available for even a small boy, a young girl, the oldest people in the tribe or the simplest of tribesmen to make the same kinds of predictions that he could of the stars and waves. And yet all these learnings did not lead him to what seemed to be a certain truth.

At long last he came over the top of the mountains in one of the driest regions of the land where there was said to live the greatest of all oracles. The religious rituals he discovered reminded him of the origin of his own tribal history. It spoke of the magic that worked for the believers. And on his journey to the land of the oracle, he heard many myths, each presented as truth for the individual that spoke it and for the tribe that believed it. He heard teachers telling stories about activities of heroes and gods, teaching their basic truths, enculturating the young, healing the troubled. He observed rituals which were designed and elaborately enacted to influence the hunts, the catches, the weather, the spirits of the ancestors, as well as the tribal members going through significant events such as birth and marriage, death and independence. When he came at long last to the feet of the oracle, he felt that his troubled heart would finally be answered, that his request for the truth would finally be given.

The oracle spoke to him of many things that he had not yet encountered, of trees that looked like carrots, of journeys to the tops of mountains from which he would find the truth. Returning daily to hear stories spoken by the oracle, he made his own plan for deciphering the wisdom hidden within the tales the oracle told. The voice of the old oracle was strong and confident. It spoke of wisdom that had been accumulated through the eyes of one who sees beyond those things that others have known.

The oracle spoke of many events that seemed to be events of the traveler's very own past. In an uncanny way, the stories woven by the oracle spoke of the places that the traveler had been and promised to be speaking of the places where the traveler would soon go. He found himself listening in awe, remembering those things from his past that were referred to by the oracle, and putting those memories together in ways that created a sense of satisfaction that made his heart sing, that filled his head with ideas and wonderment of things not yet done, and reassured him of the time that would be available to do all those things.

And the oracle, in his parting remarks, spoke at great length about a people who lived beyond the last hill, a people that he would encounter in a very short period of time. From the description the oracle gave, he could make no sense of who these persons were. It sounded terribly fantastic to him, this journey that he would have to take to discover who this incredible oracle spoke of. From the description the oracle gave, neither he nor any of his acquaintances seemed to know anything of this particular town and tribe. But, the oracle promised that the final truth would occur to him as soon as he journeyed through one more land and over the final hill. And so, confident that the oracle had given him a guide that he could follow for a short period of time, he left the oracle and the land of strange customs and ways and went on to the town of the healers and then to this mysterious town where the oracle promised he would find the truth.

CHAPTER VI THE STRUCTURE OF METAPHOR

This book is only a way of "talking about" experience. Our use of language is a metaphor for a metaphor. We select words that approximate our sensory experience, which is itself a transformation, a map of reality. It is almost as though someone with normal vision were trying to describe a *map* of California—somewhere he had once actually been—to a man blind from birth. Our sensory maps are composed of linguistic and perceptual distinctions that provide continuity to our journey through this world. Of course, paper maps are revised every few years, so sticking closely to a current version will both help one make way through a territory and may include the new discoveries and pleasant surprises that make travelling so enjoyable. Part of an individual's experiential map will be very emotional, part will embody physical sensations, part is memory, abstract verbal summary, and so on. Though all of the locations, distances, and pathways in a personal map are learned, your particular combinations and innovations are unique to you.

I will be applying the term "metaphor" to those personal maps as well as those perceptual and ideological assumptions we share collectively as members of a culture. Directly or indirectly, the term has been frequently used to describe not just the process of therapy but the way we understand reality. "I am using metaphor here in its most general sense: the use of a term for one thing to describe another because of some similarity between them or between their relations to other things." (Jaynes, 1977, p. 48)

The formation of life-metaphors starts with the complex process of learning called "socialization." What we are taught to see, hear, feel, taste, smell, as well as label and discuss is our reality or soon comes to be our reality, a fact that constrains as much as liberates us. Joseph Chilton Pearce summarizes this well:

A social world view, one shared with other people, is structured from our infant minds by the impingements on us from, and the verifying responses to us by, other people. A mind finds its definition of itself not by confrontation with *things* so much as other minds. We are shaped by each other. We adjust not to the reality of the *world* but to the reality of other thinkers. (Pearce, 71, p. 48)

Obviously this shaping of thought differs from culture to culture, and written anthropology abounds with examples of the relativity of social world views. The Plains Indians of the United States, for instance, held the belief that certain ritual ceremonies had to be conducted in an exacting and precise manner in order to prevent natural catastrophies. Any member of the tribe could bring doom upon the entire congregation by not adhering closely to his prescribed role during a ceremony. Although this belief was believed superstitious and uncivilized by the Europeans who invaded the area, the rituals kept the Indian society united; they had a very direct relationship with natural forces, a rich sense of fellowship, and no word equivalent to our concept of "crime rate."

Bear in mind the difference between the utility of a metaphor or model and the "truth" of it—that is, the process versus the content. If our emphasis is on desirable ends—a low "crime rate," social coherence, and other benign qualities—then questions of truth and falsity are useless. If we believe that "economic realism" requires that a percentage of the population be poverty stricken, then we will never imagine otherwise. On the other hand, Martin Luther King, Jr., "had a dream," a metaphor that he conveyed that evoked hope and possibility where none had existed for many people. The model of the Plains Indians was decidedly ill-suited for living in the new world the whites built around them. But the metaphor was not true or false or right or wrong—simply convenient or not for a particular situation.

As cultural metaphors vary so have the various metaphors for personality changed through time. In early Babylon demons were thought to be at the root of most human problems. Accepting the presuppositions in this model, a Babylonian doctor approached his patients with certain fixed notions. While searching for signs of demons, he would likely be oblivious to any organ deterioration or the possibility that a personal belief system was closer to the "cause" of the problem. One clash of opposing therapeutic beliefs that is well known today is between the psychoanalytic model of personality and the humanistic version. The former metaphor locates a difficulty within a person just as the medical disease pinpoints germs. The model does not allow for the influence of social interactions, treatment is lengthy, and even the practitioners believe that cures are not that common.

Both the diversity of therapeutic models and the fact that each of them in its own way helps bring about change in clients point out the power of metaphor to shape individual experience. You can harness this power in a very direct way by utilizing the formal properities of map-making to design metaphors that are tailored to fit the problems of our clients. Given that clients come to us with unfulfilled desires because of certain limitations in their metaphor of the world, we find it very potent therapeutically to create specific metaphors that expand the range of a client's map and guide him toward fruitful outcomes.

The actual "how to" of this technique is splendidly and clearly laid out in Gordon's *"Therapeutic Metaphors."* For our purposes here it will be enough to uncover the basic formal structure of such metaphors.

Many people have had the experience of being told a story by a friend and wondering if it contains a hidden meaning intended for them. The following example is from Carlos Casteneda's *Journey to Ixtlan* (pgs. 3–4):

Carlos reports that he and Don Juan exchanged greetings for a while and then Carlos confessed that he had lied the first time they met, by boasting that he knew a lot about peyote when, actually, he knew nothing about it. He noted that Don Juan simply stared at him with kind eyes. Carlos went on to explain that for six months he had been preparing for this meeting with Don Juan and that now he really knew the facts.

As the story goes, Carlos reports that Don Juan laughed and, as usual, Carlos couldn't understand what he said that was funny. Don Juan was laughing. Carlos was confused and offended. Don Juan began to reassure him that even though he had all the best intentions, there was no way that he would really have been able to properly prepare himself for the kind of experiences he was about to have. Carlos wondered again about hidden meanings and notes that Don Juan apparently sensed his curiosity because he began to explain by telling him a story.

At this point, Carlos goes into lengthy detail about the story Don Juan told. It had to do with a king who, long ago, had persecuted and killed certain people within his domain. The way the king determined who would be killed was accomplished by testing their pronunciation of a certain word. Only the people who could pronounce it in the particular manner chosen according to the king's liking were set free. So, the king went about setting roadblocks at several critical points and had officials ask those wishing passage to pronounce the key word. If they failed to do so properly they were immediately put to death. Carlos explains that, at this point, Don Juan emphasized a *certain* young man who had studied to pronounce the test word for exactly six months, hoping to master the pronunciation. When the day of the test came, the young man who had studied for so long was confident that he would pass the official at the roadblock.

Don Juan then paused dramatically, and although Carlos thought the entire enactment was a little foolish, he cooperated. At this point, Carlos thinks he is in control of the situation because he is familiar with a similar story about the Jews in Germany being apprehended according to their pronunciation of particular words. Carlos expects that the punchline will take the form of the official forgetting the key word and asking the traveler to pronounce a similar but different word which had not been studied. Since he thinks Don Juan wants him to ask what happened, he does ask, trying to sound as innocently interested as possible. Don Juan continued, mentioning that the traveler, who was indeed clever, knew that the guard had forgotten the key word and so confessed that he had prepared to pronounce that word for several months. With this, Don Juan made another dramatic pause, and because of the unexplainable turn of events, Carlos had now become truly interested in what happened to the traveler. The element of confession was something that had not belonged to the original story. So, with eagerness in his voice, Carlos asked what *did* happen to the young man. Don Juan, amidst roars of laughter, told him that the young man had been immediately executed. So, the story ends in the long run as Carlos had expected, but the process of telling it had engaged and captured his attention. Carlos particularly liked the way the story had been linked to his own situation. He even suspected that Don Juan had constructed the story specifically to fit his situation. He reports that Don Juan seemed to be making fun of him but was doing so in such a subtle and artistic manner that Carlos laughed along with him and knew that he had much more to learn from this man than he had originally believed.

Don Juan has developed a metaphor that contains all of the elements present in the actual situation between him and Carlos. The steps involved are summarized:

1. examine the problem;
2. locate all nouns (people, places, things) in the problem;
3. locate all processes (verbs, adjectives, adverbs) in the problem;
4. select the content of the metaphor (person, animal, abstract, etc.);
5. create a noun in the metaphor for each noun in the problem;
6. create a process in the metaphor for each process in the problem;
7. design the story line to provide a solution or desired response.

Thus Don Juan's metaphor can be represented visually:

SITUATION	METAPHOR
Nouns	
Carlos _ _ _ _ _ _ _ _ _ _	commoner
discomfort _ _ _ _ _ _ _ _	discomfort
Juan _ _ _ _ _ _ _ _ _ _ _	king
Knowledge of peyote _ _ _	pronunciation of key word
Appointment _ _ _ _ _ _ _	road block
Processes	
Studying 6 months _ _ _ _	studying 6 months
Meeting _ _ _ _ _ _ _ _ _	testing
Accepting/rejecting _ _ _ _	living or being killed

To establish an effective pace with a listener a metaphor must first employ the same set of representational systems, an isomorphic set of nouns, and a similiar sequence of four-tuples (i.e.

the same plot). In the example, Carlos considers his encounter
with Don Juan a test. He states that he has studied for six months
and is now ready to present himself before the old man. Don Juan
paces his client verbally; he constructs a metaphor containing a
thinly veiled reference to another person in similiar circumstances
and Carlos obviously identifies with the story's main character. In
the end, Carlos fails the test, as in the metaphor but he is left
laughing rather than dead. He has intuitively learned from the
story's lesson; his entire mood has changed and he no longer is
trapped in his presenting dilemma. The obvious irony in the contrast between the story's catastrophic conclusion and Carlos'
harmless situation is never expressed consciously. The outcome
however is that his initial apprehension gives way to humor, curiosity, and excitement.

The Strategy of Milton Erickson's Metaphors

Milton H. Erickson's ability to deliver treatment through the
form of metaphor is unequalled by anyone. He is a master in the
use of anecdotes, puns, analogies, and stories. For our purposes
here I have lumped them into the one category of metaphor.

Whether Erickson's metaphors are delivered in a deep hypnotic
trance or the "normal" mixed state of mind, the patient has the
tendency to make maximum use of them on both a conscious and
unconscious level. Stories that seem to relate to a particular problem that the client recognizes as his own will appeal to the conscious mind. The inherent surface logic of the analogy may thereby
engage the client in thinking of conscious resolutions. Also "when
the analogy refers to deeply engrained (automatic and therefore
functionally unconscious) associations, mental mechanisms, and
learned patterns of behavior, it tends to activate these internal
responses and make them available for problem solving" (Erickson, Rossi 1977, p. 225).

Having paced the client's conscious mind with an initially direct
allegory, Erickson often will then begin to vary the content of what
he says further and further from the literal and recognizable situation with which he began. The client's multi-level responses continue and now the conscious mind becomes involved in searching
out the relevant meaning of the words. Careful management of the
story's content will occupy and distract the client's conscious mind

and the fixed set of associations contained within it. Further tangents and new turns in the story leave the listener suspended and continually anticipating some direction. This state of attention allows the storyteller to access more powerful and flexible processes that are functioning out of the client's awareness but evident to the therapist's sensory experience.

An example of Dr. Erickson's work with pain control will illustrate the potency of this technique. Jay Haley has anthologized one of the articles wherein Erickson performs his "interspersal induction" in which he embeds hypnotic directives into the flow of "natural" conversation. Joe was a middle-aged florist, well respected in his community. Just prior to Erickson's first visit, Joe had lost a large portion of his face through radical therapy for a malignant growth. In addition to the operation he was told that he had only a few weeks to live. His physical pain was so severe that he could sleep very little, even with doses of morphines and demerol being administered every four hours. During the session with Dr. Erickson he even displayed the painful symptoms of drug-toxicity.

The interspersal technique was essential since Joe was adverse to even the word "hypnosis." Erickson began with a long rambling story about the growth of a tomato plant from a seed. Embedded within the story are numerous suggestions for trance induction, relaxation and comfort. Unconscious mechanisms and resources are called upon to help Joe dissociate from the pain, remain in a state of comfort, and to continue it indefinitely (post-hypnotic suggestion). At the conscious level though, the embedded messages are an acceptable part of the story content.

Interspersal Technique

Erickson began: "Joe, I would like to talk to you. I know you are a florist, that you grow flowers, and I grew up on a farm in Wisconsin and I liked growing flowers. I still do. So I would like to have you take a seat in that easy chair as I talk to you. I'm going to say a lot of things to you but it won't be about flowers because you know more than I do about flowers. *That isn't what you want.* (The reader will note that italics will be used to denote interspersed hypnotic suggestions which may be syllables, words, phrases or sentences uttered with a slightly different intonation.) Now as I talk and I can do so *comfortably,* I wish that you will *listen to me comfortably* as I talk about a tomato plant. That is an odd thing to talk about. It makes one *curious. Why talk about a tomato plant?* One puts a tomato seed in the ground. One can *feel hope* that it will grow into a tomato plant that *will bring satisfaction* by the fruit it has. The seed soaks up water, *not very much difficulty* in doing that because of the rains that *bring peace and comfort* and the joy of growing to flowers and tomatoes. That little seed, Joe, slowly swells, sends out a little rootlet with cilia on it. Now you may not know what cilia are, but cilia are *things that work* to help the tomato seed grow, to push up above the ground as a sprouting plant, and *you can listen to me Joe* so I will keep on talking and *you can keep on listening, wondering, just wondering what you can really learn,* and here is your pencil and your pad but speaking of the tomato plant, it grows so slowly. *You cannot see* it grow, *you cannot hear* it grow, but grow it does—the first little leaflike things on the stalk, the fine little hairs on the stem, those hairs are on the leaves too like the cilia on the roots, they must make the tomato plant *feel very good, very comfortable* if you can think of a plant as feeling and then, *you can't see* it growing, *you can't feel* it growing but another leaf appears on that little tomato stalk and then another. Maybe, and this is talking like a child, maybe the tomato plant does *feel comfortable and peaceful* as it grows. Each day it grows and grows and grows, *it's so comfortable Joe* to watch a plant grow and *not see* its growth *not feel* it but just know that *all is getting better* for that little tomato plant that is adding yet another leaf and still another and a branch and it is *growing comfortably* in all directions. (Much of the above by this time had been repeated many times, sometimes just phrases, sometime sentences. Care was taken to vary the wording and also to repeat the hypnotic suggestions. Quite some time after the author had begun, Joe's wife came tiptoeing into the room carrying a sheet of paper on which was written the question, "When are you going to start the hypnosis?" The author failed to cooperate with her by looking at the paper and it was necessary for her to thrust the sheet of paper in front of the author and therefore in front of Joe. Erickson was continuing his description of the tomato plant uninterruptedly and Joe's wife, as she looked at Joe, saw that he was not seeing her, did not know that she was there, that he was in a somnambulistic trance. She withdrew at once.) And soon the tomato plant will have a bud form somewhere, on one branch or another, but it makes no difference because all the branches, the whole tomato plant will soon have those nice little buds—I wonder if the tomato plant can, *Joe, feel really feel a kind of comfort.* You know, Joe, a plant is a wonderful thing, and *it is so nice, so pleasing* just to be able to think about a plant as if it were a man. Would such a plant *have nice feelings, a sense of comfort* as the tiny little tomatoes begin to form, so tiny, yet so *full of promise to give you the desire to eat* a luscious tomato, sun-ripened, it's so *nice to have food in one's stomach,* that wonderful feeling a child, a thirsty child, has and can *want a drink, Joe* is that the way the tomato plant feels when the rain falls and washes everything so that *all feels well* (pause) *You know, Joe,* a tomato plant just flourishes each day *just a day at a time.* I like to think the tomato plant can *know the fullness of comfort each day. You know, Joe, just one day at a time* for the tomato plant. That's the way for all tomato plants. (Joe suddenly came out of the trance, appeared disoriented, hopped upon the bed, waved his arms and his behavior was highly sugges-tive of the sudden surges of toxicity one sees in patients who have reacted unfavorably to barbiturates. Joe did not seem to hear or see the author until he hopped off the bed and had walked toward the author. A firm grip was taken on Joe's arm and then immedi-ately loosened. The nurse was summoned. She mopped perspira-tion from his forehead, changed his surgical dressings, and gave him, by tube, some ice water. Joe then let the author lead him back to his chair. After a pretense by the author of being curious about Joe's forearm, Joe seized his pencil and paper and wrote, "Talk, talk.") "Oh yes, Joe, I grew up on a farm, I think a tomato seed is a wonderful thing, *think, Joe, think* in that little seed there does *sleep so restfully, so comfortably* a beautiful plant yet to be grown that will bear such interesting leaves and branches. The leaves, the branches look so beautiful, that beautiful rich color, *you can really feel happy* looking at a tomato seed, thinking about the wonderful plant it contains *asleep, resting, comfortable, Joe.* I'm soon going to leave for lunch and I'll be back and I will talk some more."

The above is a summary to indicate the ease with which hypno-therapeutic suggestions can be included in the trance induction and trance maintenance suggestions which are important addition-ally as a vehicle for the transmission of therapy. Of particular significance is Joe's own request that the author "talk." Despite his toxic state, spasmodically evident, Joe was definitely accessible. Moreover he learned rapidly despite the absurdly amateurish rhapsody the author offered about a tomato seed and plant. Joe

had no real interest in pointless endless remarks about a tomato
plant. Joe wanted freedom from pain, he wanted comfort, rest,
sleep. This was what was uppermost in Joe's mind, foremost in his
emotional desires, and he would have a compelling need to try to
find something of value to him in the author's babbling. That
desired value was there, so spoken that Joe could literally receive
it without realizing it. Joe's arousal from the trance was only some
minutes after the author had said so seemingly innocuously, "want
a drink, Joe." Nor was the re-induction of the trance difficult,
achieved by two brief phrases, "think Joe think" and "sleep so
restfully, so comfortably" embedded in a rather meaningless sequence of ideas. But what Joe wanted and needed was in that
otherwise meaningless narration, and he promptly accepted it.
(Advanced techniques of Hypnosis and Therapy, pp. 516–517)

Verbal pacing occurs especially in the first five sentences: Erickson says he loves to grow flowers—in common with Joe; that Joe
can sit in that easy chair and listen—paces his physical reality; and
that Joe knows much more about flowers—deference. He also
anticipates Joe's possible suspicion with, "Why talk about a tomato
plant?"

He begins to lead Joe into a trance with embedded suggestions
to "feel hope . . . . . . bring peace and comfort. . . . . wondering
what you can really learn . . ." Suggestions are then made to induce
dissociation from the extreme pain: ". . . you cannot see . . . you
cannot hear . . . you can't feel" and, instead, a sense of ". . . comfort
. . . nice feelings. . . . peaceful. . . ." is accessed. Notice that each
step of the treatment is designed to overlap and intertwine with the
last so that the overall flow paces the literal process at work in the
unconscious.

Future-pacing is achieved in the latter part of Erickson's monologue with statements like "know the fullness of comfort each
day," and, "just one day at a time . . . sleep so restfully, so comfortably." In effect, the client is subtly encouraged to think ahead and
plan to retrieve the state of comfort indefinitely. The suggestions
are offered for Joe to accept only if they are appropriate for his
needs. It is characteristic of Erickson's artistry that he not only
provides unquestionably pertinent suggestions but leaves them
sufficiently open ended and non-directive. In fact, Joe did arrange
his own unconscious resources to continue the comfort into the
future. He also eagerly awaited Erickson's next visit.

The resources needed for Joe's problem were brought into use in a very casual manner. His capacity to remember feelings of comfort had been obviously out of reach until Erickson created a context that occupied his waking mind and evoked those experiences. The metaphor Erickson employed was a very effective vehicle for retrieving, ordering and associating the feelings that changed Joe's state.

To reiterate: metaphors organize experience. All theories are metaphors for experience. For a therapist with requisite variety, the truth of a treatment metaphor is secondary to its usefulness, to the possible changes it encourages and allows. When we encounter the suffering and unfulfilled dreams our clients have as a result of their personal metaphors we want to use anything we can that works to expand their maps. The various metaphors of psychotherapy all provide means to this end; each works well for certain groups of people. Knowing that a treatment metaphor is just that—a story designed to help expand the client's own story —sets us free to use any metaphor that is appropriate and to even make up stories that are specifically suited to a client's needs.

Metaphor Case Example

The following Metaphor was used by the author and co-trainer during a demonstration in a workshop in Colorado. The client was a man in his late forties. He was married for the second time and had children from this marriage. He was the oldest son of a farm family and was a therapist finishing his doctorate degree. He had recently moved into a neighborhood that he chose because of his school and work load. When he was away his wife and children worked to clear the yard and create a garden which they both were eager to cultivate. The problems began when the therapist realized that his stress (moving, school, income, fathering, etc.) was over-taxed. He had grown to near violence and many recent outbursts of anger were aimed at his wife and children. The incidents provoking the outbursts were seemingly out of his hands.

The family moved into the house two months before this session. For the first three weeks all went well. The routines kept the family busy, and together they pioneered this new location. But the neighborhood children and the client's children came to confrontation about "ownership" of the land being groomed as a garden. The neighborhood children had often been sent to play in this large open area. It had been the spot where forts and snowball fights, baseball, marbles, army, and science fiction were acted out. The youngsters in the neighborhood had come to think of the spot as their own, and they viewed the clients' children as the intruders.

Since the client's children knew they had a right to ownership on this precious spot; a real hostility developed in very short order. The client's children were usually the aggressors and the losers of any altercation. The client blamed his own children for their lack of psychological wisdom. He believed they set-up the difficulty as a way to get out of "work" in the chores related to the garden. He actually thought of physical violence to the children for their role in all of this. He further expected that this new home would re-move (rather than increase) some of his responsibility and stress. So, he asked for help with his tension and his ability to relax and forgive. He had not considered the plausible innocence of all the parties involved (he thought they were "playing a game") and so his solutions were restricted to disciplinary actions that seemed to place blame and add to further lowering of his sense of adequacy and self-confidence. As a man in the field of family therapy he was even more distressed and he had recently been analyzing what he called "the roots" of his "fear of success."

After I had established some initial rapport and gathered the previous information for the expressed purpose of demonstrating clinical change the client seemed alert and ready for action. My co-leader took the opportunity to speak to him in the following way. (She was seated on his left and spoke with a low tone and a tempo of speech that matched his breathing.)

> S: "Since we are yet to begin I want to *have a clear mind Bill,* and share a story I use in therapy demonstrations and work-shops. And this is one we'll use later for a new beginning."
> I: The story was told by a friend to help the participants cultivate change with a comfortable approach. He said that this story was only the beginning of the process of change now . . . and he looked the client in the eyes and challenged everyone present to consider how it might be relevant.
> (1)   There was once a garden full of all manner of beautiful vegetables and flowers. It had been carefully planned

and laid out in neat rows and graceful curves, with much thoughtful attention given to the many ways in which the plants would interact and affect each other. Everyone now knows and understands about "companion planting', the concept that some plants have beneficial effects on certain others, while *some* plants can actually retard the growth and development of other members of the vegetable kingdom.

(2) The careful and thoughtful gardeners who had laid out *this* garden had certainly considered not only the companionable aspects of the plant's positions in the garden, how they could most benefit each other by their proximity, but also how they would actually *look,* juxtaposed against each other. And they had carefully considered how to arrange the beds so that shorter plants were not deprived of their vital energy supplies from the sun by their taller neighbors.

(3) The garden was also carefully planned so that water could flow through it in the most efficient way, reaching each and every plant to bring it maximum nourishment, without leaving any pools of water at any spot in the garden to stagnate or breed insect pests.

(4) The gardeners who had planned the garden together had spent a lot of time in sharing and blending their many skills and talents, each bringing ideas from different gardens that each of them had seen in the past, other gardens that they had helped design, plant and tend. Their past experiences had taught them much of value which they had then contributed to the joint effort of making this beautiful new project flourish.

(5) Because they were experienced gardeners, they knew that gardens always include life forms other than those vegetables and flowers that are purposefully planted. Over the years they had learned not only to tolerate some of the weeds and insects that their garden contained, but to use them to maintain the ecological balance and actually profit from their presence. Many "weeds" were actually very beneficial soil-builders; others were valuable as herbal medicines. And the appearance of insects on certain plants signaled a

weakness or deficiency in those plants, alerting the gardeners to the need to tend them more closely, nourish them more appropriately.

(6) The gophers in the garden were a more serious problem. If they were allowed to get out of hand they could ruin the garden completely by cutting the roots off the plants, leaving them to wither and die. It was very discouraging to the gardeners to see their beautiful plants suddenly droop and die, knowing that the gophers had taken a small but vital part and left only a half-developed dead plant, one that would never now reach its full size and strength, its ability to provide food and nourishment.

(7) Yet the gardeners were wise and loving people and they understood that the gophers were only following their true gopher nature by eating the roots of the beautiful plants. They knew that the gophers couldn't possibly understand the results to the gardeners' hopes and dreams for their beautiful garden when they followed their true gopher nature and ate the plants' roots. The gardeners realized that life must find a balance with itself at all levels and that treating the gophers with violence would only upset the serenity and peaceful atmosphere of their lovely garden.

S: (8) So they turned in their wisdom and experience to ways of solving the problem that would allow *all* the life forms in the garden the best and happiest solution possible.

(9) They dug deep trenches all around the periphery of the garden and put underground fences of heavy wide screen in them, then filled in the trenches once again. Now there was an invisible barrier surrounding and protecting the garden from further invasion by outside gophers.

I:(10) Then they set about capturing the gophers in special traps that would not hurt them, but simply make it possible for the gardeners to put the gophers in a nearby vacant lot where they could establish a new colony, living on the roots of the hardy weeds and wild flowers that grew there.

S:(11) Eventually all the gophers had been gently caught and removed to their new, more appropriate setting and the plants were able to grow and flourish, develop and flower as they were meant to do. The gophers were happy in their new home because they were no longer bothered by garden hoses that flooded their burrows, rototillers that broke up their runs, or shovels that suddenly crashed into their tunnels.

I:(12) And best of all, the gardeners were happy and satisfied that they had found a solution to their mutual problems that required no violence, no destruction, no disruption of the peace and beauty and harmony of their garden.

S:(13) So now the garden continues to flourish at the hands of wise gardeners, bringing forth in successive seasons all manner of flowers and vegetables to delight the eye and nourish the body. And perhaps even more importantly, it stands as a tribute to the wisdom and love of the gardeners who knew how to create and maintain an important balance by understanding and respecting all the life forms that naturally co-exist with a healthy garden.

(1) Paces family units and the marital partners specifically. Language forms of each type discussed are used, but particular attention should be given to the nominalizations and referential indexes which position various processes ("thoughtful attention") and people/things ("some plants"). The relationships presupposed that "the many ways . . . plants would interact and affect each other" and the reader can recognize the use of both types of nouns and activity ("interact and effect") that is left unspecified in "verb" form.

(2) Introduces the gardener and emphasizes that the client can use a visual representational system to imagine the shapes of the plant's and the special location they have been assigned. This picturing will help the listener hold the story together and give it logic. Each suggestion builds around the presupposition of the individual differences that exist in the care of each plant. The process of transderivational search ensures

the client's participation in using his own personal history for the foundation of his understanding.

(3)   This paragraph elaborates on the special considerations and need that the plants (family members) have and in so doing it presupposes the existence of such needs with no further question about them.

(4)   Here the therapist has presupposed the "planting" of the garden and emphasized conscious intent based upon "much of value." Two gardeners were pictured, and the tale further resembles a family with two parents as the heads of house. The phrase "much of value" is particularly clever since its construction is based upon deletions (much what? and value how, to whom, in what way?) and the nominalized form (value) which the listener will be hard put to deny or ignore. Thus set up, the therapist can continue to elaborate upon the many values the parents may have had in their mind at the time of the family planning (regardless of how unplanned it may have been). Such a conversational device will make the job of developing positive resources within the client much easier.

(5)   The introduction of insects and weeds now parallels the "problems" in the family. The therapist beds these in the knowledge of ecological considerations. The conclusion that some insects and weeds are a "good" sign of a healthy garden corresponds to the novel notion that childrens' problems may be a healthy interplay with the environment. The therapist adds that the appearance of some insects signals a need for the gardener (not the plant) to take new action. The corelary, of course, is that the parents must not blame the plants but must exercise some skill and nurturing in their handling of the family.

(6)   The gophers represent the outsiders, the world where the family meets the unpredictable stranger—the neighborhood children who were plaguing the youngsters with their aggressive and incorrigible manner.

(7,8) This is an appeal to the nurturing and wisdom the client has. The therapist can now access this positive attitude as a framework for creative problem solving.

This opportunity is the result of the foregoing story line that exhausts the gardener.

(9,10)   Now the therapist presents solutions that are general and symbolic in content. They are maximally non-directive in that they allow the client an opportunity to generate their own creative and appropriate solutions. The control the metaphor provides is at the process level. Specifically, the metaphor insists that there is a solution; the solution involves mutual respect and no violence. This is exemplified in lines like this one: "Now there was an invisible barrier . . . protecting the garden . . ."

(11)   Further solutions are suggested in the form of direct contact with the "gophers," albeit gently done. Again the exact content is left to the client but the process that frames the action calls for gently catching and relocating the gophers so that they are made happy, too. This presupposes the gardener's sensitivity and awareness of the "gopher's" state of affairs.

(12,13) The summary emphasizes the success that is possible and the picturing of the family crisis as a change to demonstrate and develop parental skills and self-respect. Now the father and mother are encouraged to undertake the change as they might a challenging project about which they will later congratulate each other.

Throughout the story the therapist pauses and waits for expressions that show acknowledgement from the client. Such signals as head nods, raised brows, smiles and muscular relaxation are the ideomotor cues that give ongoing feedback for the therapist. Those signals throughout guided the speed of delivery and the amount of detail developed in each paragraph.

When the story came to the conclusion, we had no concern that it was incomplete. It was not intended to embody all of the experiences needed in the change patterns. It had become a device to urge Bill gently to be kinder to himself and his neighbors. When the group saw his cheerful and smiling face it was obvious that the mood had changed. The story had apparently initiated mental searches, associations and meanings of this man's dilemma and had let him use his own experiences to guide his readiness for the rest of the therapy session. It also became a metaphor for the experience of the other trainees present. For a time it was a metaphor for the entire group culture.

A Dream

The night before he left on his journey to the land of healers, he fell into a deep sleep and had a dream unlike any he had had before. At first, he thought that he was a sparrow, sitting on a branch, overlooking a large cavern and that this cavern represented some schism that had torn the fabric of the forest apart so that the animals on one side were not joined to the animals on the other side, and that he had been commissioned by other animals in the forest to use his ability to fly so high and sit upon the limb with such grace and security. And so commissioned, he would sit upon that limb and survey and record for them all that he could about the waterfalls, the green mist that hung over the chasm, about the activities of beavers and fish in the water. And he would be able to translate for them the activities of the animals on one side of the forest to the activities of the animals on the other side of the forest. He found himself dreaming so vividly that he actually thought he was this small bird perched on that small limb and noticing the activities with a great sense of responsibility. He must get nearly every detail right and scrutinize carefully because, somewhere in the back of the head, the dreamer knew that an answer would appear to him. And yet, in the brain of that small bird perched on a limb, still another dream emanated. The dreamer, dreaming that he was a bird found himself lost in a sequence of never ending dreams where the small bird now began to dream that it was a person traveling among other persons. And in this traveling, the bird experienced the strangest sensations, those sensations that come to people about their own beliefs, thoughts and perspectives, plans, attitudes on life, and their own memories. The sensations that the bird had were something that the bird knew nothing of. Dreaming that it was a person, the bird watched carefully as this person shook hands and smiled, sat down with, lis-

tened to, talked with others and engaged in daily activities and all
the millions of things that the bird dreamed people do, carrying
in its chest a strange feeling of compassion for the other human
beings. Soon, the bird's dream faded and the bird found itself
sitting perched on the limb once again, shaking its little head and
wondering what kind of luck had passed its way that had kept it on
that perch all night long while it fell into such a dream. And it had
the vague memory of dreaming that it had been a person with that
strange sense of compassion pounding in its chest all night long.
He wondered just what it was that this compassion had to do with
the task that it had been enjoined to accomplish by the other
animals of the forest. It flew down from its perch and joined the
other animals and spoke to them of the dream it had had of being
a person. The other animals of the forest seemed to rejoice and
share with one another something that they took from this dream,
even though the little bird still seemed uncertain as to just what
his offering had really been. All it knew was that it had shared in
great detail the contents of that dream.

Then suddenly the traveler awoke, remembering some of the
detail, but not all of the detail of this dream of a bird that had
engaged in such a strange and brave activity. He remembered the
words of the oracle, urging him to go on to the land of the great
healers before he crossed over the final hill. He paused before he
began his journey that day to think back on that dream, wondering
what the animals represented, curious about what it was that the
animals rejoiced at having learned, pleased that it had been such
a remarkable dream, that it had taken his identity from him and
carefully turned it over in the hands of the night spirit, tenderly
giving it back to him with such vivid memory of that amazing
dream. Then he set out on his way to the land of healers.

CHAPTER VII HYPNOSIS AND ALTERED STATES OF CONSCIOUSNESS

The induction of hypnosis or any altered state may strike the casual observer as an unusual or mysterious occurrence. In fact, most of us alter our states so frequently that we fail to discriminate between them.

For example, a different state of consciousness is operating while you are at work than when you are swimming, fishing, or picnicking—at least there had better be! Daydreaming is easily distinguished from the quality of attention you would bring to flying an airplane. For most people being immersed in an internal dialogue is subjectively unlike a direct conversation with a friend.

Any discussion of altered states of consciousness ought to include these every-day instances as well as less typical states like deep trance hallucination, age regression, and amnesia. It is well known that certain individuals can so alter their frame of mind that they do not suffer when they walk on hot glowing coals or recline on a bed of nails. I will provide another account of this phenomenon in the next chapter but here I want to acquaint you with the induction of altered states in general.

Charles Tart has come to classify the common altered states differently from those more rare and unfamiliar. The latter he terms "discrete altered states."

> Our ordinary or "normal" state of consciousness is a tool, a structure, a copying mechanism for dealing with a certain agreed-upon social reality—a consensus reality. As long as that consensus reality and the values and experiences behind it remain reasonably stable, we have a fairly good idea of what "normal" consciousness is for an individual and what "pathological" deviations from that norm are. Today, as many of the religious, moral, and emotional underpinnings of our civilization lose

their guiding value for our most influential people, the concepts of normal and pathological begin to lose their meanings (Tart, 1975, p. vii).

Tart questions all models of personality that lodge human behavior into the dual catagories of "normal" and "abnormal." Some tasks are performed more easily or successfully in certain states of mind than in others. The notion that there is a "normal" state for anyone is inconsistent with human behavior. The most appropriate state of consciousness for the activity of reading will depend entirely on the book. If you approach comics with the same degree of serious attention that you bring to a mathematics textbook you could endure some very tiring humor (or perhaps some enjoyable equations). The astute reader will, of course, know that these shifts in consciousness are simply what we have been calling differing strategies throughout the text.

Hypnotic Trance

There are many definitions of hypnosis. Some of these perpetuate the common superstitions and misunderstandings about the subject. Trance has been called anything from a state of stupor to more accurate, but still imprecise, definitions like "inwardly directed concentration." I want, after Tart (1975), to offer a definition that combines the elements of mental concentration, temporal functioning, and a subject's total repertoire for making sense of experience: Trance is any set of experiences that have a discrete range of externally generated stimuli and, instead, include a special temporary orientation to a specific range of experience and a fading of the general orientation to reality, in relationship with another communicator (hypnotist, parent, clergy, etc.).

In plainer words this means that as a client goes into a trance, the customary aspects of their experience (usually external) will become less vivid and noticeable while other stimuli that the hypnotist introduces will occupy the client's chunks of attention (usually internal). Maximum sensory experience before trance looks like $< V^e, A^e, K^e, O^e >$. The noise of the traffic outside, the ticking of the office clock, the visual schema of the hypnotist's office fade in the client's consciousness in proportion to the increasing intensity of a hallucination of standing on a hillside, overlooking the sea and smelling salt air. Maximum trance experience looks like $<V^i,A^i,K^i,O^i>$

The patterns of calibrated communication loops, strategy sequence and metaphor structure are the most pertinent to the task of guiding a subject to awareness of a certain range of stimuli. Therapy always requires that a client attend to specific portions of their experience be it "free association," concentration on breathing, following a continuum of internal and external sensation, or guided imagery. All of these exercises alter consciousness (induction), but let me stress that a therapist's work is not complete unless he also proceeds to retrieve resources (utilization) for the desired changes.

Keeping the above definition of trance in mind will enable you to see that hypnosis plays a role in nearly all forms of therapy. The techniques of the various schools all contain some of the patterns of hypnotic communication presented here. Proponents of each therapy have stressed to me that *their* work with clients is not hypnotic, not "manipulative," and not done unconsciously. I disagree and leave you, the reader, to determine this for yourself.

Induction of Trance and Altered States

There are innumerable books about the induction of trance. Some of the more outstanding of these are listed in the biblography. If you become familiar with very many of these books you will recognize that each approaches the phenomenon from a different angle and none of them is the definitive work on hypnosis. Complete coverage of the subject would fill a number of volumes with examples and speculation. I want to offer you a paradigm for trance induction with a transcribed example and then discuss the steps that are minimally required for you to assist your clients in reaching an altered state.

Induction Paradigm

As already noted, the hypnotist's overall behavior can be most concisely described as pacing and leading. The basic steps of the formula can be outlined as long as we remember that one category will overlap into the next.

1. Orient the client to context.
2. Pace (verbal and nonverbal/conscious and unconscious).
3. Dissociate parts.
4. Establish a learning set or context.
5. Pace the altered state.
6. Utilize trance pheonomena and change patterns.
7. Re-orient client to appropriate context.

Case Example

Before the client was seated for the induction she was talking rapidly and gesturing with her right hand. Her posture was upright and her behavior was animated. There was a great deal of activity in the muscles of her face. The color of her cheeks would be considered pale, her breathing was erratic and high in her chest cavity. Her eyes moved upward as she spoke consistent with the scanning patterns of someone leading visually.

Hypnotist	Client
1. Just sit down and	Client sits
2. can you place your hands	cheeks become slightly flattened
3. on your thighs	places hand on thighs
4. and just gaze at some one spot	eyes move to three of four locations and then fix on spot
5. I'll be mentioning something that first occurred in your childhood,	(inhale) (exhale)
6. And breathing just so . . . ,	breathing slows
7. and you want to blink	forced blink
8. and breath more deeply	deepens breathing pattern
9. as when you stared fixedly at a pebble	eyebrows move together slightly
10. you discovered	(inhale)
11. sunlight reflected in your eye	blinks slowly and exhales

INDUCTION EXAMPLE

Line 2-4

"...and just gaze at some one spot"

the process of gazing and wondering which "spot" was referred to was done with a visual mode in this example. Behavior Cues:

1) Slight muscle change denoting "search for meaning" process (flat cheeks)

2) Eye movements, breathing or other transforms such as pupil dilation

Pebble

Line 9

"...such as when you stared fixedly at a pebble"

Particular picture (s) now have been selected.

1) Slight change in body state such as in staring activity (eyebrows move together)

2) Other processing cues mentioned above continue.

Line 12

"...and you have tunnel vision and wanted to close your eyes."

Tunnel vision

Close eyes

1) Person intensifies and becomes more congruent, initiates perseveration response in flattening cheeks and double blink.

Induced experience now being stabilized, associated (and anchored) by the speaker's voice

2) Catalepsy and much muscle lassitude is displayed

Line 31

"...and you can close your eyes now."

1) Internal search is punctuated by the command to close eyes.

2) Induced experience is now being stabilized by speaker's voice tone and tempo.

12. and you have tunnel vision
    for that object   (inhale) cheeks become
                                       flattened, face becomes less
                                       red around upper lips and
                                       eyes (slow exhale)

13. and you wanted to close
    your eyes . . .   additional flattening of cheeks
14. but not just yet   (inhales slowly)
15. You may want to
16. go into a deep trance
17. with your eyes open   (exhale) double blink
18. but your unconscious
    mind
19. should do everything   inhales deeply
20. Your conscious mind will
21. do much   exhale
22. nothing of importance   inhale
23. And while I've spoken   catalepsy and great lassitude
                                       of all face, neck and upper
                                       torso
24. comfortably   exhale
25. your breathing has
    changed   inhale
26. your muscles have relaxed   exhale
27. your heart rate   inhale
28. is noticeably slowed   exhale
29. as is your swallow reflex   inhale and then a forced
                                       swallow
30. And your blinking reflex
    slower   exhale and slow blink
31. And you can close your
    eyes now . . .   inhale
                                       exhale and closes eyes

The client has been induced into an altered state with the kinesthetic components of drowsiness, heaviness of limbs, inhibition of
certain muscle groups and reflexes, and slowed deepened breathing. Prior to statement 31, the subject is staring fixedly and her
pupils are dilated. Her cheeks could now be described as
"flushed," the muscles in her face elongated and the tonus flat-

tened. The veins in her neck stand out revealing the rhythm of her heart beat. She is motionless and alert.

The transcript has been numbered so that the steps in the induction paradigm can be distinguished:

a. The client is oriented to the context with the request to be seated and the embedded commands to place her hands on her thighs and gaze at one spot. It is strongly implied in line 5 that the client will be listening closely and following an agenda.

b. Pacing statements are woven throughout the induction beginning with "and breathing just so." The hypnotist directs her attention to some thing she can verify—that she is breathing. The open-ended quality of the comment—"just so" could mean any type of breathing—will likely convince the subject that the hypnotist is somehow aware of her specific experience. Statement 7, "and you want to blink," is going to be true for anyone who is staring at "some one spot." His statement becomes as much a prophesy as an observation of fact and helps blur the line between pacing and leading. Other verbal pacing continues in statements 8, 9, 12, 13, 17, and 22. The hypnotist also paces the breathing of the client with a rising and lowering of his voice tone and pauses in tempo.

c. Dissociating parts of the subject's personality mainly means separating two functions so that they have no influence upon each other unless directed. In formal hypnosis the dissociation is always between the conscious/unconscious polarity. In the transcript, conscious function is paced up to the radical shift at line 18— "but your unconscious mind should do everything." This is again the theme in lines 20–22 and 23–30. Also notice again how the steps of the outline overlap.

d. A learning set is established as early as line 9. In line 10 the word "discovered" comes to be anchored to early attitudes of learning. That past attitude overlaps into the present context through the ambiguity presented in lines 12 and 13. "And you have tunnel vision for that object"—an object here or there? . . . "you wanted to close your eyes . . ."— then or now?

e. Pacing the altered state comes in the form of feedback that ratifies the trance. Lines 25–30 are a very straightforward summary of the physiological signs of change in the client's behavior. The pace culminates with the leading suggestion of eye closure in line 31. Again lines 25–30 are observations that will be verified by the client, so the embedded command in the last line will carry more credence.

These five steps provide us with an induction. They may be accomplished with just a few sentences and even without words. Milton Erickson has performed amazingly rapid non-verbal inductions (See Haley 1967, pp. 93–100, "the pantomime technique").

Throughout this sample induction several four-tuples were accessed that could aid the therapist. Line 5 begins evoking memories from childhood and fosters the later possible development of age regression. This is again tracked and anchored through lines 9, 10, and 11. Line 24 calls forth the feeling of comfort and anchors it to the sound of the hypnotist's voice. Obviously there is no limit to the number and type of resources that can be accessed.

How we utilize the altered state we have induced in a client depends as always upon the presenting problem and the desired therapeutic outcome. Many of the change patterns presented earlier could be used; reframing, dissociation, and metaphor are especially powerful choices, particularily when combined with anchoring. Which ever choice is the most appropriate, you would, of course, want to build upon the pacing and resources that have been retrieved or built during the initial induction.

Hypnotic Phenomena

Use of trance permits the therapist to focus upon problematic phenomenon in a sort of microscopic way, prolonging or intensifying its occurrence. Regular behavioral processes slow down as common consciousness dissolves, just as stars become visible when the sun goes down. What follows are categories of behavior that occur in trance. More detail about the paradigms used to bring this phenomena into being is the subject of another book. For now, I would like to aquaint you with the patterns that are available:

Dissociation—Known in waking states as "reverie" or "daydreaming," the term simply refers to the ability to fantasize oneself performing any manner of activity from a comfortable distance. I agree with Erickson and Rossi that "in general, a hypnotic phenomenon takes place simply by dissociating a behavior from its usual associational context" (Erickson and Rossi, 1976, p. 71). In Chapter Four I presented the steps necessary for inducing a "conscious" dissociation. The same pattern can be fruitfully applied in the context of deep trance. A woman I worked with was able to feel unusually relaxed and secure even while she visually reviewed an earlier experience in a hospital when she had nearly died from suffocation. Her former kinesthetic experience was suspended and replaced with comfort. Her memory of the incident could then be relegated to memory and cease interfering with current relevancies. The memory would thus be rechunked into a less overwhelming form.

She watched what had happened to her without reexperiencing the pain of suffocation. Occasionally, as with conscious-mind therapy, such traumatic memories will spontaneously emerge. When they do, simply use Overlap (p. 63) to bring the clients out of their painful feelings and help them begin representing visually before proceeding with dissociation. Generally, dissociation is used in trance to enable a subject to get a metaposition, that is, a different vantage with respect to memory as well as their ordinary identity.

Catalepsy—This state is characterized by uncommon muscular rigidity. It is similiar to the frozen reaction some mammals have when a bright light is suddenly shined upon them. In hypnosis, catalepsy is characteristically thought to be a clue to the subject's depth of trance. The "Cataleptic Arm" technique involves the suspension of one of the subject's arms in mid-air, moving it only when directed. The hypnotist can use this behavior to garner feedback and more precisely assess the effect of unconscious directives upon the subject. It actually has nothing to do with "depth" of trance. The total body catalepsy that may occur in clinical hypnosis is just like the immobility present during meditation and the hypnogogic state preceding sleep. When the normal associational context for the use of a part of the body is altered, the result is catalepsy. Not recognizing or being able to feel one's arm in the usual way dissociates it; the rigidity will develop naturally unless another experience is induced in its place.

Amnesia—Amnesia is a common phenomenon in everyday life. All of us have had times when we had a word on the "tip of our

tongue." Sometimes a person is introduced and we immediately
forget his name. Many people cannot recall what they wore to work
two days ago unless they conduct a laborious mental reconstruc-
tion. Amnesia is a dissociation from the ability to remember. It
serves a variety of purposes in the context of trance and is especially useful in conjunction with Post Hypnotic Design.

Anesthesia—Closely related to amnesia is a hypnotic subject's
ability to dissociate from feeling in parts of the body, to "forget"
kinesthetically.

This is a different phenomenom than catalepsy in that the body
grows numb rather than necessarily rigid. Hypnotic anesthesia has
traditionally been used to great advantage in medical and dental
practice.

Age Regression—Reliving or revivifying the past in a present context is yet another form of dissociation. When a subject modifies
his total self-presentation and displays the behavior and mental set
of a small child he may be described as "age regressed." As we
shall see, many established therapies, most notably Gestalt and the
"scream" therapies, age regress their clients as a matter of course.
The techniques differ and none of them is "formally" hypnotic,
but the outcome is the same: anyone who is fully reexperiencing
a painful limiting childhood experiences (four-tuple) has temporarily adopted the mind frame of a pre-adolescent. But age regression in hypnosis, formal or otherwise, also allows for the seemingly
unheard of choices of personal resources inherent "in" childhood.
The mental set of a grammar schooler is characterized by a greater
openness to experience, both tragic and nourishing. For certain
complex tasks, children learn faster and more profoundly than
most adults; whatever the adulthood limits your client has learned,
his roots of creative learning are only a heartbeat away and can be
relearned given the proper inducement and context. Further, the
many joys and satisfactions common to childhood can be evoked
via age regression. These four-tuples can be used as resources to
help change other painful memories. *Patterns II* contains a lengthy
transcript (pp. 121–169) in which Milton Erickson's expert use of
age regression in trance is brought to light repeatedly in just this
way.

Negative and Positive Hallucinations—Negative Hallucination refers to a trance subject's ability to delete some of the sensory
information available in the immediate physical environment. At

the hypnotist's suggestion a client might, for instance, be unable to see a nearby object or her own hand. She can also be taught to delete painful stimuli in her environment. A "positive Hallucination" is the experience of stimuli that are not present—that is, what I have just described with age regression and dissociation. This is sometimes useful for simply convincing a subject that he is in a trance, and to stop noticing anchors to undesirable experience.

Ideomotor Activity—This refers to the involuntary capacity of the muscles and nervous system to respond to external stimuli. It is useful in enhancing suggestibility ("I'm wondering which of your hands will move slightly first. . . .") and provides the therapist a reliable alternative to communicating with a client's conscious mind. Very often clients will first respond to a question with a head shake or nod before verbally "catching up" to their message. A hypnotist/therapist while gathering information may get finger twitches or other body movements that consistently correspond with "yes" and "no" replies to questions. Like any communication offered by the client, these messages can be utilized ("If that part's answer is 'yes' have it continue to signal me in the same way. . . ."). There is thus no need for the therapist to force information into the client's consciousness and, as I demonstrated in the reframing example on page 115, the desired changes can occur without the client even knowing what they are. Of course, out of respect for the client's desire to have answers and in the interest of sustaining the changes you have brought about, the client should be allowed decide what is of conscious use to them. Milton Erickson states that

> '. . . in some aspects of the patient's problem, direct reintegration under the guidance of the therapist is desirable; in other aspects, the unconscious mind should merely be made available to the conscious mind, thereby permitting a spontaneous reintegration free from any immediate influence by the therapist. Properly, hypnotherapy should be oriented equally about the conscious and unconscious, since integration of the total personality is the desired goal in psychotherapy." (Erickson, 1948, pg. 576)

Hypermnesia or Memory Recall—In deep trance people can recall events from their past in much greater detail then they can while the "normal" waking states distract them. The subject may not

remember an event "accurately"—i.e. as verified by others who
were present in the client's past. But, since you as a therapist are
working to alter a map rather than a territory, this distinction is
largely irrelevant; what the client experienced was real for them at
that time. In trance these realities can become especially vivid and
detailed.

Time Disorientation or Pseudo-Orientation in Time—A person absorbed in a good concert will experience the passage of time much
differently from someone taking a very difficult test. All of us have
felt or seen our sense of time change in differing circumstances.
In trance, this phenomenon can be accessed and employed in a
direct way. The hypnotist can progress the client into the future,
past the barrier of chronological age and determine how he might
actually respond to possible circumstances and events. Not only do
distinctions like "past/present/future" become blurred but trance
subjects typically have no idea how long a session has lasted upon
awakening.

Post-Hypnotic Design—is a special case of Pseudo-Orientation in
Time. After discovering how a subject will respond to future stimulus the, therapist can design post-hypnotic programs (leading) that
are consistent with the client's present behavioral predispositions
(pacing). Ordinary waking activities like setting goals, budgeting
money, and mental rehearsing for upcoming encounters are not
dissimiliar to this; the advertisements we see and hear daily very
cleverly employ this strategy: "Next time you're shopping, remember to bring home a case of Blahblah," "Buy some today! Your
family will love you for it!" "You deserve a break." Post-Hypnotic
Design is, in other words, future pacing. It is most effective when
it is a) specifically tailored to the subject's needs and b) communicated by implicit rather than direct suggestion. A series of
initially general statements that gradually begin to build toward
more particular suggestions will be the most effective. The mind's
ability to preconceive the sensory cues (anchors) that will later
trigger desirable behavior is an enormous aid to implanting
suggestions. As always, the real test of treatment will happen when
the client carries what is learned with the therapist into the "real
life" contexts where it is needed.

Milton Erickson's Utilization Strategy

A comprehensive discussion of Erickson's skill at utilizing the above phenomena would require several volumes. Certain aspects of his work are dealt with in the *Patterns* series and Erickson's own published writings. In one of his articles he outlines what he considers to be the four stages present in nearly all of his hypnotic encounters:

1. hold and fixate the client's attention.
2. present comprehensible ideas which are not, in content, relevant to the therapy context.
3. create or foster the client's readiness to respond and find meaning.
4. access and direct behavioral potentialities which can be employed in a helpful way within and after the therapy session. (Erickson in Haley, 1967, p.510).

The steps are similiar to those presented for constructing a metaphor: delivering a story that initially paces as well as distracts the conscious mind, leading it further away from direct comprehension, then accessing resources that will unconsciously concur with elements embedded within the metaphor. The major goal in approaching problem solving this way is to involve the client in a search for meaning that bypasses their usual conscious processes. After all, a client is in therapy because his conscious attempts have failed to solve a problem. As Erickson says, distracting the conscious mind serves to prevent the client from "intruding unhelpfully into a situation which he cannot understand and for which he is seeking help." (Erickson in Haley, 1967 p. 510)

Erickson elsewhere has described much the same process in working with families:

I do certain things when I interview a family group, or a husband and wife, or a mother and son. People come for help, but they also come to be substantiated in their attitudes and they come to have face saved. I pay attention to this, and I'm on their side. Then I digress on a tangent that they can accept, but it leaves them teetering on the edge of expectation. They have to admit that my digression is all right, it's perfectly correct, but they didn't expect me to do it that way. It's an uncomfortable position

to be teetering, and they want some solution of the matter that
I had just brought to the edge of settlement. Since they want that
solution, they are more likely to accept what I say. They are very
eager for a decisive statement. If you gave the directive right
away, they could take issue with it. But if you digress, they hope
you will get back and they welcome a decisive statement from
you." (Erickson, in Haley, 1973, p. 206).

This description follows the first three steps in Erickson's outline
above. The utilization step then depends upon the client's presenting problem. Erickson's ability to use the hypnotic phenomena
outlined in the last section to secure outcomes for his clients is, to
my knowledge, unequalled by anyone.

The application of hypnosis in therapy is the most highly sensitive free-form and, therefore, challenging way of working with
clients. To those of you for whom learning to do hypnosis seems
an awesome task allow me to suggest gently that, according to the
definitions I have offered here, you as a therapist, already practice
it to some degree. To communicate is to influence someone's
experience. Therapeutic communication directs the client's attention to a specific range of their experience. How you specifically
utilize the experience you access depends on your personal style
of working and the therapeutic metaphor that you operate from.

Each school of change has its own induction process and collection of techniques. The following chapter outlines the process
patterns evident in a variety of therapies. Whether the mode is
understood at the conscious level to be Gestalt Therapy, Transactional Analysis, scream therapy, Psychosynthesis etc., the operations I have offered throughout this book are employed in each
dicipline, as I will show. The formal aspects of hypnotic induction
and some trance phenomena are also present, as we shall see.

Truths

The traveler had but this one last land to visit before the promised truth awaited him over the final hill. In the land of healers he discovered that an entire community, busily bustling about, going from here to there on special assignments, existed as a tribe of enormous size. And in the council of those who were the rulers of the tribe of healers, he discovered healing techniques such as the use of herbs and clays, metals, of special exercises, pilgrimages, massages, incantations, of giving offerings and baths, use of steam and use of fasting, techniques to alter and increase awareness, techniques of special dance and speech. The healers were many and varied, and yet something he had taken in all his travels and which had been encouraged by the oracle was that he needn't worry about the fine details of each of these healing techniques. He need only expose himself to the various methodologies and learn each of them because the structure of each of those techniques was knowable and learnable. None contained the entire truth. With the wisdom of a traveler, confident in his mind that the world of each individual is only his own personal world, he set out to learn what was important for him from each of the healers. He translated what they told him into a knowledge of experience which would be useful for him, that would include for him the special wisdom he had gained in traveling throughout the country. Unlike the healers themselves, he knew of lands where people never engaged in practices that they used and he knew that people engaged in diverse practices were able to obtain similar results. So from each healer he separated the personal and extraneous embellishment from the task of healing itself.

CHAPTER VIII PROCESS PATTERNS IN THE METAPHORS OF PSYCHOTHERAPY

Each school of psychotherapy is a metaphor designed to help expand the limitations of its client's personal metaphors. Some of these theories are simple and some of them are complex. Each has its own set of tools, conceptual labels, presuppositions and techniques. A lot of them have the same stated goals and intentions and yet are considered rival theories by their respective proponents. As we shall discover, though the content of these stories of personality may differ radically, the processes by which they effect change in their clients are formally identical. Just as the form and organization of an individual's map of existence deeply affect his experience so, too, do the different treatment metaphors offer hosts of limitations as well as ways to learn and grow.

Most of the metaphors of personality that have come out of the Human Potential Movement underscore the importance of having sensory experience. An ongoing and increasing ability to use one's sense of sight, hearing, touching, feeling, smelling and tasting to contact the present external world is what Fritz Perls (1969) meant when he said, "Lose your mind and come to your senses." Transactional Analysis defines mental health as a capacity for spontaneity, awareness and intimacy. Eric Berne, in particular, defines awareness, as "the capacity to see the coffeepot and hear the birds sing in one's own way, and not the way one was taught" (1964, p. 178): to see and hear birds without having "helpful" father's advice as to which label to apply to which bird, whether he be a sparrow or a robin. The popularity of therapies spawned by Wilhelm Reich (1945), Alexander Lowen (1958), Ida Rolf (1962) and the high running interest in yoga, Tai Chi, and other forms of body work have been fostered by the desire for greater sensory experience.

In a sense, the Human Potential Movement can be thought of as one vast polarity response to the more traditional metaphors of personality that had come before it. When a metaphor of personality becomes so wordy and entrancing that the graceful art of change is buried by concepts and analysis, then a reorientation must take place.

As a therapist, your own ability to make refined sensory distinctions is the basis for your work. Your effectiveness depends, in part, on how well you notice the multitude of messages a client offers and how accurately you can observe your own influence upon a client's experience. Different therapies tend to emphasize certain sensory channels over others. Someone who works with altering the musculature of the body is going to be forever directing his clients into the kinesthetic channel. This can certainly be effective: many people have limited resources available kinesthetically. However, in my experience, there are also individuals who are *too* in touch with their feelings. Whatever problem they are faced with they cast for resources kinesthetically even though "getting a clearer perspective" or "sounding things out" might be a more efficient, effective, or desirable way to cope. Ideally, everyone including therapists ought to have as much sensory range as is available. If I subscribe too closely to one orientation I may be limiting my own sensory experience and be missing the vast amount of information that my clients are endlessly offering.

Your willingness to attend to and trust your sensory experience will determine your success with the powerful methods of change offered in this book. Your senses can be limited to perceiving how a client's behavior corresponds with the rules of a metaphor or you can pay attention to the process of that behavior and how your own communication influences it. You can "diagnose" a problem based on what someone has told you elsewhere or you can act on your own immediate perceptions, limiting yourself only to doing whatever is appropriate and easiest to bring about quick, effective, and painless change on your client's behalf.

Represenative Examples

The goal of this chapter is to bring forth representative examples of the change patterns initially identified and modeled by Bandler and Grinder that lay implicit in various therapies. Each of these therapies typically, employs several process patterns each and this presentation is not fully comprehensive.

Each example is meant to be representative of the major patterns used in the particular therapy.

Process Patterns in Gestalt Therapy

Fritz Perls imagined that when the client encounters the therapist, he asks the therapist for the very resources he lacks, hoping to find in the therapist "the environmental support that will supplement his own inadequate means of support" (*The Gestalt Approach*, 1973, p. 45). Perls wrote at length about "the neurotics' " attempts to "manipulate the environment." Keep in mind the power of metaphor to shape experience as you read the excerpt below. There is a certain bias to the observations made by Perls in the example and that bias is an interpretation of manipulation and deceit. Although it may be harmless and may be intended to be illustrative and descriptive, it seems to me to be an unnecessary turn of perception that may only further some clients' sense of self-doubt, self-evil and lack of self-confidence.

> However, he does not come empty-handed. He brings with him his means of manipulation, his ways of mobilizing and using his environment, to do his work for him. And let us not delude ourselves into thinking that these manipulatory techniques are not clever. The neurotic is not a fool. He has to be pretty shrewd in order to survive since in fact, he is lacking, to a marked degree, one of the essential qualities that promotes survival—self support. He literally has a handicap, and it takes considerable ingenuity to get along with it. Unfortunately, however, all his maneuvers are directed towards minimizing its effects instead of overcoming it. The maneuvers may have been deliberate at one time and by now are so habitual that the neurotic is no longer aware of them. But that does not mean they are not maneuvers and that they are not clever . . . The neurotic's problem is not

that he cannot manipulate, but that his manipulations are directed towards preserving and cherishing his handicap, rather
than getting rid of it. If he learns how to devote as much intelligence and energy to becoming self-supportive as he does to
making his environment support him, he cannot but succeed
(1973, p. 46).

Consider this paragraph in light of the trance induction paradigm offered on page 174. Perls orients the client to the context
by stating that he is there to "manipulate" the therapist into providing support, to go "preserving and cherishing his handicap."
For Perls, that is what the therapeutic context means. He paces the
client's presenting problem and probable sense of inadequacy attached to it with statements like, "he literally has a handicap" and
"he is lacking. . . . self-support." Step 3 in the trance induction
outline is to dissociate parts. The paragraph above presupposes a
handicapped part that wants "support" from the environment and
a part that could bring "intelligence and energy" to the aid of the
handicap. This both dissociates the parts and verbally anchors
them. The "learning set" is also established by the principle of the
remark, "If he (the neurotic) learns how to devote as much intelligence and energy to becoming self-supportive as he does to making his environment support him, he cannot but succeed." To this
end Perls advocated the use of frustration to thwart the "handicapped" part's "manipulations" therefore forcing it to mobilize
and contact resources inherent in the client's personality. In turn,
Perls would work with a client until an integration had taken place
(collapsing anchors). He insisted on the curative power of conscious awareness: "when he (the client) becomes aware of his
manipulatory techniques he will be able to make changes." Otherwise, "without awareness there is no cognition of choice" (Perls
1973, p. 65).

Perls' famous technique utilizing the "hot seat" and projecting
incongruities into empty chairs might be best explained in terms
of anchoring. A client's metaphor or experience would be sorted
into two polarities. Perls would ask the client to play one polarity
where she was sitting and project the other into an empty chair
facing her. The client would move back and forth between the two
chairs and, aided by Perls, work to give full expression to the two
conflicting "parts" of her personality. The polarities are thus pow-

erfully anchored to two spatial locations in the room. The fact that the client has to move to a different spot and posture to express each polarity constitutes a kinesthetic anchor alone; this is strengthened by the therapist's encouragement to adopt appropriate body expressions. The polarities are also associated visually to the two different views from the two chairs as well as to the internal imagery that the client frequently produces when looking at the empty chair. Finally, there is usually a difference in the speaking voices of the two parts and this constitutes an auditory anchor.

Once the conflicting parts have been allowed to express themselves fully, an integration is thought to take place and the polarities, typically, lose their distinctness from each other. Sometimes an "exchange" of resources will have been effected, with each part "giving" to the other a resource they had "held back"; sometimes, once the polarities have been fully expressed, a client will experience himself as being somewhere between the two chairs, no longer able to adopt either polarity with any consistency. In other words, the two anchored polarities have been sorted and paired as in the paradigms for collapsing anchors or dissociation and a new set of four-tuples has been created. This may lead to a new experience of conscious awareness and choices, but given the limits of conscious attention, it is reasonable to assume that the major changes arising from the operation take place at the unconscious level. Perls himself, from time to time, stressed that the most salient changes happen without volition or effort (Perls in Fagan and Sheperd, 1970, p. 26).

Fritz Perls often used a client's words and labels when working with them. The following is a description of Gestalt Therapist Jack Downing in practice:

> What Jack Downing brings to these sessions is an unusual openness, a receptivity, an awareness of every breathing as well as nonbreathing thing around him. You could call it empathy, but it goes much deeper than empathy. I have watched him closely at work and *have noticed that the rhythm of his breathing often matches that of the subject in the hot seat*—Downing does not merely understand the subject, he becomes the subject. (emphasis mine) (Downing and Marmorstein, 1973, p. 3)

This is a very fine sensory based description of the process pattern of pacing. Pacing is implicit in most of the forms of Gestalt Therapy. Perls once said that when he worked with a client he was "no longer Fritz Perls." In other words, he gave as much of his attention as he could to the individual in the "hot seat." Pacing at its most impeccable and most effective level is tantamount to "becoming" the subject in this special way.

Perls's metaphor of personality contained presuppositions that necessarily limited his sensory experience, though. His paragraph above makes the therapeutic encounter sound like an act of war between client and therapist. On the one side the client—a "neurotic"—is handicapped and trying to "manipulate" the therapist into doing something for him that he could easily do for himself. The therapist, in turn, fights back by keeping alert to the client's "shrewd" and "ingenious" methods for "taking" something away from him. Any of you who have ever had a client who congruently and believably wanted to effect a change in his life might find this metaphor rather narrow and, possibly, paranoid. Again: why go get therapy in the first place if you want to keep your "handicap"? Perls claimed that clients merely wanted to find ways to remain "neurotic" and be more comfortable with it. If a client actually believed that he could not solve a problem, wouldn't trying to be more comfortable with it be one good choice?

Let me caution you once more about the power of metaphor: you can induce all kinds of behavior in your clients and yourself by not questioning your therapeutic presuppositions. If you want to see "manipulators" everywhere, you may find them and, perhaps you have some excellent choices for creating change once you have. There also might be a great number of other effective and less stressful ways of gracefully securing the same outcomes on your client's behalf; ways that do not require that he meet you at your model of personality. . . . or that do not negatively bias the client as a human being in his effort to enhance himself.

Overlap Gestalt Therapy and Collapsing Anchors

The diminished situation moves naturally into completion when resistances are redeployed and when inner stimulation propels one toward completing the heretofore unfinished business . . . The next example illustrates how sensations rather than mere words may lead the way to the reawakening of a past event which is still influential.

Joan, whose husband had died about ten years previously, had spoken often about her relationship with him but had never conveyed a sense of the profundity of their experience together. In one session, a series of awarenesses evolved including the experience of her tongue tingling, a burning feeling around her eyes, tenseness in her back and shoulders and then dampness around her eyes. Finally, she caught a deep breath and realized that she felt like crying. There was a sense of tears in her eyes and a sensation in her throat that she could not describe. After a very long pause, she felt an itch which she concentrated on at some length. With each new sensation the silence and inner concentration were lengthy, frequently lasting for minutes. Silence—when joined with "focused concentration"—has the effect of building up the intensity of feeling. Soon Joan began to feel itchy in many places. She found it difficult to stay with these sensations without scratching, but she did. She felt somewhat amused about the surprising spread of her itching sensations, but she also began to feel frustrated and sad again, as though she might cry. She mentioned an irritating experience she had had the previous evening at the home of her parents where she had not been able to show her irritation. Then she felt a lump in her throat and after a period of concentration on this lump, a palpitation appeared in her chest. Her heart started beating quite rapidly and this made her very anxious. She verbalized the *pump, pump, pump* sounds and then became aware of a sharp pain in her upper back. She paused at length to concentrate on the pain in her back, then said under considerable stress, "Now I remember that horrible night that my first husband had a heart attack." Another lengthy pause followed in which Joan appeared under great tension and absorption. Then she said, in a hushed tone, that she was aware of the pain, the anxiety and the whole experience of that night. At this point she gave in to profound heartfelt crying. When she finished, she looked up and said, "I guess I still miss him." Now her vagueness was gone and she could convey the seriousness and wholeness of her relationship with her husband. The clear transformation from conventional superficiality to depth was brought on by the build-up in sensation. Through self-awareness and concentration she let her own sensations lead the way rather than her ideas or explanations. (Gestalt Therapy Integrated, Polster, 1977, pp. 221–222).

In this example, Polster and Polster demonstrate the "completing of unfinished business" in the common therapeutic form it takes. In dealing with her memories the client is systematically guided from her presenting auditory digital representations into a kinesthetic experience of them. The Polsters' rationale is evident when they state that the example "illustrates how sensations rather than *mere words*" may lead the way to the reawakening of a past event which is still influential." As in scream therapies, the assumption is that the way to integrate pain is to experience it again. A difficult memory that is stored visually or auditorily is to be overlapped into a kinesthetic representation.

We are told by the Polsters that Joan had often recounted the circumstances surrounding her husband's death and their life together but always in "mere words." In this session she is encouraged to attend solely to body sensations. This therapeutic choice adds to her congruent expression by mapping her Auditory digital to kinesthetic. This produces, at first, a rather random series of feelings—of wanting to cry and itching. She then begins to pay closer attention to the sensations and with each new one "the silence and inner concentration (are) lengthy." That is to say, with her limited conscious attention fixed upon the kinesthetic element of the four-tuple, she could no longer go on processing information, specifically her memories, through her auditory digital system. The Polsters comment, in their own way, upon the same process: "*Silence*—when joined with focused concentration—has the effect of building up the intensity of *feeling.*"

The overlap from Joan's auditory digital system into kinesthetics, then, becomes more consistent. She *mentions* an irritating experience that leads to her *feeling* a lump in her throat and heart palpitations. She *verbalizes* the "pump pump pump" sounds and then is aware of "a sharp *pain* in her upper back." She *says* that she remembers the night of her husband's heart attack, describes it verbally and then gives in "to profound heartfelt crying." In sum, then, we see the process pattern of overlap, and the temporary use of a kinesthetic to auditory tonal processing strategy during age regression.

The other phenonenon implicit in Joan's behavior is what Bandler and Grinder have called the "Transderivational Search" (Pattern I, p. 219). While Joan is attending to the series of body sensations—existential time/space events—she is continuously associating them with memories, searching to connect her present

experience with events from the past. While Joan is making meaning out of her sensations, none of her attention is on her immediate physical surroundings as her consciousness is elsewhere. Hyp-
notists often "send" their clients on Transderivational Searches,
choosing the words they use so that the subject must work to make
meaning of them. This overloads and distracts the client's dominate hemisphere functioning—in Joan's case, the auditory digital
system. As we defined the word earlier, Joan might well be said to
have been in a trance experiencing an age regression during her
session with the Polsters.

Scream Therapies—Collapsing Anchors

There are several schools of therapy that find an intrinsic value
in having their clients relive painful experiences from their personal history. Primal Therapy (Janov, 1970), the Radix school,
some forms of encounter and body work, all invest the act of
painful catharsis with curative power.

The paradigm for inducing these cartharsis employs the techniques of both overlap and age regression. Any presenting problem from the client's current experience is assumed to be associated to some buried traumatic incident in their past.

A client may speak of a recurrent internal image, a sequence of
words or sounds, or an interpersonal conflict; all will be taken by
the therapist to be caused by something in the client's early childhood intruding into present sensory state to form kinesthetic explosions. The therapists of these schools, presupposing causality,
structure their language to encourage age regression, frequently
asking binding questions like "How old are you *now?*" and generally helping to induce in the client a congruent four-tuple for being
a small child who feels anything from abject abandonment and
primitive rage to various childhood joys. The client is then aided
in reliving whatever past experience in which he is absorbed, and
this often leads to quite dramatic expressions of emotion. As in the
hydraulic pump metaphor, here the "unexpressed emotion" is
thought to be sort of clogging the client's system and the cathartic
release is assumed to clean the client out, freeing him to live more
fully in the present. Subsequent to the explosions, it is thought that
an equilibrium is regained by the natural forces of a client's personality.

Although catharsis is certainly spectacular, I want to refer you to the dissociation paradigm I presented as an alternative. Changing a four-tuple does not require reliving it. If the client *is* fully age-regressed he is no more going to be able to cope with an impossible situation in the therapy session than he was when it first occurred. He may be able to express it more eloquently and, no doubt, sooner or later, some change will arise out of doing so but why put someone through a process that is painful and inelegant if there is a choice?

For some reason, dating far back into unwritten antiquity, change has been associated with effort and suffering in the European tradition. I want to suggest that, though pervasive, this marriage of pain and growth is purely a matter of programming. I doubt very much that a flower screams when it opens its petals to the morning sun. In my opinion, a therapist encouraging clients to revivify past traumata kinesthetically, without mustering the adult resources the client has to change the four-tuple more easily, is analogous to a surgeon neglecting to sew up an incision. The body's natural forces will eventually close the wound but not without the possibility of pain and scarring.

What follows is an example of a well known scream therapist whom I witnessed at work. He was consistent in his approach to any problem presented by a client and he often got results. His technique also contains the process patterns of both overlap, collapsing anchors, and age regression. Please note that this man's way of working has already greatly reduced the degree of age regression it encourages, compared to other scream therapies.

A man came to this therapist because, he reported, he had been passive and depressed for most of his adult life. The therapist did not gather much information about the structure of this experience but he did quickly uncover an image the client had of his father which the client said was an element in his depression. The therapist asked him detailed questions about the content of the eidetic image and found that the man was specifically able to see a scene of his father departing for the armed forces. The client was very young, as he remembered the incident, and he had then thought of his father's departure as "abandonment." The father had left him to live with his hostile mother.

Having found all this out, the therapist then proceeded: he encouraged the client physically to take hold of and hug him, look over his shoulder, and reaccess the eidetic image of the father, seeing it *there in the room.* Through a judicious choice of words, he helped the client express feelings of anger (*"beneath* your feeling of abandonment there is a lot of rage brewing"). Having overlapped the feelings of depression and helplessness to the visual eidetic image, he began to presuppose, induce and overlap the more active and incompatible feelings of rage.

Before long the client was yelling at the picture of his father. Thus anger and abandonment were both anchored to the therapist's hug, words, tone, and the picture of Dad. The pairing of incompatible experience in this way constitutes the paradigm for collapsed anchors. The feelings of helplessness generated by the eidetic image are less intense than the congruently screamed anger, and the change occurs. The end result was that the client had a new choice about his kinesthetic response to that old picture of Dad.

To summarize the process patterns used:

1. Identify the limitating representation.
2. Use overlap to obtain much fuller description of the content of the limiting four-tuple.
3. Induce the client to hug the therapist and anchor resources needed for the collapsing.
4. Retrieve an incompatible four-tuple by inducing the client to produce an incompatible feeling state compared to the one triggered by the representation. In the case of the scream therapy, this is fostered by having the person scream angrily. This particular pattern of screaming is usually sufficient to produce partial age regression four-tuples in the client.
5. Collapse anchors by pairing limiting representation with the kinesthetically anchored resources at the same moment.

Transactional Analysis—Dissociation

In the Transactional Analysis (Berne 1964, 1972) metaphor the personality is divided into three basic parts: the Parent, the Adult, and the Child. Human behavior is explained as an ongoing interaction of the three. In a healthy personality, the Parent, Adult, and Child make decisions collectively, taking each parts' needs into account. Some conflicts are explained as one collection of parts begin acting on its own behalf without respect to the others' needs. A family member metaphor such as this is a convenient metaphor to teach because everyone who hears about a Parent, Adult and Child can relate to and remember the categories easily.

Implicit in the technique is "sorting"; the therapist is encouraged to make sensory-based observations of the client's behavior and to classify the behavior according to the three subdivisions. Sorting categories are, of course, dictated by the metaphor so the client's behavior must easily fit the model. There are always attempts to expand the number of distinctions possible in a metaphor when it is observed from the level of content. At the level of process structure T.A. treatment or therapy displays the same formal patterns.

To refresh the reader with the T.A. vocabulary—interpersonal incongruities are explained with the concept of "ulterior transactions." If someone's behavior is incongruent it is said to be because he is "up to something," (an unconscious "con"). This something could be a "game" the person is playing that has rules known only to him—for even symbolic intangible secondary gains. They could be "collecting stamps"—amassing undesirable feelings so as to later be justified in losing their temper, bullying someone, or acting "helpless" in some situation.

Still again, I want to reiterate my assumption that everyone makes the best possible choice for himself given how he has come to map reality. Obviously the behavior the T.A. metaphor describes does go on—I differ with any antagonistic motives, and not the utility of punctuating social reality in that way.

The following transcript is an un-edited report from a woman who worked with a certified Transactional Analyst. She later said that what came out of the session for her was a "redecision" to act and feel in new ways that were forbidden in her experience of her family. The accompanying commentary in the margins will show how the change patterns of, first, Collapsing Anchors and then, Dissociation were used to bring about the "redecision" (Goulding and Goulding, 1976).

When I came to our group Wednesday evening I was feeling good and thinking I probably wouldn't work. Then another woman was getting into her feelings of pain for her children's having to suffer through a divorce and I found myself identifying with her distress and responding to my own similar feelings. The therapist noticed my tears and asked me what was going on and when I mentioned my similar painful feelings he helped me to focus on them and just get into them and feel the pain. Then I was standing in front of my therapist who was seated, and weeping with my head up. Somehow then he actually looked like my father, rather stern and somehow detached, and I wanted to talk to him. So I told the therapist (my father) that I was "OK," that I could cry, I could be happy and silly, but most of all that I could and would be me and not his quiet, sweet little girl.

client has problem in kinesthetic system overlap

age regression

referential index shift

this woman's usual state of consciousness is visual

the problem is an unpleasant feeling experience

an anchor from therapist triggers a calibrated loop established as early as in her family

At that point I began to cry harder, very noisily and easily as I hadn't before and wanted him to hold me. I cried in his lap for a while and then I actually began laughing as loudly and relaxedly as I had just cried—I felt fine—had no lingering tension, no headache as I usually have after I have cried.

client behaves according to a different representation than that previously used during the calibrated loop

collapsing anchors occurs to the extent that client uses the age regression 4-tuple to access feelings that were incompatable with the painful ones

My feeling, looking back on this experience, is that I got into my Natural Child and really experienced some of the feelings so long locked up, thereby hopefully breaking a few of the rigid controls my Adapted Child is so full of; e.g., BE GOOD, BE QUIET, BE HAPPY and above all, BE REASONABLE.

Now she can *see* the previous problem (which was in the kinesthetic representational system) and the new position is dissociated from the other. She has come to label (anchor) the experience with the triple nominalization "Child Ego State," in a visually-dissociated diagram containing three stacked circles

Psychosynthesis—Reframing

Roberto Assagioli developed a system of psychotherapy that rests upon a rich anthropomorphic metaphor. In his model, the total personality is comprised of various "sub-personalities," each of whom has his function and a benign intention. The treatment Assagioli advocated is a very elegant example of the change pattern of Reframing. His first step is to introduce the metaphor to the client:

"At first glance it might appear difficult to the therapist to introduce the concept of sub-personalities to the 'innocent' patient. But practice has shown that the concept is easily accepted by him if presented in the same way similar to the following: 'Have you noticed that you behave differently in your office, at home, in social interplay, in solitude, at church, or as a member of a political party?' In that way he is easily brought to recognize the differences and even the contradictions in his behavior." (Assagioli, 1965, p. 74)

These contradictions are interpreted as the simultaneous or sequential expression of the various sub-personalities:

"These differences of traits which are organized around a role justify, in our opinion, the use of the word 'sub-personality'.

Ordinary people shift from one to the other without clear awareness, and only a thin thread of memory connects them: but for
all practical purposes they are different beings—they act differently, they show very different traits." (Assagioli, 1965, p. 75)

The metaphor of "sub-personalities embodies both the possibilities and constraints present in human social behavior. Each
sub-personality in effect, has volition. Since Assagioli's metaphor
limits itself to a social anthropological scope, the sub-personalities
he identifies have a propensity for conflicts similiar to the prevail-
ing code of regional social conduct. They break normative rules
and quarrel with each other; each sub-personality is, in some way,
limited by the social constraints that restrain whole people in society. As Assagioli lays it out, the sub-parts *must* take on some recog-
nizably human form. It would be alien to the metaphor were a
sub-personality to act like a visual image, a low back pain, buzzing
in the ears, or a cancer.

The client whose sub-personalities are in conflict will, obviously,
be incongruent in his outward behavior. The parts would be said
to be "competing for control" in this metaphor and this could be
expressed in a myriad of ways. The job of the therapist is to
socialize and politicize the conflicting parts, to "synthesize these
sub-personalities into a larger organic whole without repressing
any of the useful traits." (Assagioli, 1965, p. 75)

So the metaphor of Psychosynthesis, like many others, induces
and encourages a kind of controlled psychodrama; the client is
introduced to the notion of sub-personalities, told that they are all
interacting in some way on his behalf, and given a conflict—that
they are competing with one another. Having established this dissociation, the therapist can then guide the client through a mental
play theater and allow the various actors on stage to express their
individual purposes. Since the parts are framed in a social context,
their differences are analogous to the quarreling factions of a political party. "Synthesis" is accomplished when these factions are
able to work cooperatively toward a mutual goal.

Once the sub-personalities are functioning in harmony, the individual, Assagioli submits, will begin to experience growth and
integration at a higher level. The client's energy is then turned
away from personal conflicts toward more spiritual levels and mature social involvement. Assagioli himself was aware of the danger

of narrowing a metaphor of personality to the sole treatment of remedial personal conflicts:

> "However, this pathological approach has, besides its assets, also a serious liability, and that is an exaggerated emphasis on the morbid manifestations and on the lower aspects of human nature and the consequent unwarranted generalized applications of the many findings of psychopathology to the psychology of normal human beings." (1965, p. 35)

I heartily agree with him in this spirit. He thus broadens the scope of his metaphor to emphasize the value of "creativity, intuition, will and the Self." He holds the "Self" to be a higher organizing principle for experience and encourages his clients to recognize and use this higher order as it exists within themselves. He further proposes that the yearning toward higher "plateaus of self-realization" is, to some extent, "fostered by the manifold experiences of life" (1967, p. 24), so that built into the very process of living and aging is a constant movement toward "individual expression of a wider principle, of a general law of interindividual and cosmic synthesis." (1967, p. 31)

Applying the reframing paradigm to the technique of Psychosynthesis is an easy matter given the latter's theoretical premises regarding an underlying positive motive in human behavior. The process of coordinating and uniting a person's sub-personalities is presented in five phases: recognition, acceptance, coordination, integration, and synthesis. (*Synthesis,* Spring 1974, WB p. 19)

Recognition: This first stage requires that the client focus in upon one or two of the most "important" personalities—"perhaps those that seem to have the greatest energy, now emerging qualities that one wants to develop or the most acute need: those that, in other words, seem more central or more important at the moment."

Acceptance: This and the first stage may go hand in hand. Acceptance primarily means evoking an attitude of objective observation and non-judgment toward the sub-personality even if its behavior is considered "bad" by another part or the individual's overall value system.

Coordination: This phase involves locating the positive intent behind the part. "Whenever we go deep enough toward the core of a sub-personality we find that the core—which is some basic urge or need—is good." (*Synthesis,* Spring 1974, WP p. 39) Once this basic need is uncovered the goal becomes finding new and more acceptable ways to fulfill it.

Integration: This deals with the responsible expression of the conflicting sub-personalities. Special attention is paid to the reconciliation of any opposite urges and to finding them means of expression that are acceptable to the other sub-personalities. This can be done by "time sharing," where each part is insured an occasional opportunity to express its needs; by "cooperation," in which two or more parts become aligned toward the same goal; and by "fusion," when two or more parts develop into a new sub-personality.

Synthesis: This stage is the culmination. Once the client has fully integrated the changes into his total personality, he can move from an intra-personal focus to interpersonal changes.

The following transcript shows how the above five stages are manifest in a therapy session. The approach is congruent with the reframing paradigm presented on page 115. It is a real tribute to Roberto Assagioli that he independently developed a system with all the basic steps of this powerful change pattern and made them explicit. As with the reframing paradigm, there is considerable overlap between the categories in actual practice:

Recognition: Reframing step number 1
Acceptance: Reframing step number 2
Coordinate: Reframing steps number 3,
Integrate: Reframing steps number 4, 5, 6
Synthesis: Reframing step number 7 and Future Pace

All quotes below are from the *Synthesis Journal,* Spring 1974. They published an extensive transcript of a session with a 23 year-old woman who was depressed and continually overeating. She said she felt badly blocked by "anxiety" and desperately wanted to develop more fulfilling ways to express herself.

The therapist's first move was to help the client, Sharon, identify the problem and make contact with the part of her that is generating it. "Close your eyes . . . relax . . . take some deep breaths . . . (pause) . . . and now let yourself experience again those feelings of anger and disgust. Tell me when you are in touch with them." Sharon contacts the feelings and identifies them as a sub-personality she calls the "Hag." The therapist has paced her so far as she has represented her dilemma kinesthetically. He has then led her into contact with the part. This accomplishes the first and second step in reframing, identifying the problem part, and establishing contact with it. The therapist (representing visually, by the way) comments:

> "So the first step is to establish clear and open communication. One can then focus on what the sides want from each other." (*Synthesis,* Spring 1974, p. 30)

He next asks Sharon to ask the Hag part if "there's anything she'd like to tell you." Sharon answers: 'She said to stop being so phony. . . ." He has thus led her to the third step of reframing: to separate the problematic behavior from the positive intention that lies behind it. The "Hag" sub-personality is found to be helping Sharon to recognize and overcome her phoniness.

Stage four in reframing is to access resources that will help bring about the changes. In the transcript, the therapist suggests that Sharon ask the Hag "if there's anything she needs from you." Sharon responds: "Yes, she says there is. . . . she needs understanding and help." The therapist organizes his own perceptions by explaining that the "Hag" that wants Sharon to stop being phony is competing with the part of Sharon that needs "to be accepted, then helped so as to move out of her twistedness and to grow." He spends some time with Sharon sorting out these parts so that they are clearly identifiable. What she needs is to get the "understanding and help" (resources) to the part of her she calls the "Hag."

The next stage is to generate new ways to satisfy the problem part's positive intention. Sharon is encouraged to do this by the therapist in the transcript and produces several options. She can generate "positive energy" a little more often, and also "take things one step at a time" and not criticize herself verbally. A third was what she called "accepting ideals." She said: "I have to *look* at her and accept her ideals and her desires to be pure and help her realize them." Sharon here gives herself congruent and resourceful responses in all three major representational systems: "positive energy"—kinesthetic; verbal criticism—auditory; looking at ideals—visual. Having choices in all three sensory channels is a powerful option to the feelings of depression, anxiety and blocked growth.

The therapist says to Sharon: "Okay, in the future, then, how can you get Sharon's attention when you need help or feel you can help her?" This is clearly a move toward crystalyzing the agreement of the original problem part to use, outside of the therapist's office, the alternative choices she has generated. This is step six from the reframing paradigm, also what we have been calling future pacing. Sharon responds with: "I can ask her to send some of her energy, some of her ideals, some of her will . . ."

Therapist: "Why don't you do that now . . ." (long pause)

Sharon: "I asked her for some positive energy, for some will, and she said, 'Yes, okay'." (Synthesis, Spring 1974, p. 24)

So the reframing is completed and all that remains is the ecological check, to discover whether there is any other part that may object to Sharon implementing the new choices in her behavior. Sharon's next comment begins this process:

Sharon: "But then something started nagging at me . . . something new . . . and now I feel different."

Therapist: "What is it?"

Sharon: "I don't know exactly, some kind of negative feeling, possibly doubt or something." (Synthesis, Spring 1974, p. 24)

So the therapist cycles back through the entire sequence again, reframing the objections of this new part.

Summary of Special therapeutic operations and the change patterns

The following charts are intended to help the reader recognize the logic of certain psychotherapy operations in the context of this book's "chunking" of experience. The chart is largely developed from the information and training of the author and hundreds of workshop participants who helped in its completion. Each practitioner, no doubt, takes certain liberties and adds certain stylistic modifications to his own performance of these operations. Hopefully, the general breakdown offered here will enrich the choices of any practitioner and help every reader gain an appreciation for the effect he can and does have on the experience of others. This appreciation and awareness may lead to a more sane and humane treatment of people who seek change in their behavior.

The following charts are not thought to be all-inclusive. One noticeable deletion from the charts includes several psychotherapies (new and old). The reason for the absence is that many of the operations listed are the same in other therapies and this broad group is expected to guide the reader's thoughts in the direction of making his own ongoing analysis of useful communication and change patterns. This chart helps to enrich the foregoing simplification which generalized about the representative patterns used by each approach. The more specifically and elegantly a pattern is reduced or modeled, the more learnable and usable it becomes.

Gestalt Therapy Operations

Techniques	NLP Counterparts
Awareness continuum	Pacing/identifying calibration meta-commenting
Shuttling	Fractionate/sort polarities
Dialog parts	Establish meta-position/pattern disruption/sort incongruities
Exaggerate symptoms	Pattern disruption/produce congruence or access polarity
Speak here/now present tense	Produce living metaphor
Replace the "it"	Referential index shift/access polarity
Switch "can't" to "won't"	Switch modal operation of possibility to necessity
Double chair	Kino sort of polarities (pattern disrupt calibration)
Enact a fantasy (dream)	Living metaphor/referential index shift/kino sort
Own projection	Referential index switch
Enact retroflexion	Kino enactment of unspecified verb/Role switch on the referential index
Throw out introjection	Auditory digital dissociation for lost performatives

Define boundary of confluence	Produce and sort polarities of experience (Auditory Digital)
Explosive layer	Emergency response due to pattern disruption of kinesthetic representation of collapsing anchors
Finish unfinished business	Overlap to K and collapse anchors
Gestalt body work	Overlap to K and denominalize

Transactional Analysis Operations

Techniques	Change pattern counterparts
Interrogate	Meta model questioning/develop Auditory digital representations of experience in a causal-model
Confront	Meta comment/pattern disrupt
Explain	Metaphor and anchor
Illustrate	Metaphor and access experience
Contract	Outcome specification/induction
Structural analysis	Family member metaphor/teach V. dissociation and incongruity sorting
Transactional analysis	Future pace V. dissociation
Game Analysis	Produce meta-position with Aud. digital and Visual from undesirable kinesthetic punctuation point/identify the calibrated communication
Blackboard	Pattern Disruption/anchor for dissoc.
Think Structure outline	Pattern Disruption and metaphor
Parent interview	Dissociation and polarity sort

Rubberband	Transderivational search (TDS for short) on undesirable K
Locate early scene	Overlap to complete 4-tuple
Redecide	Collapse anchors
Complementary transactions	Pacing
Turn-over	Speak for presupposition/polarity request usually creating uniform anchors Aud.Tonal or Aud.dig. for certain experiences
Options	Teach beh. choices anchored to V. dissoc.
Dream work	Referential index shift or living metaphor
Script Analysis	Tracking 4-tuples for metaphor
Crossed transactions	Pattern Disruption and access incompatible 4-tuple
Discount confrontation	Metamodeling some modal operators, lost performatives, generalizations, universal quantifiers
Redefinition confrontation	A specific use of metacomments about how the client failed to pace the therapist, inducing them to take the therapist's metaphor
Reparenting	Age regression/pattern disruption/Anchoring/building new behavioral programs/rechunking old experience
Stroking	Anchoring (very often Aud.dig. or K)
Homework	Future pace
Spot reparenting	TDS to early scene (overlap to complete 4-tuple, collapse anchors and usually, rechunk Aud.dig. channel)

Cathexis to Child	Age regression/overlap
Deconfuse Child	Rechunk pieces of 4-tuple that create incongruence
Decontamination	Use V.dissociation as a metaposition to sort incongruities
Permission	Conversational postulate/embedded commands (usually with tonal anchor)
Protection	A congruence statement re: availability of/therapist's aid and time
Potency	A statement about the therapist's congruence and requisite variety

Family Therapy Operations

Techniques	Change Pattern Counterparts
Making contact with members	Pace and anchor
Defining session	induction/defining outcome
Family sculpting or enactment	Make living metaphor/gather meta model data
Restructuring boundaries or Create dyads or sub-groups	Pattern disrupt calibrations/new anchors
Individual "working through"	(Variety of patterns from Gestalt, T.A., etc.)
Unbalancing	Pattern disruptions of various types
Relabel	Relabel
"Reframe"	sometimes relabeling and anchoring/sometimes reframing
Homework	Future pace/create contextual experiences
Family geneology chart	V. dissoc. to access resources and develop ideosyncratic

| | family metaphor/anchors resources of fam. to the office |
| Challenging assumptions | Breaking calibrated loops, mind reading and complex generalizations |

Psychodrama Operations

Warm up	Access needed resources (k. induction)
Double	Speak for polarity
Protaganist directs	V dissociation and meta position
Soliloquy	Aud.dig. dissociation and TDS
Fantasy scene (enactment)	TDS to accessed 4tuple/living metaphor
Behavior rehearsal	Build behavioral programs
Alternate w/double	K dissociation

Esoteric Schools

There are many schools of thought and secret "knowledge" that have been traditionally labelled "esoteric" by European culture. They range from the study of the Tarot, to alchemy, to the techniques of Yoga. Many of the Esoteric metaphors date back into the mysterious darkness of pre-history. Others arise from the times and locations of Hermes Trismegistus, Imhotep, Aristotle, Pythagoras, and Paracelsus. Although the connection is not often obvious, many of our modern scientific forms are heavily indebted to these ancient traditions. The disciplines of astronomy, chemistry, medicine, the study or agriculture and philosophy were begun in this antiquity. (See Kippner and Villoido, 1976, pg. 149). The often accurate weather predictions that are still published yearly in the *Farmer's Almanac* are made entirely with the ancient tools of Astrology.

In the preface, I noted that the historic roots of the contemporary theories of personality and treatment are deep. The relativity of these metaphors should by now be obvious. They induce behavior as much as they model and represent it. It is like the old debate about whether the egg or the chicken came first. The map is not the territory, but creating a map gives us the impression of territory. Whatever can be said about "absolute reality" is ultimately unknowable. Pearce echoes this when he says, "Science and common-sense inquiry do not discover the ways in which events are grouped in the world. . . . they *invent* ways of grouping. Newton was a creative inventor, if unknowingly." (Pearce, 1971 p. 81)

In a way, the Esoteric schools can be thought of as keepers of knowledge that the metaphor of modern science has not wanted to claim and incorporate. The following is only one powerful example. In my opinion, it shows how an esoteric metaphor creates change by virtue of its congruence and formal pattern.

Senoi Dreamwork—Reframing

The Senoi tribe of Malaysia is reputed to operate out of an extremely effective holistic system. The tribe has had no armed conflict, violent crime or insanity for the past three centuries (Johnson, 1975). The Senoi recognize that their model of personality—based on dreams—is metaphorical. As in Gestalt Therapy, the characters and elements in a person's dream are thought to be aspects of his character.

According to the Senoi, each dreamer must conquer the hostile spirits that frequent his dreams. To this end they have developed a particular therapeutic technique that anthropologists have called "Senoi Dreamwork."

The procedure is inextricably linked to all aspects of the culture. For our purposes here it will be enough to lay out the stages of the Dreamwork.

According to Jack Johnson (1975), the healer begins the process by telling the dreamer to "close your eyes and let me know when you are in the dream." When this is accomplished, the dreamer is led through six typical stages: Key, Embellishment, Main Figure, Trophy, and Quest.

Briefly, the dreamer is led into the reality of the dream and aided in contacting the evil spirit. Once done, the dreamer then induces the spirit to give him a gift. When, in the dream, the gift is manifest the dreamer then proceeds to go about creating a tangible replica in his physical world. Sometimes this requires a lengthy physical journey which is referred to as the "quest."

The stages are:

Key: The key is the memory of the dream and the unfinished situation(s) that may be apparent within it.

Embellishment: This is the reliving of the dream itself in waking life. The dreamer is led into the state by the healer with the consensus assistance of the entire tribe. Often other tribal members will take on the various roles.

Main Figure: the spirit is identified and communication is opened.

Gift: the benign power of the spirit and a symbol of the spirit's lifelong allegiance with the dreamer is created and identified.

Trophy and Quest: these stages involve the dreamer in physicalizing the spirit's dream gift. When this is accomplished, the spirit is considered to be integrated into the dreamer's personality.

Phrased another way, of course, this procedure is a reframing of the problem part of the dreamer's personality. Step 1 from the reframing paradigm, identifying the part, corresponds with the Senoi stage of Embellishment. Once the part is identified, a positive intent is presupposed even though the part is regarded as an evil spirit. This is isomorphic with the third step of reframing. Jack Johnson, following the Senoi, in a session with a client who had developed hives, told her that "her physical self might be giving her a message and asked if she would be willing to meet the "Live Spirit," discover the message, and, making the spirit her ally, ask it to suggest what she could do in her waking life to be rid of the hives." By implying that receiving the message will lead to the problem's resolution, Johnson presupposes a positive purpose for the spirit as well as the hives.

The Trophy and Quest assume the existence of a creative part of the personality—step four of reframing. The dreamer is then set into new behavior in the physical world. In addition to the personal strength and unity that the quest stage brings to the dreamer, he also gains secondarily from the tribal recognition he is accorded. Reframing step six is completed when the dreamer successfully manifests the dream gift in the material world. The Trophy, whose powers are meant to last a lifetime, will forever enable the dreamer to call upon the aid of the spirit. It is, in other words, an anchor. When so controlled, the spirit can act as an ally in dealing with any other hostile spirits. This latter group may correspond with the objections found in step 7 of reframing: the ecological check. They

can then be dealt with in the same manner, with the added resource of the dreamer's new spirit ally.

Other Maps for Other Territories

Even the surreal effectiveness of Senoi Dreamwork is surpassed
by the metaphor of experience that allows certain people to walk
on burning coals. Accounts of fire-walking have appeared in Atlan-
tic Monthly (May 1959) and National Geographic (April 1966). In
the latter article, the author says that the heat of the coals measured 1328° Fahrenheit. Almost twenty people, including men,
women and children, were seen crossing the coals. Some of them
dug in their heels as they walked and even picked the coals up and
tossed them over their shoulders. Upon examination, the soles of
their feet showed no damage. How can such an event occur? It is
totally at odds with apparent physical laws. Pearce has written on
other less spectacular but equally improbable events. He postulates this model:

> "Is there a pattern? Yes. There is the conscious desire for the
> experience, the asking of the question. There is the detachment
> from the commonplace; the commitment to replace the conven-
> tional with a new construct; the passion and decorum—the in-
> tensive preparation, the gathering of materials for the answer;
> the freedom to be dominated by the subject of desire—the sud-
> den seizure, the break-through of mind that gives the inexplica-
> ble conviction that it can, after all, be done; and then the serving
> of the new construct, the instant application. (Pearce, 1971, p.
> 107).

Summary Incantation

In this chapter I have presented a number of operations from
several therapeutic schools and shown how they are but variations
on the process patterns delineated by on approach emphasizing
modeling and the reliance upon an elegant model.

Since I have repeatedly suggested to your conscious and unconscious mind that the assumptions, categories, and labels in the
different schools of psychotherapy constitute merely a version of
the story of human behavior, continuing to embrace one metaphor

over another will become an increasingly difficult task. Once you
have absorbed the fact that the map—personal and clinical—is not
the territory, you might first experience some uncertainty as you
wonder whether the presuppositions in your own thinking have
been limiting your range of personal and professional choices. In
fact, many clinicians tell me that once this information has taken
root they sense that they can no longer proceed as they once had,
believing in the ultimate veracity of their theoretical orientation.
They worry that they may have to give up what they already know
and start over again. In reply, I usually tell them to take a deep
breath and relax. The dilemma is easily resolved: "You already
know how to operate at the level of process," I tell them, "you just
haven't known it consciously . . . now you not only still have your
original skills but an awareness of how you use them that can lead
you to further develop even more choices."

The information in this book can only produce a dilemma if a
therapist is bound to the content of his particular metaphor. Once
you begin to see, hear, and feel the fact that there are identical
process patterns implicit in the techniques of therapy, you are free
to expand your limitations and utilize whatever new choices come
to you most easily in working most effectively with your clients.

A Realization

When he had acquired the certainty that his learnings had allowed him to accumulate a large body of wisdom about healing
from all the healers, and when he began to get diminishing returns
from the instructions of the various healers, he knew that it was
time, as the oracle had mentioned, for him to journey over the final
hill. With great excitement in his heart, he set out through the final
pathway across the mountains, streams, and plains that lay between him and the final village, the village of people who he had
never known. The strange description given by the oracle did not
help him navigate to this new land at all. Time passed for the
traveler and here his diary is not specific. Many sunrises and moon-
rises came. He passed across many fields, many rivers, and a few
mountains. And though time passed, back in those days, one is
never certain whether the time that is spoken of is the time that it
takes a hawk to fly across a river or the time it takes for sunlight
to twinkle in the eye of a deer, or whether it is nearly a generation
passing. One thing is certain; eventually, he climbed down from
the ridge of the final mountain that separated the land that was
promised to him by the oracle. As he walked into the new village
with his experiences and varieties of skills, looking for the people
that he had heard described by the oracle, he was surprised, bewildered, and delighted to discover that he had returned to his own
village of origin! He was astounded that this familiar setting could
have seemed so totally different when it came from the eyes and
the ears of the oracle who had described it to him long ago. And
as he looked at the people of his own tribe through the eyes of
others and through the eyes of the oracle, they looked and
sounded much different. And then he realized that this was the
wisdom that he had gone seeking, that he could only find it upon

his return and that the oracle had instructed him wisely. And now his mind was at ease once more since his journey was over, and he had set about the task of returning to become part of his community once again.

Tales of his travel and his wisdom began to spread out from his community to other places and other lands that he had traveled. The joy in finding this truth of which the oracle spoke reached the ears of those he had learned from, studied from, and those that he had aided, and even those that he had passed by as a friends and acquaintances.

In his own city and in his own tribe, he was excited to share what he had learned about the changes and strategies and rituals, practices, family structures and the roles that were played by the various persons that he had encountered on his journey. He became a shaman of his area.

Like other shaman, he knew that periodically he would undertake a similar voyage of discovery to refine his sensitivities and his noticings. Like most travelers returning from their journeys, he didn't inquire when he would journey again. It was enough to know that a completion had taken place, that a period of implementing the wisdom and knowledge gained must come before he journeyed again. And yet, that ever present cycle of discovery and journey remains as a possible future in the mind of all travelers who have returned from journeys. Just how each traveler goes about implementing the truth he discovers is a personal matter that will be shared as he engages in other journeys or as journeyers come to them.

With that, the traveler unpacks his bag, to once again find his familiars, to water plants, to gather and place the herbs in his kitchen that he will use in his own growth and day to day living. He finds places to hang those paintings that Indians have given him and those statues he has gotten from the land of people who believe in demons, and a place for the katchina dolls given to him by plains people, and seashells given to him by peoples on the shores. He finds a place for the butterflies that he has collected in the fields. He finds a special place for the music that he has gathered on his journey and a special place to enjoy the comforts of those that have taught him comfort along his trail.

The traveler grows older and wiser, having found contentment and release, remembering contentment with each breath and speaking it with each heartbeat, keeping it as a precious memory forever through teachings, keeping it through children's learnings and through the place that he makes in the community and world in which he lives and will again eventually leave.

Chapter IX: Concluding and Continuing

Everything is metaphor and in a certain sense everything is a half-truth. At one glance something may seem to be a truth and at the next turn it seems only to be a very small chalice shining in the sun. So now what? People seem to hold onto certain half-truths and defend them "at all costs" even though they bring pain and limit choice. This is true for short descriptive metaphors and for longer more intricate metaphors. These longer ones include conclusions about one's past, predications about one's own future, theories of psychology, theories of any kind (religious, science, world views, cultures and the one you are reading).

So, what is one to do? People are burdened or blessed with the most creative opportunity: the opportunity to create. Man is endowed with a mind that presupposes any manner of processes and things. Man invents the existence of "time," "space," "consciousness," and even "existence" itself, and then projects his reminders of it onto the situation. He gives it meaning and convinces himself that it is, to some degree, not his creation at all. He is an actor on a stage that he created complete with many of the trappings and sets.

There is no way to tell if the person prefers the part(s) that he plays unless he has a choice to change any and every part as easily as possible. And who is to say what is possible and what is not? What one believes in the metaphors of his life comes true including imagined limits. Furthermore, the parts of his metaphors that are most detailed and specified in sensory-based noticings become "more true" to him than other parts of the metaphor. The detailed parts seem to become "more true" in that the "protagonist" reports he senses them being real. Other people in his life are induced to consider them "real" or "real for him" as well.

The choices and qualities of living are most easily enhanced when a person finds the talents and resources within his world view, metaphor or map. Using the talents and resources that exist is a matter of detailing them, expanding them, or breaking them down into specific sensory-based perceptions and memories and applying them. Meta-model (question) your metaphor and that portion will become the "reality."

Should the person who is changing and discovering talents and resources find instead something that at first seems like a limitation or shortcoming, he only needs to reapproach this same "reality" from a position that makes it understandable as an opportunity, or a resource after all. In electronics and in other sophisticated circuitry, "easy is best" (providing the circuit does its job with utmost quality). In mathematics "the shortest distance between two points is a straight line." With people the straight line is not always obvious. The therapist can't use his own life or anyone else's to decide about the client's life. The client knows best and makes the best choice to get there "in a straight line" and "easiest" from his set of choices. Therapists are advised not just to accept the clients' conscious explanations: it is just content, the form of the process, and the structure of the experience is honestly offered up by everyone's unconscious. It is the map of both the limiting and the openings. This offering is like handwriting on the wall. The answer is there to be found. There are "no hidden meanings." John Grinder put it precisely when he said, "It is most useful to assume that every communication has a positive intent, to assume anything else is to create another intent."

Others (Toffler, 1970) have spoken of our world as one in which rapidly changing stimuli and a certain sensitivity (or insensitivity?) to these prevail. We are assaulted at every turn by ecological pollutions and artificial environments. Musak, artificial flowers, auto fumes, T.V. violence, and other contemporary irritants are an inexorable part of our Western Culture. We are responsive, each in our own way, to these various stimulants. And even though "what's music to one man may be noise to another" there is one thing we can be sure to agree upon . . . too many songs played at once will be noise to all. All media participate in programming people.

In the technological jungle the symphonies are less common than the sirens. Man has very likely "suffered" a desensitizing of his five sensory input channels. In this regard he has lost some of his common sense. He has lost some of his potential to experience, as well as to store, code and comprehend all the experience he can receive. Man has argued or imposed certain limits upon the variety of experiences he can see, hear, smell, feel, taste and put words to.

Perhaps, man gains in the variety of internal experience the equivalent of what is lost in the variety of externally generated experience . . . but that is doubtful. His internal thoughts (kinesthetic, tonal, visual, verbal, olfactory experience) are not under his direction to any large extent. Many people follow the biddings of the words, feelings and/or pictures that they make and have no awareness of either the thoughts or of the control they can have over them.

Man is growing in sophistication about his ability to direct his thoughts or awareness of his on-going production or his internal experience. It seems that the person who has a problem is sometimes the only one who can't understand how he creates or continues it. It usually seems like everyone else is more aware of the way a depressed person makes himself get that way than the depressed person himself.

Our cultural wisdom is only recently overcoming its ignorance about effects of the sight and sound pollution. The various organizations and media (T.V., radio, families, schools, therapies, clubs, cults, etc.) program us, reinforce programs and interfere with existing programming everyday. Those who have more choice in expression and experience become leaders (and programmers) and those who have less choice in perception and expression become the "followers" (programmees) to use a simple formula. It is the law of Requisite Variety taken at a cultural level of analysis. Those who try to remove violence from T.V. are themselves an example that T.V. violence influences large numbers of people. Whether it induces them to violence or to protest T.V. programming is not really the point. It influenced them either way.

Man lives in a culture where others program his neurology (as he programs others) from crib to casket. Hardly an inch of his body or personality is sacred. The media alone (without considering the similarity of contrast of schools, families, churches and factories) address all aspects of experience in either program content or commercial advertisements. We are told and shown what to eat, wear, brush with, smile at, and strive for. Much of the output from the television medium is intended actually to motivate the viewer to do something or to buy something. Some is meant to "entertain" and some is meant to "inform." But all of it operates to influence the experience of the viewer. Much of it later becomes part of some person's internal memory, feeling, thought, and so on. Someone looks in a mirror and matches make-up to a memory of the latest model. Someone throws a basketball and imagines a game on channel 5 last night. Someone kisses his mate and compares the moment to a feeling that was elicited during a daytime soap opera. The list is long, and what is true about this influence from a passive television set is even more true about family, school, club and cult activity. This programming is not always expected to have such long lasting effects . . . but it happens that way, anyway. Man is programmed more by others than by his own action whenever the programming occurs without his awareness or beyond his range of skill in self-control and choice.

When a child imagines a boogeyman (boogeywoman?), everyone except the child realizes that it exists only in the child's mind. And just who is it that educates the people in our Western Civilization about the thoughts they think or how they think the thoughts? Is it the family, the schools, the universities, the streets, the "yoga" teachers, or the media? Education about our ability to control and regulate our experience is not systematically taught to modern man. "Ancient man" had the inclination to regulate inner experience. Ancient mental health practices stressed pilgrimage, "right thinking," and meditation as an intervention or cure for ailment of non-physical origin. But we seem to have a lot to learn about our own experience and their structure.

Prayer, meditation, social congregation, postures, breathing, and concentrated participation in ritual redundancies are some of the religious paths to "healing" human troubles. Traditional psychotherapists, Freudians to "post-avant guard" humanists, each prescribe that we restructure certain of our perceptions, associations, behaviors, internal dialogues and images, tensions, diets, and social ties. It seems that the same or similar cures have been prescribed for ages in the history of psychiatry, and the secrets have been sort of "written on the wall." It could be that the reason people tell one another the same information repeatedly is that it is not communicated the first time.

The limitations many of us experience about the control of our thinking process has been the subject of modern psychology and psychotherapy, as well as the ancient science and occult. Meditation practices today invite many persons to the possibility of turning off the internal dialogue and replacing it with mantras of various sorts. Man controls his thinking in a fashion by changing his environment. If he begins to socialize with mantra users and studies and practices the mantra he may become adept at the replacement of an internal dialogue with an auditory tonal substitute. This does not teach him to control his experience—it teaches one particular state of consciousness. Other people find *their* state of consciousness changes in disco, drugs, or dogma.

We can make a distinction between environmental variables and control variables. The class of events which a person can directly act upon or implement can be called control variables because they change when we exercise our ability to control them. Those events which we do not directly effect or do not seem to effect at all are environmental variables. They are under the control of others, or of a deity or chance, etc.

This dichotomy is most useful in considering the changes that occur in aging or "growing up," socially and technologically alike. Man strives to make the elements which are important in his life come into his self-control. To the extent they remain under the control of the environment he is a victim of circumstances (beyond his control!).

When people fail to change their experience and believe they can do so only by changing their environment then they have lost some of their control. The environment is empowered with the responsibility for their experience and they must remain powerless if the environment is beyond their control. The clinical psychotherapist has usually supported the notion that man has choice and can use it to his own betterment. But man only has choice to the extent that the outcomes he seeks are decision variables instead of environmental variables.

We now have a new set of tools to convey specific understandings to our clients. This is a tool box to do *practical* Magic: another public announcement of the celebrated value(s) called by various names (freedom, choice, self-control, autonomy, and mental health). The particular difference in this writing is the advancement and emphasis upon the "how" and the "what" (and not the "why") of subjective experience. The special emphasis here has been a sensory-based discription of what to notice and an explicit set of prescriptions about how to respond to the noticings.

This book has not introduced any new or mysterious ways for

change to occur. It has, however, introduced some new words to pinpoint existing patterns of change that are found in various therapies, and in many households, corporations and information /entertainment media. The vocabulary used here has been taken from linguistics, cybernetics, and in some cases simply invented by neuro-linguistic programmers. As with most jargon, it is meant to mark out an experience so that experience can be made noticeable and learnable. Reading a book such as this is part of that process of learning and is by no means a substitute for actual participation in therapist training groups. Seeing, hearing, feeling and smelling the actual people in the course of learning is the best (the only) way to learn the artful and stylistic balance that this otherwise mechanistic approach requires.

To reach and support these conclusions, this book has been making and building several points: Communication is most useful and perhaps most understandable when it is approached from a position of modeling (how it is structured) and not from the position of a theoretical explanation. Communication rests upon feedback. When we communicate without information from the person(s) in the relationship with us, we do not know anything about the meaning that is conveyed. Richard Bandler stated this to be one of the cornerstones of NLP: "The meaning of a communication is in the response that it elicits!"

The feedback mechanisms between the writer and the reader of a book are slower than the feedback mechanisms between face-to-face speakers. The duration of the circuit changes the usefulness of the feedback. However, even in face-to-face exchanges the feedback circuit is variable. Some people (including some therapists) don't use the responses of the client to modify and shape what they imagine they are communicating.

Behaviors that interfere with feedback are easy to identify. Interupting, re-labeling several words, looking away for extended moments at a time, talking to oneself or picturing to oneself while the other is acting and speaking are all common methods of poor communication. The effect that these behaviors have upon the use of feedback from the "listener" by the "talker" account for the poor communication.

Even when two or more individuals do attend to one another during the communication process, the feedback is affected by more subtle phenomena. Some of the variables affecting the communication process are at the input stages and some are at the output or response stage of communication. Still other factors are those that effect the processing in between. This book has been about those variables.

Accessing Cuss	Input Mode	Representation System	Syntax and Coding Choice	Strategy Sequence	Behavior
predicates	visual	visual	linguistic	series of	all
eye scan	auditory tonal	auditory tonal	packaging	rep. sys.	channels
skin color	auditory digital	auditory digital	Meta-Model	congruence	congruence
breathing	kinesthetic	kinesthetic	violations	polarity	congruence
locus		visual constructed	calibrations	meta-	
tone/tempo			Metaphor and	positions	
			belief system	designed outcome	lateralixatic

Communication-Feedback Variables

The above chart is a quick summary of many of the items presented in the previous pages. The input portion of the feedback-communication process is enhanced or limited depending upon which of the sensory bits are noticed. If the bits noticed make a difference that is significant, they will be of some aid in communicating. Accessing cues offered here and elsewhere are intended to make that kind of significant difference for the reader. The noticing of such significant cues can help refine and advance the skill that we all seek as communicators.

The behavior choices at the output stage of communicating are also important. If the communicator is flexible enough in his behavior to alter their communication, he can use the input information (whether this is accessing cues or otherwise). Utilization of the input information can be immediate or postponed. The more immediate the use of the information the more sensitive and flexible the communicator will seem to be. Rapport and understanding are thus enhanced. When a lecturer has bored his class he is not so easily able to turn the lecture into something interesting. If he notices the beginnings of questions, comments, stirrings, objections and misunderstanding early enough in the presentation and if he can vary his course of delivery, he may divert and forever delay the experience of boredom.

Saying *"if* he can change the course of his lecture" is no small matter. Many persons get feedback about their presentations from themselves. They "feel" finished or they "see" that they have covered the material or they "heard" themselves make their point. They do not vary from their proposed course until *they* inform themselves that they arrived at the goal. This type of behavior detracts from their ability to lecture longer or to shorten their presentation. It makes it less likely that they will give more detail or less detail as the situation requires. The inflexibility rules out the possibility of going on tangents that may enrich the experience and mutual understanding of those involved. It is such behavior that seems to preclude certain people the choice of switching predicate systems, visual, auditory, kinesthetic, or unspecified verbs and adjectives, when they are hearing the person in front of them.

The ability to respond in several different ways to express the same intention is a matter of how many different response patterns one has learned. In some families the children learn a broad range of acceptable packages for their self-expression. Many of the more discreet and important ones have been discussed and exemplified earlier. These consist of pacing, polarity response, meta-commenting, meta-model type questions, induction type suggestions, and metaphor. Some people automatically and gracefully use those patterns which initiate transderivational search processes and various presupposition operations in their audiences. This book has specified several of these operations so that they can be practiced and learned as automatically as those that you already have. The reason for acquiring such choices is, of course, to increase your own ability to respond in a sensitive and effective manner during the communication-feedback cycle.

In addition to this aspect of reducing and changing response patterns, still another dimension contributes to the person's ability to communicate. Internal processing is the large category for this set of variables. Internal processing, as explained here, consists of the sequencing of representational systems, the linguistic packaging used to code the representations, and the fabric of belief or metaphor that the person uses to relate the various pieces to one another. These have each been examined in several chapters. The changes that can be achieved with each and within each of these areas is perhaps the most fascinating and exciting news.

As therapists and professional communicators (or as parents!) each of us have proceeded to help change the "maps" from which people operate. Changing the behavior attached to the map is really no different from changing the map, thus producing bodily expression of the map. The map is not hidden or "cognitive;" it is the entire language, verbal and non-verbal, the person speaks. The language of family "A" or the language of family "B" differ as greatly from one another as the verbal difference between English and German.

In the clinic or the family where behavior, feeling, thinking and learning are changed and shaped, our ability to communicate flexibly is one important variable to success. The pattern of communicating what we communicate is still another. The change patterns described here by no means constitute a complete list of possible operations. They do, however, encompass many therapeutic operations that otherwise seem to be mutually contradictory or perhaps unrelated. The change patterns related in this writing are like blueprints. They are not encumbered with the specific content that each theory uses to explain the operations. Each therapist will be free to add any personal style that makes the blueprint into a comfortable and beautiful home. These paradigms and patterns are expressed as the nucleus of the change operation. They are like the bones that hold the body of change together. They are also like the biologists' taxonomy for categorizing all birds in one group, all reptiles in another, and the differences between them ecologically. One sparrow is much like one cardinal and much like an eagle in the way it is constructed and in the habitat it selects. The actual differences between the birds (color, size, domain, etc.) are like differences between theoretical explanations in two different approaches, both of which rely upon collapsing anchors, dissociation, or reframing as their particular change pattern. Different species of collapsing anchors exist and many have theoretical names and many don't. Many species of dissociation exist and some are named and some are not explicitly named. Many species of reframing exist, although that is rarer in the change kingdom, and they too go by different names.

The change patterns will be valuable guides as the architects of experience. These patterns will be changed and embellished and will be expanded and others added. The minimum number offered here are those which have been found to be among the most different and most profound in creating change. And what they change depends upon who uses them, how well that person can notice subtle indicators of client response, and how flexible the person is packaging behavior to fit the client's particular needs.

The change patterns can alter the input variety, the form and content of the representational systems, and the output behavior. They are the building blocks which facilitate the change in sequencing and processing strategies.

Changes in the processing that is done internally will change several items of the person's experience. It might be that such a change of the series of experience modes called "strategies" in this writing will create changes in every aspect of the person's life. It most certainly will change the bits of sensory datum that are apprehended from the environment. The difference in data and in data-to-data associations during processing will change the explanations used to verbalize those bits of sights, sounds and feelings. The different explanations require different metaphors and beliefs (both in words and internal pictures). The changes in the metaphors and beliefs will certainly support changes in behaviors that are anchored and conditioned to the internal map. Changes in the behaviors can be used to shift the existing social systems and networks in which the person lives.

It is not as if such changes didn't happen for the individual even before he visits a therapist. It was, in fact, by observing common situations and normal range of personal styles that inhabit those common situations that these patterns were learned and verified. Many of the change patterns exist systematically in the habits of only a few therapeutic wizards from various disciplines. Often top managers and salespersons, attorneys, and architects will display a similar range of useful and rare patterns. These tools are to be used to identify and recreate these patterns to increase the broad range of available options people may use.

The use of such patterns and operations as these presented here does not require a particular I.Q., aptitude, college degree, occupational niche or otherwise. They are useful to therapists because they, more than others, spend their professional lives addressing the concern. Therapists also have the belief that people can change. Styles are learned and acquired and they can be changed. Most of all, therapists have the conviction that personal experience is the result of all of these factors of living. They are not willing to think that people can't change some behavior, feeling, thought, skill, etc. They are not willing to stop improving upon the decency, duration or diversity that goes into creating change with others.

These patterns are learnable by each person I meet and train. Each person wants to acquire and use different ones and various quanties for his personal needs. Some trainees can't help but wonder about the individual freedom that would be available when each person is prepared to take charge of his own experience. Of course, the speculations that can be thought to answer that question are as unlimited as each of us is unlimited in the ability to demonstrate choice ourselves. The tools and techniques offered here are specific and sensory-based. Labels and logic have been provided for man's processing and use of experience and for the structure and story of his words. Such specifications as these allow the work of learning, training, teaching, researching, and tabulating the rich and wonderful possibilities which are available to be shared.

The reader is urged to journey through his world as he did through this book, finding, at each turn, a rich variety of flora and fauna and a wide spectrum of species among each. When you return to your training practices, your offices, your clinics and universities, you will take with you many of these new learnings. You return from this journey and you are able to experience your world in a new way. You return to the same world and find that it or you have changed. You are at a crossroad. Bits noticed and techniques found carry into the world to which you return and find you older and wiser.

In the course of this journey you have learned to survive and thrive in a world that you may not have known before. You have learned to pack your luggage and backpacks more economically and to pace your own travel. When you know of this new world that you find waiting back in your office, and when you know of it in a way that delights and surprises you, you can either stay and appreciate your participation in it or you can journey out again into the world of "truth seekers." There you will find an infinite variety of illusions and myths that will only make your own private world much more compatible with tradesmen, shamen, nobility and townspeople you encounter at each crossroad in the future.

Learn from each of them in a manner that best suits you and change your manner when you wish. Learn too that new ways can be learned and you will have no prior knowledge about their suitability. Each moment that you live you can use the core of the sorcerer's explanation: You are a co-creator of your world. You are forever at a crossroad. "At this precise point," Don Juan said to Carlos (*Tales of Power,* p. 227), "a teacher would usually say to his disciple that they have arrived as a *final* crossroad. To say such a thing is misleading, though. In my opinion there is no final cross-road, no final step to anything. And since there is no final step to anything, there shouldn't be any secrecy about any part of our lot as luminous beings. Personal power decides who can or who can-not profit by a revelation."

APPENDIX I

Study guide for Magic I and Magic II

Modified from *The Structure of Magic Vol. 1*

DELETIONS

Verb   Step 1:   Listen to the Surface Structure the client presents;

Step 2:   Identify the verbs in that Surface Structure;

Step 3:   Determine whether the verbs can occur in a sentence which is fuller—that is, has more arguments or noun phrases in it than the original.

Step 4:   Ask for the deleted material. (p. 60)

     Example: "My father was angry." He was angry at whom/what?

Adverbs   Step 1:   Listen to the client's Surface Structure for -ly adverbs.

Step 2:   Apply the paraphrase test to each -ly adverb —paraphrases with "it is . . ."—and check for the equivalence of the new sentence.

Step 3:   If the paraphrase works, examine the new Surface Structure.

Step 4:   Use the normal methods for recovering the deleted material. (p. 69)

     Example: "Unfortunately, you forgot to call me on my birthday." It is unfortunate to whom?

Adjectives that compare

Step 1:   Listen to the client, examining the client's Surface Structure for the grammatical mark-

ers of the comparative and superlative construction; i.e., Adjectives plus -er, more/less
plus Adjective, Adjective plus -est, most-
/least plus Adjective.

Step 2:   In the case of comparative occurring in the
client's Surface Structuring, determine
whether the reference set is present.

Step 3:   For each deleted portion, recover the missing material by using the suggested questions. (p. 67–8)

Example: "She is most difficult." The most difficult with
respect to what?

Modal Operators   (such as "I must work hard", "One ought to do
it")

Step 1:   Listen to the client; examine the client's Surface Structure for the presence of the cue
words and phrases identified in this section:
must, ought, etc.

Step 2:   (a) If modal operators of necessity are present, use a question form asking for the deleted consequence of outcome of failing to
do what the client's Surface Structure claims
is necessary, and (b) if the modal operators
of possibility are present, use a question
form asking for the deleted material which
makes impossible what the client's Surface
Structure claims is impossible.

Example: "A person can't just go and cry when they feel
like it." What would happen/what prevents
them from doing this?

DISTORTIONS

Nominalizations   (representing a process with a noun)

Step 1:   Listen to the Surface Structure presented by
the client.

Step 2:   For each of the elements of the Surface
Structure which is not a process word or
verb, ask yourself whether it describes some

event which is actually a process in the world, or ask yourself whether there is some verb which sounds/looks like it and is close to it in meaning.

Step 3:   Test to see whether the event word fits into the blank in the syntactic frame, an ongoing _____. (p. 74)

Step 4:   Change the noun back into a verb and ask for the deleted portion when possible.

Example: "The decision to return home bothers me." How is your deciding bothering you?

Presuppositions   (basic assumption that must be true)

Step 1:   Listen for the main process word or verb in the client's Surface Structure—call this Sentence A.

Step 2:   Create a new Surface Structure by introducing the negative word in the client's original Surface Structure on the main verb—call this Sentence B.

Step 3:   Ask yourself what must be true for both A and B to make sense.

Step 4:   Ask the client to explore this presupposition or accept the presupposition and ask the client to specify the verb and replace the deleted material. (p. 92, 94)

Example: "My wife will probably be as unreasonable as she was last time." What specifically seemed unreasonable about your wife to you?

Implied Causatives   (using the word, or implying the word, But)

Step 1:   Listen to the Surface Structure for the report of a causal connection in his model—usually this occurs with the conjunction "but."

Step 2:   Ask the client to specify this relationship more carefully.

Step 3:   Ask if this causality is always this way or in some other way challenge the cause-effect relationship.

Example   "I don't want to get angry, but she's always
                        blaming me." Then, if she didn't blame you,
                        you wouldn't become angry, is that true? (p.
                        100)

SPECIAL CASES OF DISTORTIONS

Cause and Effect and *Mind Reading*

Step 1:   Listen to the client's Surface Structure;
Step 2:   Determine if it involves (a) a claim that one
            person is performing some action which
            causes another person to experience some
            emotion or (b) a claim that one person
            comes to know what another person is think-
            ing and feeling:
Step 3:   Respond by asking, how, specifically, these
            processes occur. (p. 104)

GENERALIZATIONS

Referential Indices (connections of specific experience)

Step 1:   Listen to the client's Surface Structure, iden-
            tifying each nonprocess word.
Step 2:   For each of these, ask yourself whether it
            picks out a specific thing in the world.
Step 3:   Ask the client to supply the specific referent.

Example: "She doesn't pay attention to what I say."
            Who, specifically, is not attending? (p. 80)

Universal Quantifiers   (everybody, no one, always, etc)

Step 1:   Listen to the client's Surface Structure iden-
            tifying universal quantifiers.
Step 2:   Challenge the universality of the generaliza-
            tion.

Example: "Nobody pays any attention to what I say."
            You mean NOBODY EVER pays attention to
            you AT ALL? (p. 83)

Incompletely Specified Verbs

Step 1:   Listen to the client's Surface Structure, iden-
            tifying the process words of verbs.

Step 2:   Ask yourself whether the image presented by
          the verb in its sentence is clear enough for
          you to visualize the actual sequence of events
          being described.
Step 3:   Ask for a more fully specified image. (p. 90)

Example: "My mother hurt me." How specifically does
                  your mother hurt you?

Lost Performatives   (generalizations about the model of the world)
Step 1:   Listen to the client's Surface Structure for
          generalizations about the world—these are
          identified with the words "crazy, bad, good,
          correct, right, wrong, only, true, false."
Step 2:   Identify that this is a generalization about the
          client's model of the world.
Step 3:   Since this is a generalization about the model
          and not about the world, the therapist may
          help the client develop other options within
          his model. (p. 106)

Example: "It's wrong to hurt anyone's feelings." How
                  could you tell him what you want in another
                  way?

Complex Generalizations—Equivalence
This is a more complex generalization in which the client typi-
cally says one generalized Surface Structure, pauses and adds an-
other that he considers to be equivalent. They have the same
syntactic form.
Step 1:   Listen to the Surface Structures that are sep-
          arated by a pause—one involving mind-read-
          ing and the other one not;
Step 2:   Ask the client to verify her equivalence;
Step 3:   Shift the referential indices in an attempt to
          get the client to deny the equivalence of the
          new sentence.

Example: "My husband never appreciates me . . . My
                  husband never smiles." Does your not smil-
                  ing at your husband always mean that you
                  don't like him? (p. 89)

Modified from *The Structure of Magic Vol. 2*

REPRESENTATIONAL SYSTEMS

INPUT CHANNELS: There are three major input channels by
    which we, as human beings receive information about the
    world around us—vision, audition, and kinesthetics (body
    sensations). Each of these three sensory input channels pro-
    vides us with an ongoing stream of information which we use
    to organize our experience. Information received through
    one of the input channels may be stored or represented in a
    map or model which is different from that channel. (p. 4,5)
    Gustatory (taste) and olfactory (smell) are also input chan-
    nels.
    Examples:

>   When two people transact, one may be responding pri-
>   marily to what he sees (as opposed to hears)—such as the
>   frown on the other's face. The other person may respond
>   to what he hears—such as a grating voice tone and not to
>   the smile on person's face.

REPRESENTATIONAL SYSTEMS: We have five recognized
    senses for making contact with the world—we see, we hear,
    we feel, we taste and we smell. In addition to these sensory
    systems, we have a language system which we use to represent
    our experience. We may store our experience directly in the
    representational system most closely associated with that sen-
    sory channel. However, we tend to use one or more of these
    representational systems more often than the others. We also
    tend to have more distinctions available in this same repre-
    sentational system to code our experience, which is to say that
    we more highly value one or more of these representational
    systems. (p. 7, 8)
    Examples:

>   When a person remembers an encounter, it can be via
>   pictures of the person he was with, while another person
>   may recall the words spoken and the harmonious voice
>   tones.

IDENTIFYING THE MOST HIGHLY VALUED REP SYSTEM:
In order to identify which of the representational systems is the most highly valued one, the therapist needs only to pay attention to the predicates which the client uses to describe his experience. Predicates appear as verbs, adjectives and adverbs in the sentences which the client uses to describe his experience. (p. 9)
Examples:
Listen for words:

(1) *Auditory:* hear, say, tell, spoken, yell, loudly, softly, harmony, peace & quiet—"I *told* her not to *yell.*"

(2) *Visual:* see, show, point out, focus, clearly, foggy, grey, blackness, distance. "I don't *see* why we have this distance."

(3) *Kinesthetic:* (feelings); feeling, pounding, heavy, solid, sensation, experience. "I *feel solid* with this decision."

OUTPUT CHANNELS: Communication occurs in a number of forms such as natural language, body posture, body movement, or in voice qualities, etc. We call them output channels. (p. 12)

META-TACTICS

MATCHING PREDICATES (p. 16.)
Step 1:   Listen to the client's Surface Structure for predicates;
Step 2:   Identify the most highly valued predicate group, i.e., visual, auditory, kinesthetic;
Step 3:   Select predicate from that group and utilize them when responding to client.
Examples:
Client: "I can't get the *focus* on this problem." (visual)
Therapist: "I *see* what you mean."
Client: "I'm so *down* and out of *touch.*" (kinesthetic)
Therapist: "I understand that you have a part which is *unsolid* and *feels down.* What does that down part do for you?"

Client: "She just *yells and yells* at me."

Therapist: "I hear that her *yelling sounds* bad to you. What do *hear* yourself *saying* to her next?"

SWITCHING REPRESENTATIONAL SYSTEMS (p. 19)

Step 1:   Identify the client's most highly valued representational system (Meta-Tactic 1);

Step 2:   Identify the rep system that the client experiences pain with:

Step 3:   Create an experience wherein the client will re-map from the rep system in which she has discomfort to the most highly valued rep system, i.e., K to V:

Step 4:   Guide the client (using predicates from the discomforting rep system) to describe his discomfort in her most highly valued rep system (using predicates of that system).

Example:

Client: "I have a headache."

Therapist: "Identify the location of the *tension* in your head. Now continue to locate the exact location and *picture* your head with each *tension* just *as you feel* it. Continue to describe what your head *looks* like with tension. What *color* is it, etc."

ADDING REPRESENTATIONAL SYSTEMS (p. 24)

Step 1:   Listen to the client's Surface Structures:

Step 2:   Identify an experience which is registered in representational system X with which the client is having difficulty coping:

Step 3:   Finding a point of overlap between representational system X and representational system Y pertaining to that experience;

Step 4:   Repeat Step 3 with all other common representational systems.

Example:

Therapist: *"See* (visual) the *tension* (kino) as it is near your ears and begin to *hear* how the *sound* (auditory) is different. Keep listening for the how *sound* changes *as the feelings and pictures* of your headache change."

INCONGRUITY

PARAMESSAGES: The client presents a set of messages, as many as one per output channel. These messages we call paramessages. The paramessages may be either congruent or incongruent with respect to one another. Paramessages are always messages of the same logical level, expressed in different representational systems or output channels. (p. 30, 46)
Example:
> When the therapist sees and hears: voice tone, speech rhythm, volume, facial expressions, left and right hand and feet gestures, posture, head and shoulder tilt, etc., each of these is considered a valid expression of some part of the client and none is to be considered more valid or important than any other. Read the next example also.

INCONGRUITY: When the client is communicating congruently, each of the paramessages matches, fits with, is congruent with, each of the others. . . . When the client is communicating incongruently, we know that the models of the world which he is using to guide his behavior are inconsistent.
Example:
> Client: "I don't know why my head hurts." (while signaling with left palm up and right hand pointing "critically")
> Therapist: Sees the mis-match between the messages that are expressed by the client's hands and also hears the words used.

GENERAL STRATEGY FOR RESPONDING

When a client communicates incongruently, presenting a set of paramessages which do not match, the therapist is faced with an existential decision. The therapist's actions in responding to the incongruency of the client will have a profound effect upon the client's subsequent experience. Within a client who has conflicting parts, there are (at least) two incompatible models or maps of the world. (p. 44)

PHASE 1: IDENTIFYING THE CLIENT'S INCONGRUITIES
Checking for visual paramessages
1. the person's hands;
2. the person's breathing;

3.   the person's legs and feet;
4.   the eye fixation patterns;
5.   the head/neck/shoulder relationship;
6.   the facial expression, especially the brow, mouth, cheek.

Checking for auditory paramessages
1.   the tonality of the person's voice;
2.   the tempo of the person's speech;
3.   the words, phrases, and sentences used by the person;
4.   the volume of the person's voice;
5.   the information patterns of the person's speech.
Example:
> Therapist needs to see and hear what is being done by
> client. The client's hands are incongruent when one palm
> up and one has a "blaming" finger pointing. Or a soft
> voice tone with critical words. Or the client's body and
> face don't seem to organize into an expressive message.

PHASE 2:   SORTING THE CLIENT'S INCONGRUITIES

It is at this point—when the therapist has identified the Incongruities in the client's communication—that the therapist will
begin to work actively to convert the client's incongruities
into identifiable, fully expressed parts. The most common
sorting of a client's incongruities is a sorting into two parts
. . . we call these two parts "polarities." (p. 62)

1.   The therapist selects one of the groups of paramessages
     which fit together and assists the client in fully expressing
     it as one of the polarities.
2.   The therapist does the same for another polarity.
3.   The therapist will usually have to have the client switch
     from polarity to polarity a number of times before he will
     be able to express himself congruently in each position.
     It is important to use Meta-Model questions and re-check
     for visual Incongruence.
4.   The situation has changed from one of simultaneous In-
     congruity to sequential incongruity, or alternating polari-
     ties. When this occurs, the second phase of the incon-
     gruity work is accomplished. (p. 63-5)
Examples:
> The therapist can match the critical words with the
> "blaming" finger pointing into one "polarity." Then the

combination of the left palm and soft voice can be sorted into another polarity (victim). Therapist says: "Sit there and point and blame the 'other part of yourself' as if it were sitting in this empty chair. Then switch chairs and respond." (Or continue the sorting in any of the following ways.)

SORTING SYSTEMS

SPATIAL SORTING—this is like the double-chair technique in gestalt work.

It always involves the client kinesthetically.

Example:

Therapist: *"Sit there* and point your finger and criticize the 'other part of yourself' as if that part were *in the other chair.* Then *switch chairs* and talk softly with your palms up."

FANTASY SORTING—this is useful with clients whose most highly valued representational system is visual. Here you have the client imagine both polarities in detail, one at a time.

Example:

Therapist: "Close your eyes and *get a picture* of two parts of yourself. *Imagine* one as pointing a finger and criticizing, and one part with your palms up and with a pleasing voice tone."

PSYCHODRAMA SORTING—the client first selects members of the group to act as each pole. At some point, the client replaces each and experiences the pole visually, auditorially, and kinesthetically.

Example:

Therapist: "Pick out someone here who can act like you when you point your finger and criticize". Then the therapist would procede with any one of the psychodrama techniques as appropriate: role reversal, alter ego, soliloquy, etc. (consult Ira Greenberg's *Psychodrama*).

REPRESENTATIONAL SYSTEM SORTING—In conjunction with any of the other sortings, the therapist directs each polarity to use predicates of different rep systems.

Representational System Polarities:

Visual-   -Kinesthetic
Visual-   -Auditory
Auditory-   -Kinesthetic
Kinesthetic -Kinesthetic

Example:

The therapist says: "I want this critical part to *watch* and *see* the other part of you sitting over there. Then switch chairs and *get in touch* with the *feelings* you have as the criticized part."

SATIR CATEGORY SORTING—this system uses the Blaming, Placating, and Super-Reasonable categories developed by Virginia Satir.

Satir Category Polarities
Blaming-   -Placating
Blaming-   -Super-Reasonable
Super-Reasonable--Placating
placating-   -Placating

Representational System	Satir Category
Kinesthetic	Placating
Visual	Blaming
Auditory	Super-Reasonable (p. 69)

Example:

Therapist says: "Sit here and point your finger and raise your voice as you *blame* that part you *see* over there. Then play the placating part and kneel on one knee with your palms up and try to please the first part as you *feel* your response to the blame."

PHASE 3:   INTEGRATING THE CLIENT'S INCONGRUITIES
Contact between the polarities
1.   choosing the representational system for contact
2.   fully express polarities during contact
   a.   Meta-Model questions (Vol. 1)
   b.   Polarity Questions
   What do you want, how does other stop you, what does other want, how can you use other, how can other use you, what would happen if other went away, how can you help each other? (p. 83)
3.   check for a solid contact Achieving Meta-Position—a sin-

gle rep system will now include all of the paramessages
of both, and will be itself greater than the sum of the two.
Example:

"Let this *dialog* continue between the critical part (visual,
blamer) and the pleasing part (kinesthetic, placater) until
you *hear* some possibility of agreement spoken on the
questions of how these parts can help each other."

Bibliography

1. Arnold, M.B.: "Brain function in hypnosis." *Int. J. Clin. Exp. Hypn.,* 7:109, 1959.
2. Assagioli, Roberto, PSYCHOSYNTHESIS, The Viking Press, New York, 1965.
3. Bandler, Richard and Grinder, John, THE STRUCTURE OF MAGIC I, Science and Behavior Books, Inc., Palo Alto, Ca., 1975.
4. Bandler, Richard and Grinder, John, THE STRUCTURE OF MAGIC II, Science and Behavior Books, Inc., Palo Alto, Ca., 1976.
5. Bandler, Richard and Grinder, John, PATTERNS OF THE HYPNOTIC TECHNIQUES OF MILTON H. ERICKSON, M.D., Vol I, Meta Publications, Cupertino, Ca., 1975.
6. Bandler, Richard, Grinder, John, Satir, Virginia, CHANGING WITH FAMILIES, Science & Behavior Books, Inc., Palo Alto, Ca., 1976.
7. Bandler, Richard, Grinder, John, Delozier, Judith, PATTERNS OF THE HYPNOTIC TECHNIQUES OF MILTON H. ERICKSON, M.D., Volume 2, Meta Publications, Culpertino, Ca. 1977.
8. Bateson, Gregory, STEPS TO AN ECOLOGY OF MIND, Ballantine Books, New York, 1972.
9. Berne, Eric, GAMES PEOPLE PLAY, Ballantine Books, New York, 1964.
10. Berne, Eric, WHAT DO YOU SAY AFTER YOU SAY HELLO, Bantam Books, New York, 1972.
11. Berne, Eric, TRANSACTIONAL ANALYSIS IN PSYCHO-THERAPY, Grove Press, 1961.
12. Bettelheim, Bruno, THE USES OF ENCHANTMENT, Vintage Books, Random House, Inc., New York, 1975.

13. Brown, Michael, & Kahler, Taibi, NOTATIONS: A GUIDE TO TA LITERATURE, Huron Valley Institute, Dexter, Mi. 1977.

14. Cameron-Bandler, Leslie, THEY LIVED HAPPILY EVER AFTER, Meta Publications, Cupertino, Ca. 1978.

15. Casriel, Daniel, A SCREAM AWAY FROM HAPPINESS, Grosset & Dunlap, New York, 1972.

16. Castaneda, Carlos, JOURNEY TO IXTLAN, Simon & Schuster Inc., 1972, NY, NY

17. Castaneda, Carlos, TALES OF POWER, Simon and Schuster, New York, 1974.

18. Charny, Joseph, "Psychosomatic Manifestations of Rapport in Psychotherapy", *Psychosomatic Medicine,* Vol. XXVIII No. 4, 1966, 28, 305–315.

19. Downing, Jack & Marmorstein, Robert, DREAMS AND NIGHTMARES, Harper & Row Publishers, New York, 1973.

20. Ellis, Albert, GROWTH THROUGH REASON, Science & Behavior Books, Palo Alto, Ca., 1971.

21. Erickson, M., HYPNOTIC PSYCHOTHERAPY. The Medical Clinics of North America. 1948.

22. Erickson, M., Rossi, E., Rossi, S, HYPNOTIC REALITIES, Halsted Press, John Wiley & Sons, New York, 1976.

23. Erickson, Milton H., Hershman, Seymour & Secter, Irving, THE PRACTICAL APPLICATION OF MEDICAL AND DENTAL HYPNOSIS, The Julian Press, Inc. New York, 1961.

24. Fagan, Joen & Shepherd, Irma Lee Shepherd, GESTALT THERAPY NOW, Harper Colophon Books, New York, 1970.

25. Fenichel, Otto, THE PSYCHOANALYTIC THEORY OF NEUROSIS, W.W. Norton & Co., Inc., New York, 1945.

26. Freud, Sigmund, M.D. *Group Psychology and the Analysis of the Ego.* The International Psycho-analytical Library. London: Hogarth Press, Ltd., 1922.

27. Gazzaniga, Michael, "The Split Brain in Man," *Scientific American,* Aug, 1967 Vol. 217, No. 2, PP. 24–29.

28. Gordon, David, THERAPEUTIC METAPHORS, Meta Publications, Cupertino, Ca., 1978.

29. Goulding and Goulding, 6:1, January 1976, "Injunctions, Decisions, and Redecisions," pp 41–48, *Transactional Analysis Journal.*

30. Greenberg, Ira, PSYCHODRAMA, Behavioral Publications, New York, 1974.

31. Haley, Jay, STRATEGIES OF PSYCHOTHERAPY, Grune & Stratton, New York, 1963.
32. Haley, Jay, UNCOMMON THERAPY, W.W. Norton & Co., Inc., New York, 1973.
33. Haley, Jay, PROBLEM SOLVING THERAPY, Jossey-Bass Publishers, San.Fran., 1976.
34. Haley, Jay, CHANGING FAMILIES, Grune & Stratton, New York, 1971.
35. Haley, Jay, ADVANCED TECHNIQUES OF HYPNOSIS & THERAPY—SELECTED PAPERS OF MILTON H. ERICKSON, M.D., Grune & Stratton, New York, 1967.
36. Hart, Joseph & Corriere, Richard & Binder, Jerry, GOING SANE, Jason Aronson, Inc., New York, 1975.
37. Janov, Arthur, THE PRIMAL SCREAM, Dell Publishing, New York, 1970.
38. Johnson, Jack, SENOI DREAMWORK IN A WESTERN CULTURE, California School for Professional Psychology, San Francisco, Ca., 1975.
39. Krippner, Stanley, and Velloldo, Alberto, THE REALMS OF HEALING, Celestial Arts, Mullbrae, Ca., 1976.
40. Kurtz, Ron, & Prestera, Hector, THE BODY REVEALS, Harper & Row, New York 1970.
41. Langs, Robert, PSYCHOANALYTIC PSYCHOTHERAPY, Jason Aronson, Inc., New York, 1973.
42. Lazarus, Arnold, MULTIMODAL BEHAVIOR THERAPY, Springer Publishing Co., New York, 1976.
43. Lowen, Alexander, THE LANGUAGE OF THE BODY, Macmillan Publishing Co, New York, 1958.
44. Lowen, BIOENERGETICS, Coward, McCann & Geoghegan, Inc., New York, 1975.
45. Miller, George, "The Magical Number Seven, Plus or Minus Two: Some Limits on our Capacity for Processing Information," *The Psychological Review,* Vol. 63, March, 1956.
46. Minuchin, Salvador, FAMILIES & FAMILY THERAPY, Harvard University Press, Cambridge, Mass., 1974.
47. Moreno, J.L., PSYCHODRAMA, Beacon House Inc., Beacon, New York, 1972.
48. Pearce, Joseph Chilton, taken from THE CRACK IN THE COSMIC EGG, used by permission of Crown Publishers, Inc., New York, New York, copyright © 1971 by Joseph Chilton Pearce.

49. Perls, Frederick, GESTALT THERAPY VERBATIM, Real People Press, Lafayette, Ca., 1969.

50. Perls, Fritz, THE GESTALT APPROACH: EYE WITNESS TO THERAPY, Science and Behavior Books, Inc., 1973.

51. Polster, Erving and Miriam, GESTALT THERAPY INTE-GRATED, Brunner/Mazel Publishers, New York, N.Y., 1973.

52. Reich, Wilhelm, CHARACTER ANALYSIS, Simon and Schuster, New York 1972.

53. Rolf, Ida, STRUCTURAL INTEGRATION, Rolf Institute of Structural Integration, Boulder, Co., 1962.

54. Satir, Virginia, PEOPLEMAKING, Science & Behavior Books, Inc., Palo Alto, Ca., 1972.

55. Shannon, C., & Weaver, W. THE MATHEMATICAL THE-ORY OF COMMUNICATION. Urbana: University of Illinois Press, 1949.

56. Skinner, B.F., BEYOND FREEDOM & DIGNITY, Alfred A. Knopf, New York, 1971.

57. Tart, Charles, ALTERED STATES OF CONSCIOUSNESS, John Wiley & Sons, Inc., 1969, New York.

58. Tart, Charles, STATES OF CONSCIOUSNESS., by permission of E.P. Dutton & Co., Inc., New York, copyright 1975 by Charles T. Tart.

59. Toffler, Alvin, FUTURE SHOCK, Random House, Inc., New York, 1970.

60. Vargiu, James, "Subpersonalities," SYNTHESIS, volume I, number 1, 1974, the Psychosynthesis Press, San Francisco, CA.

Index